CH00858274

All This and Free Boots Too

TONY RATTIGAN

Copyright © Antony Rattigan 2018

All rights reserved.

The Cosford and Stanbridge photos are courtesy of the Trade Group 11 Association website.

In the 100th anniversary year of the RAF, it's time to tell of my small part in its operation and my 22 year's service during the Cold War.

At last it can be told, the true story of what really happened when I walked out the door in 1972 saying, 'Just popping out for some milk. Shan't be long.'

WARNING – this book is not "politically correct" and contains some adult content. The views expressed are my own and have not been sanctioned by the UK government or its military.

This book is dedicated to Samuel Finley Breese Morse, without whom we would all have been merely Wireless Voice Operators.

In remembrance of our most famous RAF Wireless Operator and funny man, Eric Sykes 1923 – 2012 and other airmen that I met along the way, who are no longer with us – Pete Broster, Reg Howarth, Dave Lewington, Ken Pavitt and "Captain".

CONTENTS

INTRODUCTION

First of all, why did I write this book when I always claimed I wouldn't? Once I started writing novels it did cross my mind about writing my memoirs but I discarded the idea.

Then in 2016 one of my old buddies from my RAF training days, Dave (Dafydd) Manton, mentioned on Facebook that his regular publisher had no wish to produce Dave's RAF memoirs, *I Was a Cold War Penguin*. As I had just published my latest novel, I had free time on my hands and was looking for a new project, so I offered to help him publish it through Amazon. We did this and produced an ebook and a paperback. Dave generously donated the royalties to the RAF Benevolent Fund, which encouraged sales, and eventually the proceeds ran into the thousands.

Despite working together on this project, we only communicated by phone and email and never actually met up until later in the year. By sheer coincidence, that summer I happened to rent a holiday chalet just 16 miles away from his home. Once I realised this, we arranged a meeting and Dave came to the site and bought me lunch (and drinks!) So we finally met face to face for the first time in 43 years.

Of course Dave and I swapped stories of our time in the RAF (our careers had taken vastly different courses so our paths had never crossed) so we had lots to tell. Unfortunately for Dave, I had read most of his stories in the book. Having spent so much time working on his book only months before, at that time I was probably more familiar with his life than he was.

But he hadn't heard *my* stories before and after a while he suggested that I write my own book about my career. 'Well, maybe. I'll think about it,' I told him and put it on the back burner.

By a curious coincidence 2016, the year in which I started work on this book that you are holding, also happened to be 22 years after I left the RAF, following 22 year's service. 11th December 2016 marked the day that I was OUT of the Air Force *exactly* as long as I had been IN it, so now seemed an appropriate time to tell my story. (*The years of therapy having finally paid off.*)

So for me, what with first producing Dave's book, the anniversary I've just mentioned and then writing my own Air Force memoir, 2016 was for me, the "Year of the RAF".

Before you go any further, I should point out that this book isn't about aviation heroes or flying aces. If you want to read about one, I recommend *Wings on My Sleeve,* the autobiography of Captain Eric "Winkle" Brown RN, a navy test pilot. Apart from all the other amazing things he did, he holds the world record for making 2,047 landings on aircraft carriers. The Americans deliberately set out to beat his record but their man had a nervous breakdown after only 1,600 landings. (*Ha Ha!*)

Rather, this book is about an ordinary communications guy who didn't go anywhere dark or dangerous, wasn't anyone special or did anything unusual, who spent most of his time working in nice, air-conditioned Communication Centres (Commcens) of one sort or another. Much as I'd liked to have been, I was never the guy that got posted into a new camp, sorted out everyone's personal and professional problems, then rode off into the sunset while the townsfolk looked on, saying, 'Who was that masked telegraphist?'

But along the way I went to some interesting places and met some interesting people and they're who this book is really about.

I should also make it clear that this book is about my "professional" life and not my "personal" one. (*Dozens of WRAF's heave a sigh of relief! – I wish.*) In fact I only mention my marriage and subsequent divorce to explain why on various postings I go from living in married quarters, to my own house, back to living in barrack blocks. Apart from that – mind your own business!

To quote J. R. R. Tolkien – 'This tale grew in the telling.' When I set out to write this book I didn't imagine it would be so long. (I actually think my Word Processor was typing stuff long after I'd gone to bed.)

I didn't realise that so much had happened to me during my life, as the more I reviewed the different periods of my life; the more stories floated up from the memory banks that had been forgotten for so long. I know from relating some of my RAF stories to people I've worked with in civilian life, that some of them can sound quite exciting to someone who's never done that sort of thing. But as a wise man once said, 'It reads better than it lives.'

When I told a member of the writing group that I belong to, I was toying with the idea of writing my RAF memoirs he asked, 'Will they be funny?' (He and I are usually the ones making jokes in the class.) I replied, 'I hope so.' But thinking about it later, I realised I should have said, 'Not necessarily.' The point being these are not *The Comic Adventures of Airman Rattigan,* rather it's the story of my life in the Air Force. Like everybody's life, it's not an endless series of thigh-slapping, side-splitting, knockabout romps – it's just life, with all its ups and downs.

Not that my life was particularly hard, I hasten to add (compared to other servicemen that is) there are tough, funny, ironic, sad parts to everyone's life and that's what I've put down on these pages. I'm also sorry if it gets a bit philosophical at times but what is the point of life if you don't learn anything along the way?

I'd like to apologise to the people I don't mention in this book. I've met a lot of people and I can't remember them all. Faces I'm good at but names … unless I use them regularly, I forget them. Also, as I get older the fresh information is overwriting the old memory banks. If you were a friend or did me a service, I have used your real name where I could. If you were one of the 'bad 'uns, then for legal reasons I have made up a pseudonym for you or just not bothered to name you.

Apologies also to readers who were in the forces, for over-explaining technical details as they are already familiar with those and it will bore them. But apologies to civilian readers for probably not explaining enough. It's a fine line between the two.

There's an old saying in the forces – 'Pull up a sandbag and I'll tell you a story.' It evokes images of old black and white war movies, where the squaddies are sat around their tank/trench/gunpit/fortified defence, the Hurricane lamp swinging gently in the night breeze, as the grizzled old Sarge tells them about his previous adventures. So, telling your mates about the things you got up to on other postings, to pass the night shift or an evening in the bar, became known as "Sandbagging".

Needless to say those stories were not necessarily 100% accurate all the time. As long as it was entertaining, a certain amount of embellishment was allowed, nay, expected. "Sandbagging" (it was a verb as well as a noun) was a socially acceptable habit.

So, Dear Reader, I invite you to, 'Pull up a sandbag,' and I'll tell you *my* story.

Training

"Only the Beginning is Difficult"

Okay, let me start off by admitting to something now and get it out of the way, so I don't have to keep apologising for it throughout the book. I was cocky and arrogant as a youngster. (*Some will say I still am ... but don't listen to my mother, she's biased.*) Always thought I knew more than my elders and betters. On my telegraphist course I even gave myself the nickname "Super Rat". I was 18 when I joined up and like most 18 year olds; I thought I knew it all. Later, when you are in your 20's, you realise you don't know the half of it. And that's the beginning of wisdom.

I've said and done some stupid things during my life (haven't we all?) but the point of this confession, right here at the beginning, is so I don't have to qualify each episode by saying, 'I was young and stupid.' You get this one explanation/apology now and that's it for the book. Okay? Good, now let's move on.

***

So there I was in 1972, 17 years old, with a failed Gas Board apprenticeship and a job selling carpets behind me, currently unemployed. Having left school at 15 with no qualifications except a swimming certificate, I didn't fancy working in one of Coventry's many car factories, so there weren't really a lot of options open to me. I could have become a postman I suppose – it's not much of a job but it keeps you off the streets.

I had planned with friends to go backpacking around Europe but I could see that within a couple of weeks we would be begging on the street of Paris, so I gave up that idea. Then I thought that if I wanted to see the world, I could do it on "the queen's shilling" as I came to know it. In other words, let the government send me around the world and they could feed and clothe me at the same time. So I thought I'd look into joining the RAF.

I duly toddled off to the Careers Information Office (CIO). In the Coventry's shopping centre precinct there are a row of shops on the ground floor, above them is a balcony with another row of shops, with offices above them. On the balcony level was the Joint Services CIO. You went in there and they told you that the RAF office was up another several flights of stairs. Their standing joke was that if you had a nose bleed before you reached the office, then you were no good for the RAF.

I made it without any medical problems and met a man in RAF uniform. On his arm he had the 3 stripes of a Sergeant, with a propeller in a circle, above them. As we talked I asked him what that meant, it denoted a Chief Technician, apparently.

Anyway, we talked about joining the RAF, he took my details and gave me some brochures on the jobs available, depending on my score in the aptitude/intelligence tests which I came back and took a few days later.

I finished the tests and he added up my score and then told me which trades my results qualified me to enlist in. Apart from the obvious ones like cook, fireman, clerk, I didn't know what most of them were or what they involved – except for one, Teleprinter Operator. I'd seen enough TV programmes to know what a teleprinter was and what it did. (*And it sounded just my sort of job – indoor work with no heavy lifting!*)

'I'll have that one,' I said.

He checked my score and told me that I had actually qualified for a higher trade in the same field, a Telegraphist.

'What's the difference?' I asked.

'Telegraphists learn teleprinters AND radios and Morse code. The training is longer, 6 months as opposed to 14 weeks, but you end up in a higher pay band.'

Sold! To the man in the blue uniform.

(*When the Data Protection Act came in, one of the things it stated was that any organisation that stored information about you had to give you a copy of that data on request. When the RAF computerised all our records many years later, we were told that we could request a computer printout of that data, but only ONCE. I wisely saved mine up until my last year of service so that I would have a complete record of my career. I still have my printout and used it to check my recollection of dates of postings, promotions, etc. and was surprised to discover that it even included the scores I achieved on the entry exams. I'm not going to disclose them here but they weren't good. I'm surprised that they even offered me a position as anything higher than a police dog! But there you go; they did, so they must have been desperate.*)

We agreed that I would enlist as a telegraphist. It seems that at that time you could sign on for as long as you liked, even the full engagement of 22 years. Who walks in off the street and signs their life away like that, without knowing what they are getting into? Personally I figured I'd do the minimum, 3 years, and see how it went. Unfortunately the recruiter told me that as the Air Force was spending a lot of time and money training me, the minimum engagement for my chosen trade was 6 years.

Fair enough, I suppose. I reckoned that if I really hated it and bought myself out, I would do it long before the 3 year deadline, never mind the 6. As I was only 17 and a minor, I had to get my mum's signature on a form, giving her permission. So he gave me the forms, arranged a medical for me and off I went.

I duly passed the medical and it was arranged that I would join up in December as the basic training schedule had to fit in with the trade training schedule and the next telegraphist courses weren't until January.

I had a few months to myself to kill (this was the middle of the year) so I got a book out of the library and taught myself Morse code, as I would have to know it in my new career.

Eventually, they sent me a rail warrant and asked me to attend Birmingham CIO for my "Attestation ceremony". On the 12th December 1972, with my best suit on, I made my way to Birmingham on my own, I was 18 by then, so I didn't need Mum to sign any more forms for me, and along with a few others, I took "the queen's shilling" and swore my oath to the queen.

Not the government, not politicians, but the queen. Did you get that you slimy politicians who have sold the UK out to the EU over the ensuing years? I and my fellow troops didn't take our oath to you. So if the military ever do circle our tanks around Westminster, I assure you the guns will be pointing INWARDS not OUTWARDS.

They did actually give us £5 cash each for expenses, I often wonder if it was meant to be the modern equivalent of "taking the shilling". They also gave us a rail warrant to Newark railway station for the day after next, the 14th and instructions to report to RAF Swinderby.

***

RAF Swinderby

14 December 1972 – 6 February 1973 School of Recruit Training

I arrived at Newark railway station in Lincolnshire to find dozens of others milling around, looking for someone from the RAF to tell us where to go next. There were buses waiting to take us to RAF Swinderby. When we got there, I think the first thing they did was take us into the barrack block to drop off our cases and find the bed space that would be home to us for the next 6 weeks.

I can't remember if we chose our beds or if we were allocated them but I was in an upstairs room, first on the left at the top of the stairs and my bed was half-way down on the left hand side. The bed space consisted of a bed, a bedside locker and a wardrobe type locker, single.

At some point our new sergeant introduced himself to us, Sergeant Bastable. *Oh come on,* I thought. *Am I in a Carry On movie? Sergeant Basta**? Who's next, Corporal Punishment?*

He assembled us outside and marched us off to the barbers. As it happens, I was the first one in the chair. I'd had long hair for years but several weeks before I had sensibly had it cut short, so I could at least get some attempt at styling it, before the RAF got their hands on me. Others though had turned up with long hair and they just basically got it all shaved off.

The barber gave me a short, back and sides and then charged me five bob (25p). I'd have thought if they were going to butcher us like that, they could at least do it for free! I thought he was joking so I told him to charge it to the MOD but no, he wasn't joking and so, to add insult to injury, I had to pay up.

Then we were lined up outside again and marched off to the clothing store, to get our kit. We were told that from now on wherever we went, we would have to march there, for it is written, 'Whenever 2 or 3 are gathered in my name, then verily, they shall march everywhere.' Of course at this stage we weren't actually marching as such, we were just all walking in the same direction, in 3 orderly lines.

We were given our kit, everything for the "Airman to be" except underwear. Shirts, ties, beret, shoes, belts, braces, boots, jumper, raincoat and the old "Hairy Mary" battledress. They felt like they were made out of old Army blankets. You know what I mean when I say battledress. Go on, you've all seen *Porridge*, that's what our uniforms looked like, as if we were all inmates of Slade Prison.

We were also measured up for our No 1 uniforms. Our battledress was our every day, working outfit, our No 2 dress. The smart uniforms, made of a material called Barathea (*no, me neither*) for best and parades and such like, were our No 1 uniforms or "Best Blues". We had to wear those whenever we left camp i.e. to go on leave.

We shoved all this kit into the holdalls we had been issued and were shown the best way for 2 men to carry their holdalls. You place one on top of the other (holdalls that is, not men) and put the handles from the bottom holdall through the handles of the top one and then you stand either side of it and each of you grabs a handle.

Over the next week or so they taught us all the basics such as how to iron a shirt, how to press your uniform, how to tie a Windsor knot in your tie and so on. I had been a salesman in a carpet showroom and always had to wear a suit and tie, so was quite familiar with how to use an iron on my shirt and trousers, and how to tie a knot correctly. Many hadn't so they had to pick up these life skills quickly. They also taught us to lace our shoes and boots straight across instead of criss-cross, as most people do. Try it, it looks a lot smarter.

People came from all sorts of backgrounds and previous experiences. As this was basic training, all trades were present, I got pally with an armourer. I didn't really know the guys who would be on my Trade Training course, I don't even know if they were on the same flight as me but you just got along with whoever was around you. Usually the people in the surrounding bed spaces or the ones who stood next to you when you lined up for drill practice.

One of the more dastardly things we had to learn was how to "bull" your shoes. This isn't just polishing them; it meant applying layer after layer of polish, then, using a duster or a piece of cotton wool dipped in water, you would rub and rub in tiny little circles until the leather shone. Shoes had to be bulled all over but boots only had to have the toecaps and heel parts bulled. The rest of it was dimpled so couldn't be bulled anyway.

Over time as the polish built up, everyone's toecaps shone but on some people's, they positively gleamed. With enough effort some people could get it to look like black glass and you could actually see your reflection in it, but that was going too far for me. I had neither the knack nor the patience. We had 2 pairs of shoes, one that we wore every day and one that was laid out at the end of the bed for inspection, which we were saving for our "passing out" parade. Always looking for the easy way around things, I didn't even apply polish to that pair until the final week. I reckoned that they were shiny enough the way they had been issued. Apparently the Sgt agreed because he never picked me up for it.

Another odious task was the "bed pack". We each had a counterpane, top and bottom sheets and a couple of blankets. When we got up each morning, we were expected to fold and stack these into a square shape, the same size as the top of the bedside table, the sheets and blankets layered in a particular order, with the counterpane wrapped around the outside, so that it looked like a large, liquorice allsort. This was then placed on the bed for morning inspection. After breakfast we would have to stand by our beds while the Cpl inspected us, our bed packs and bed spaces before the day's fun began. If he didn't like what he saw, he would often tip it on the floor. I heard that some poor devils had theirs thrown out of the window, but it never happened in our room.

After a while I just slept under the counterpane in my overalls, it saved so much time in the mornings. Getting to sleep was never difficult, we were so exhausted that staying awake was the problem.

A week and a bit after we arrived, they sent us all away on Christmas leave. I wondered why they'd bother bringing us in before Christmas at all, but I suppose everything had to work to the Trade Training camp timetable. We all proudly put on our No 1's and headed off home. A chap got chatting to me on the train and I'm telling him all this guff about the RAF I had picked up in my WHOLE WEEK in the Air Force, and he asked me how long I'd been in. Well, I could hardly say just a week, could I? I'd look such a fool. So I blithely told him I been in 11 months.

***

We came back after Christmas refreshed and ready for anything. That was when we started in earnest.

We had regular "bull nights" where the whole block

had to be scrubbed and polished. All brass was polished as were all floors, tiled floors in the bathrooms were scrubbed, windows were cleaned until, well … you could see through them.

We had lino on the floor and it had to be polished every bull night. We didn't have the luxury of electric bumpers, oh no, it had to be done by hand. They gave us liquid polish and a hand polisher. It was a rectangular block of metal with a soft pad underneath. Sticking out of the top was a broom handle on a pivot, so you could swing it from side to side and lay it almost level with the floor. It was known as the "Brick on a stick". The idea was that you would slide the brick backwards and forwards but not like a broom, you could swing it in front of you, and then because of the pivoting handle, slide it behind you. Or you could stand there and swing it from side to side.

Some idiots thought it would be cool to polish the soles of their shoes. There is nothing more soul destroying than to watch someone who has done that, walk across the floor you've just spent half an hour polishing and leave footprints behind. Fortunately the Sgt soon put a stop to that foolishness.

The food was passable, we ate in the Airman's Mess. I don't know what it was like in the Officer's or Sergeant's Messes but in the Airman's they served Breakfast, Lunch and Tea in that order (according to the Recruit's Handbook of which I have a copy, thanks to Steve Hughes). It was fine by me because calling the evening meal "Tea" was what I was used to at home (although we called the midday meal "Dinner" not "Lunch") but I bet the posher ones amongst us had a fit of angst and had to adjust. So that's why I shall refer to the meals as they were advertised in the Mess. (*So don't go thinking it's because of how uncouth I am.*)

Supposedly, if you skipped breakfast and ended up passing out, you could get charged for it, but you would have to be stupid to pass up food like that. It was the middle of winter and they worked us hard, so you needed all the fuel you could get, just to keep going.

Every day they would march us around and teach us the finer points of drill and then for a break, would take us into the cinema to try and teach us stuff. I doubt if anyone learnt anything though, because as soon as the lights went down, everyone immediately fell asleep. Sometimes they wouldn't show us a film but talk to us, so we couldn't kip, but sitting down, indoors, in the warm, it was a major struggle to keep your eyes open.

We learnt about the RAF rank structure: (*Pay attention, there'll be a test later.*)

We mainly wore rank badges on our uniform upper sleeves to denote our rank.

AC – Aircraftsman (What we were.)

LAC – Leading Aircraftsman (What we would be when we had finished our Trade Training.)

SAC – Senior Aircraftsman (What we would be after a year as an LAC, subject to us passing our promotion exams.)

J/T – Junior Technician (Only for technical trades, which didn't apply to me.)

Cpl – Corporal

Sgt – Sergeant

C/T – Chief Technician (Again, only technical trades.)

FS – Flight Sergeant

WO – Warrant Officer

Then the officers:

They wore rings of varying thickness on their uniform forearms.

PO – Pilot Officer
FO – Flying Officer
Flt Lt – Flight Lieutenant (Although, because us Brits are ornery, we pronounce it Leftenant.)
Sqn Ldr – Squadron Leader
Wg Cdr – Wing Commander
Gp Capt – Group Captain
Air Cdre – Air Commodore

I stopped paying attention after that, on the grounds it was getting too confusing as the stripes on their sleeves started looking like supermarket bar-codes (thin one, thin one, thick one, thin one, thick one, thin one). Besides, I was probably never going to meet them in person and if I was, somebody would tell me who they were beforehand.

They also taught us about the history of the RAF. It was formed on April 1st, 1918. An apt date, I reckoned, "All Fools Day". Probably explains why over the years I have heard it referred to as the Royal Air FARCE.

***

After a while they reckoned that we were well disciplined enough to carry sticks with us as we marched around. Dummy rifles actually, to get us used to the weight. We had to learn the basics of rifle drill before they would let us carry the real things. Not just carry them but how to do things like salute officers and also do a General Salute when you are parading in front of really high ranking officers. That's tricky. From the rifle standing on the ground, you have to flick it up into the air, catch it with both hands, swing it around in front of you one-handed as you slap your other hand into it, so it makes a bang. Finally, you hold it out in front of you, while simultaneously slamming one foot down behind the other. It's like doing a curtsy in boots. And as it was winter, you had to do all that whilst wearing woollen (sometimes wet) gloves that have absolutely no grip at all.

But as well as marching with the rifles they taught us how to shoot them!!

So began our introduction to the L1A1 Self-Loading Rifle commonly referred to as just the SLR. Based on the Belgian FN FAL rifle, it was a semi-automatic weapon. Nice piece of kit. Weighed 9 pounds, fully loaded with a 20 round magazine of 7.62mm bullets.

Most military men of my generation preferred the SLR to the toy plastic rifle, the 5.56mm SA80, which replaced it some years later. Reputedly some innocent civilian got hit by an SLR round once, and when they tracked it back to where it had been fired, it was 2 miles away. It could supposedly fire through a brick wall, if you put several rounds in the same spot. *That's* the sort of gun I want to be holding if I'm fighting the queen's enemies. As they say, 'When you hit someone with a 7.62 round they develop an uncanny knack of staying still, on a permanent basis.'

As an aside, it took me ages to figure out what the difference was between a semi-automatic and a fully automatic weapon. (There was no Google in those days.) Don't know if you're interested but …

Semi-automatic means when you pull the trigger, the round (bullet) in the chamber is fired. Some of the blast is diverted to push back a piston that forces the breech-block mechanism back, to the rear of the weapon. This ejects the empty cartridge case. Then a spring forces the breech-block forwards again, which automatically pushes another round into the chamber. That's it. One pull of the trigger, one shot. Even if you hold it back, only one shot is fired. To repeat the process you have to pull the trigger again.

Fully automatic means you pull the trigger and as long as you hold the trigger back, the above process is repeated again and again. Fire, eject, reload, fire, eject, reload, until you run out of bullets. That's the difference.

Sadly, although the original Belgian FN rifle on which the SLR is based had a fully automatic setting, that was disabled on our weapons. The British method of combat is single, aimed shots. It's meant to instil accuracy and firing discipline instead of just "blatting off" everywhere (and saves money on bullets). The Americans however, believe in throwing everything they've got at the enemy in one go. They even have a thing, "Reconnaissance by fire" which means when they see a suspicious bush or something, the whole patrol (or whatever grouping of soldiers they have) fires at it until their magazines are empty, to see if there is anyone there. Yes, well, no comment. But they're Americans, they can afford it.

***

Of course it wasn't all bulling and marching, marching and bulling. They let us go free in the evenings (once we'd finished our bull night). We could go across to the Newcomers Bar in the NAAFI, to have a pint or two to relax.

Sometimes they put on a disco and brought over the WRAF's from RAF Spitalgate, some miles down the road from us, where they were doing their basic training, or we'd go over to visit them.

I should mention at this point – once upon a time there was the Women's Auxiliary Air Force (WAAF) and its members were known as WAAF's, (pronounced "Waffs"). At some point after the war they changed it to the Women's Royal Air Force (WRAF) but its members were still known as "Waffs" because "Wurraffs" sounds silly. Some of them used to complain about this but there was no way your average airman was going to identify them as "Double Yew, Ar, Ay, Effs" every time we spoke about them. "Waffs" it was and "Waffs" it stayed. Call me a sexist pig if you want ... no, seriously, go on, I love it when you talk dirty!

***

This was also where we had our introduction to the concept of Nuclear, Biological and Chemical (NBC) Warfare and how to protect ourselves in those environments. We were trained in how to use gas masks and protective NBC suits lined with charcoal that was supposed to absorb all the "nasties". (Noddy suits we soon learned they were called.)

They also took us into the dreaded "gas chamber" filled with CS gas (tear gas) to show us that A) our gas masks did work and we could have faith in them. Then later, when they deliberately caused us to get a lungful of tear gas that B) it wasn't really that bad and it wouldn't kill you. So if we ever had to face it for real – in a riot situation, maybe – if we caught a whiff of it, it wouldn't be the end of the world.

They would take you into the gas chamber, let you stand around for a while to show that you were safe with your mask on. Then, one by one, you would have to take your mask off, recite your name and service number, and then leave by the door. Most people can do that by holding their breath but then the instructor would go, 'Sorry, didn't catch that. Could you say it again?' by which time you've breathed in again and got a lungful of gas.

This was done for a purpose, they weren't just being

cruel, you *had* to experience the effects of the gas. Once you started coughing they threw you out of the door.

At the time I had a really bad head cold. An unexpected side effect of the gas chamber was that all the snot in my nasal passages relocated to the front of the overalls I was wearing, and my cold miraculously cleared up. Never bothered me again during the rest of my stay at Swinderby!

N.B. In those days we wore gas masks and went into gas chambers. In later years, along came Political Correctness and it was decided that the term "gas chamber" had negative connotations, so from then on we had to call the things covering our faces "respirators" and we tried them out in the "respirator testing facility".

The instructors used to get a strop on if we pointed out to them that the motto we had to remember was, "Mask in nine, to stay alive." (Nine seconds that is.) And not "Respirator in nine to ..." well, let's just not go there.

***

To make men of us and toughen us up, they sent us camping in nearby Sherwood Forest. The only camping I'd done before was a family holiday, on a beach, at a campsite in Italy, so I was hardly experienced in that sort of thing. *Where was the beach? Where were the ice-cream salesmen? Would I need sun cream?* It turned out that one of our number used to go poaching in Sherwood Forest. *Right, I'm sticking next to him,* I thought.

I don't remember much about it to be honest – I think we went on map marches and were given exercises like tying rope bridges between trees. Mind as they invariably ended up about 6 inches off the ground they weren't much of a challenge or a danger.

It was also our introduction to composite rations (compo). They gave us several packs of 24 hour rations each (24 hour rat-packs as they were known) and we had to use our own judgement to stretch them out over the time we were in Sherwood, so if you just ate all the chocolate or ate all the main meals on the first day, more fool you. (*You know, like when you're a kid on a school outing and you've eaten all your packed lunch before the coach has even left the car park.*)

We also learnt how to re-heat the food by burning Hexamine blocks set on a folding, tin frame. I don't know what they're made of (Hexamine presumably) but they looked suspiciously like those blocks you find in the bottom of urinals, and taste just like them too. (*Only kidding ... they taste completely different.*) They smell horrible when they are burning and taint the flavour of the food, but they do the job.

The easiest way to cook the compo rations was to light the "Hexi" block in the tin frame and put your mess tin on the top, filled with water. You would make a hole in the top of a can of food (24 hour ration packs only contained half-sized tins) and stand it in the water which heated the food as it slowly boiled. The food was already cooked and could, if necessary, be eaten cold. All we were doing was reheating it. You could of course empty the can into the mess tin but that involved washing them out afterwards, which isn't always viable in the woods.

We were warned not to drink the water we'd used for cooking as chemicals could leach out of the tins as they were heated. Ironic really, as the mess tins that they gave us were made of aluminium. Every item for cooking food issued to us (mess tins, frying pans, pots and pans etc. in quarters) or used by the RAF for about the next 20 years, were made of aluminium, which it is now believed can cause Alzheimer's disease. We might as well have been licking lead pipes.

Anyway, overall it made a pleasant break from drill-practice and at least we didn't have to polish any trees!

***

Finally, all good things must come to an end. (*Ha!*) We'd polished everything that we could till it shone, marched around the world 3 times and learned how to press a razor sharp crease into our trousers. (The trick is to turn them inside out, run a bar of soap down the crease, turn them the right way then press them. The heat melts the soap, it's pressed into a sharp crease, which then cools into a fixed crease). There was nothing else they could teach us. The time had come for us to graduate from Swinderby.

They "lent" us greatcoats as it was still mid-winter, white gloves and white plastic belts. (Which was annoying. Before I joined the RAF I actually owned an RAF greatcoat which I gave away, as I assumed I would be issued one when I joined up. Instead they gave me a raincoat.)

People's families came for the big day and we went out and marched up and down to impress some top brass who had come along to wave us off. After all the pomp and ceremony was over, as we marched off the parade square for the last time, the RAF band that was there played the theme music from the film, *The Great Escape*. I often wonder if that was chosen because it's a nice tune or was it an "in-joke" from the band. Whatever.

We handed in our rifles, greatcoats, white gloves and belts, said our goodbyes to each other and went off to our new lives.

***

People ask me why I chose to join the RAF instead of any other service. Apart from the fact that I preferred their uniform to the others – after giving it a lot of thought in my early years I came to this conclusion:

Royal Navy – the officers and men are all on the same ship (literally all in the same boat). If the ship sinks, they all go down together.

Army – the men get sent off to war while the officers sit back at headquarters.

RAF – the officers fly off to war while the airmen go and have a cup of tea, read the paper and wait to see if they come back or not.

Which service would you rather be in?

***

RAF Cosford

7 Feb 73 – 21 Aug 73 No 2 School of Technical Training.

So, after a few days off, I arrived at RAF Cosford and was put in an upstairs, 24-man room, overlooking the carpark behind station headquarters. Alas, that was where the station band used to practise of a Sunday morning, while you were still in bed, recovering from Saturday night.

Next day, along with all the other newbies, I was marched down to the hangar marked "No 2 School of Technical Training". There we were divided up into groups according to what training course we were on. I was on Telegraphist course number 12, or Tel 12 for short, and met my fellow inmates (*sorry, trainees*). They were:

Les Davidson, Mark Seddon, Mick Spensely, Mal Gray, Steve Knight, John Goody, Roy Hannis, Cedric Francis, Ken Jones, Sandy Riach, Jeff Kewin, Dave Manton, Mick Moore, "Gunner" Duxbury, Lawrence Hopkins, Steve Hughes and Bob Oldershaw.

Our instructor for the course was Roger Elliott. Most of us arrived at the same time from Swinderby, with the exception of Steve Knight who had been there for a week already, waiting for us.

"Gunner" Duxbury was so called as although he had joined as a telegraphist, he really wanted to join the RAF Regiment (the Air Force's soldiers). I think that the recruiting office had told him that there were no vacancies at that time but if he joined as a telegraphist, he could switch later (which was a lie, they only every let you change trades upwards, not downwards.) Eventually he got his way and went away, never to be seen by us again.

The hangar was enormous. All the classrooms were around the edges with more upstairs but the hangar floor was empty except for a couple of odd, little buildings in the middle. These we learnt were "Outstations", more of which later. There was so much empty floor space because they often had parades and inspections there.

***

We settled in to what would be our home for the next 6 months, while we learnt everything they could teach us about our "Bibles" whose rules we would practice our craft by. They were Allied Communications Publications or ACP for short:

ACP 121 Communications Instructions General (how a message is created).
ACP 124 Radio Telegraphy Procedures (sending signals by Morse code).
ACP 125 Radio Telephone Procedures (sending signals by voice procedures).
ACP 127 Tape Relay Procedures (sending signals by teleprinters).

Basic message procedures apply to all methods of transmission, such as when a person writes out a signal, he decides the precedence i.e. how fast it is to be handled throughout the system, based on the content of the signal. This is also dependant on a person's rank or the position they hold. There were four precedences Routine, Priority, Immediate and Flash! (*A-ah, saviour of the universe.*) All of those should be self-explanatory. They also taught us the various security classifications we would normally see, Unclassified, Restricted, Confidential and Secret.

Alongside all this theoretical stuff we had to learn the practical side, namely Morse code and typing. They taught us the Morse characters by making us listen to tapes day after day until we remembered what each sound meant. Typing we learnt by sitting in front of typewriters, while a graphic of a keyboard hanging on the wall, lit up a key at a time and a voice droned on in our headphones, 'A now, B now, C now …' and so on. We had to press the identical key on our typewriter.

Once we had learned the Morse characters we were then put into different rooms playing tapes of dummy Morse messages, which we had to transcribe. Each room had its own speed and as you progressed, they moved you into other rooms where the Morse was faster.

Personally I always struggled with Morse code. Learning it before I joined didn't seem to help me at all, in fact I think it slowed me down. I had learnt it from a book, so I knew what it LOOKED like written down, not what it SOUNDED like. So when I heard it I think there was always a built in delay while my mind translated the sound to the visual image of it, then I could write it down. (*At least that's MY theory.*) For the first month or so this caused me a lot of grief. I never really "mastered" Morse, shall we say? The speed we had to achieve to pass the final exam was 18 Words Per Minute (WPM) and I only got into the 20 WPM room a week before our final exams, whereas the others had raced ahead. Some were up into the high 20's by the time we finished the course.

I wasn't much better at typing to be honest. Once we had learned the keyboard on a typewriter we transferred to teleprinters. Judging the speed on those was different, we didn't do WPM as typists normally do. The ultimate aim is to produce a paper tape that has been perforated with punch holes for the different letters, to be fed into a Tape Relay machine. So, producing that tape was known as "perforating" or "perfing" for short and we did "perf" practice not typing practice.

We also had to learn how to read all those little holes in the tape. The western military comms networks use the Murray Code system of a paper tape 5 holes wide, and different combinations of those holes produce different characters or machine instructions such as carriage returns or line-feeds.

The keyboard layout is different on a teleprinter, there are only capital letters, no lower case, lots of keys are doubled up, for example all the numbers are on the QWERTYUIOP top line keys. To differentiate between a figure 4 or the letter R you had to either press the figure key first or the letter key. Each of these key presses or "depressions" as they were known, were counted when you were being assessed.

By looking at a page copy of a signal you could count up all the times a key had been depressed, as well as the individual characters, there were letter shifts and figure shifts to carriage returns and line-feeds, and that was how a test was judged. A perfing test would contain so many depressions and we had to reach the perfing speed of 1125 depressions in 5 minutes, without errors, to qualify at the end of the course.

Now me, I can either perf *fast* or I can perf *accurately*, but apparently I can't do both at the same time. You can either have it fast or you can have it correct. Which do you want?

You can correct mistakes on the paper tape so that they don't appear when the tape is run through a tape reader and your effort is printed out, but those corrections take extra depressions which aren't counted in the final analysis.

To be honest, when it comes to my Morse taking and perfing, although I managed to achieve the required speeds *during* the course ... I'm pretty certain that I actually failed my final exams in those subjects.

There, I've said it. If you want to take back all the salary and pension you've paid me over the past forty odd years, I'll see you in court.

The instructors obviously didn't want to waste the 6 months of their lives spent training me, so they entered results from earlier tests that I *had* passed. This in a way is fair, if like me, you had proven you could do it but just couldn't manage it on the day.

Fortunately I was better in the theoretical subjects.

***

There were a couple of cafes outside the camp but the nearest place to go for a drink if you wanted to get away, was the village of Albrighton. It was a bit of a walk, half an hour maybe, but as long as it wasn't raining or if you were thirsty enough, it wasn't too bad.

The one thing I remember most about it was, as you made your way up the country lanes, if you looked carefully, across the fields you could see a church in the distance. Easy to miss if you weren't looking for it. It had a cut-out in the front of the steeple in the shape of a cross. Nothing unusual about it, during the daytime.

When they closed the church up at night, they left a light burning inside. As you walked back from the pub along the dark, unlit country lanes, you would see this glowing cross hanging in the air, shining across the fields, like a sign from above. Unless you knew what it was it would *literally* put the fear of God into you. I'm sure there was many an airman that swore off alcohol after seeing that.

***

At some point during my time at Cosford, we had the misfortune to have an AOC's inspection. I say misfortune as I ended up getting charged for the first time in my career.

(*I'll own up, I seem to remember having been charged twice in my whole 22 year career but I can't for the life of me remember where or what the other one was for. Strange but there it is.*)

Every year the Air Officer Commanding (AOC) visits each camp under his jurisdiction. With mature hindsight I can see that it is a good thing really. It's like having occasional bull nights in the barrack block. If you let it go too far then the place (camp or block) gets shabby and untidy. AOC's is an excuse to give the camp a wash and brush up. A fresh coat of paint everywhere it is needed and the place scrubbed clean.

It happened at Cosford while I was training there. They kept us so busy with bull nights and practising parading that I never had time to get a haircut. (*Okay, so lots of other people on camp managed it, yeah, yeah. Tell it to someone who cares.*)

Come the day of the parade, on a pre-parade inspection, I was deemed "too scruffy" to be inspected as my hair was too long, and told to go and fall in with Pool flight. This was where all the misfits were gathered. The scruffs like me or people who had 2 left feet when it came to marching, that sort of thing. I think you'd actually have to be on crutches not to be in Pool flight. Next to me was a guy that was also thrown off the parade for being scruffy. Why they didn't just leave us out of the parade completely I'll never know, but they insisted on us marching on as well and making us stand off to one side of the parade ground.

The AOC duly turns up and decides he wants to inspect Pool flight!

I nearly laughed out loud as I imagined the blood draining from the face of the idiot who said we weren't decent enough to be inspected.

So the AOC wanders up and down our ranks looking us over, and stops to speak to the guy next to me (who, you'll remember, was told that he wasn't fit to be inspected by the AOC) and the AOC *actually compliments him on his appearance!*

The parade finishes and those of us sent to Pool flight were all charged. Now, if I'd have been the guy standing next to me, I would have said, as the charge was being heard, that if the AOC considered me to be acceptable then it wasn't up to a junior officer to call him wrong.

I'd have even been prepared to request the AOC as a witness, as is my right. (I know it wouldn't have happened but it might have stirred up enough trouble that they'd have dropped the charge.)

I of course, didn't have the AOC as a character witness and so got awarded 7 days Restrictions (or Jankers as it is commonly known). Jankers is designed just to mess a person around so that they will never, willingly, put himself in a position ever again, where they might have to serve Jankers.

You have to report for inspection early in the morning, before work. After tea, you report again to the guard room to be detailed some boring duty like scrubbing pots in the Airman's Mess. Then you return to the guard room at 10 pm in your best uniform to be inspected again. During your time on Jankers you are not allowed to use any of the station bars. The irregular times you have to attend inspections eats into your rest time, so it is really wearing and believe me you would never want to do it again.

But at least they don't flog you these days.

***

As well as learning all the procedures (the software, you might say) we also had to learn the hardware we were likely to come across. That meant a radio. The RACAL RA17 to be precise. It was a, "32 valve, triple superhetrodyne radio receiver capable of receiving CW, SSB and voice," according to Dave Manton's book, *I Was a Cold War Penguin*. Dunno if all that's true, but I'll take his word for it.

It had been around since the 50's and we were in the 70's but it was still going strong. I see it from time to time in war movies where they are trying to look authentic. It even features in the first James Bond movie, *Dr. No*.

When I had a NATO posting to Belgium in the 80's, they told us that we would be getting a "new British radio" installed. The old RA17 turned up and they were duly impressed whereas all of us Brits were rolling around on the floor, slapping our thighs, laughing at this "new" radio.

***

I'll admit that when it came to the theoretical side, I got a bit of a reputation, both with my class colleagues and the instructors, as someone who was always asking questions instead of just accepting what the instructors told us. I wasn't being awkward or just liked the sound of my own voice; rather it was that fact that I needed to get my head around what I was being told. I've never liked, 'Well, it's just that way because it is!' I always want to understand why it is that way. Either the others in the class got it straight away (in which case they were cleverer than me) or they weren't brave enough to speak up.

Sometimes I even pointed out the mistakes in the instructor's teaching or logic if I thought I saw any (which they didn't appreciate). One case in particular stands out in my memory. I remember one time they were teaching us about two-way authentication from a code book and how it was uncrackable. I argued a case against this which they flatly denied was possible. The scenario went like this:

The instructor told us that radio stations A and B want to talk to each other but they make each other prove who they are first, to make sure they are not the enemy.

A challenges B with a 2 letter code from his code book, B replies with a single letter from his code book. A is happy as he has received the correct answer.

B however does not know if the challenge is genuine –

A might have simply picked 2 letters at random, so for his own piece of mind the procedure is to challenge him back.

B challenges A with a 2 letter code and A replies with the correct single letter.

Everyone is happy as they have both proven who they are.

Job done, according to the instructors, safe as houses, can't be beat as the challenge and reply are used one time only.

After thinking about it I asked, 'Well, what about this?'

2 radio stations A and B are trying to communicate with each other but for whatever reason, geographical, power issues, frequency issues, whatever, cannot make contact.

Station C (who happens to be a bad guy) can hear them both clearly. (Before anyone denies this can happen, I have had it happen to me in real life. I was station C and relayed traffic between A and B who could not hear each other.) Of course I wasn't a bad guy.

So station C passes the challenges and authentication between A and B and they both end up believing they are speaking to each other and send their signals to C.

So then C sits in the middle, passing traffic between the 2 stations A and B and copying it all and sending it to his intelligence people or even altering it as necessary. *Voila!* Uncrackable system cracked!

'That's not possible, you're talking nonsense,' I was told. *Oh well,* I thought, *you believe what you want and I'll believe what I want.*

Fast forward 30 years and I'm in the IT business and learn about a situation in computer networking where someone can sit in the middle of a network and copy authentication signals from one part of the network and then pass them on to another part, *pretending* to be the originator. They even have a name for it *"Man in the Middle Attacks"*.

See, I was 30 years ahead of my time but no one appreciated that.

***

Of course it's all very well learning about these highly technical ways of sending signals but sooner or later you have to stop the book learning and get out there and do it for real. This is where "Outstations" came in.

They had various rooms and the odd buildings in the middle of the hangar floor, which contained various dummy communication setups. Sometimes they were simply a cubicle with an RA17 in, where we practised sending and receiving messages in CW (Morse) or R/T (Radio Telephony or Voice, in other words).

For your information – in R/T:

OVER means, 'I have finished speaking, please send your reply.'

OUT means, 'I have finished speaking and the conversation has ended.'

So I don't care what you've seen in the war movies or the cop shows, you NEVER say, 'OVER and OUT.' They contradict each other.

Of course even using the correct procedures you can have fun. The R/T sessions were often full of nonsense transmissions such as …

'THE LAND ROVER IN THE ANDOVER, OVER DOVER, HAS FALLEN OVER, OVER.'

'REQUEST YOU SAY AGAIN WORD AFTER OVER, OVER.'

'I SAY AGAIN, WORD AFTER OVER IS OVER, OVER.' And so on.

Yeah well, training can be boring sometimes.

And then there were the more elaborate Outstations that were fitted out as full Tape Relay centres or standalone Commcens. They were all named after real RAF camps and we had our own mini-network to play with and we sent signals to each other. I was put in one on my own. I remember it was upstairs in one of the buildings in the middle of the hangar and I think it was named after one of the RAF bases in Germany.

Being on my own was a bit hair-raising at first, but once I got into the swing of it, it was good fun actually. Perfing up dummy signals and sending them, receiving signals in and having to distribute them correctly. Okay, that sounds boring I admit, but there was more to it than that. It sounds silly I know but it was good to finally practise what we had spent so many months learning.

***

Towards the end of our course, when our friends and girlfriends on shorter courses had left Cosford, Tel 12 started socialising with each other more. I started hanging around with Dave Manton. (*Nothing to do with the fact he had a car. Absolutely nothing. I promise.*)

He had this wonderful cream-coloured Austin A35 van. Like me he never seemed to go home at the weekends, so we would hop in his motor and take off.

It used to be great fun driving out to country pubs, or just going for a drive to break the monotony of a Sunday afternoon. One time we were out, driving down a country lane and some idiot overtook us and cut us up, so Dave had to brake sharply to avoid running into them.

Dave gave the driver the old "Agincourt Salute" and stuck 2 fingers up to him. As his fingers rose above the level of the dashboard, the bonnet of the car in front flipped back, covering the windscreen and 2 insulating pads flew into the air and over our car, landing on the road behind us.

That car skidded to a halt and we drove past, laughing at them. (*Karma's a b*tch, ain't it?*) Mind you, I was always extremely polite to Dave after that and made sure never to get on the wrong side of him.

***

We'd also gelled together as a group by this time. We called ourselves "Rent–A–Crowd" (available for birthdays, weddings, bar-mitzvahs, etc.). We used to joke that we could be hired to make parties and social get-togethers look as if they were well attended and popular.

We even had plaques made which read:

19   TEL 12   73

RENT-A-CROWD

RAF COSFORD

~*Seul Le Premier*~

(*I'm looking at mine now as I type this. Still got it after all these years.*)

Some wag on the course had told us that the bit of

French at the bottom meant, "Only the finest" or "Only the best" but while I was researching this book I found out that the station motto for RAF Cosford is:

"Seul Le Premier Pas Coute" which means "Only the Beginning is Difficult".

So I think he was telling us porkies.

***

Our final paper exams were of the "multiple choice" variety – known in the RAF as "Vote for Joe" tests. To each question there were 4 optional answers and you put your cross in the box next to the one you thought was correct, just like on a ballot paper.

RAF Urban myth stated that if you were in any doubt about which was the right answer, choose option 'C' as that usually turned out to be correct.

Thankfully we all passed, so no one had to face the embarrassment of being kept back or worse, kicked out. We were all now fully paid up members of Trade Group 11 (TG11) and were entitled to wear the "Fist and Sparks" badge. This was worn by all RAF tradesmen who had anything to do with electronic communications (ranging from Telephonists to Radar and Aircraft Avionic techs). It is a fist holding 3 lightning bolts and was worn proudly on the right arm, under the rank badge. LAC propellers, "props", were also handed out. Our postings were then given to us, Les Davidson, Steve Knight and I were to go to the big tape relay centre at RAF Stanbridge, near Leighton Buzzard. The rest were sent off to the four corners of the UK.

Anyway, the last day at Cosford came; we all hugged each other and promised that we'd be friends for ever … then promptly went off and never saw each other again for the rest of our lives.

Well, that's not strictly true – I remained life-long friends with Steve and Les. I never saw the others again during my career but due to the wonders of Facebook, I have reconnected with some of them in recent years and others from my days in "the mob". As I said in the introduction, I met up with Dave Manton again, and by the time you read this, Tel 12 will have had a reunion with those who could make it. (We're all still alive thankfully.)

Tel 12 Rent-A-Crowd.

Cosford Outstations.

RAF STANBRIDGE

"LACking in ambition"

Arrived 22 August 1973 Communications Control Centre, RAF Stanbridge.

So Steve Knight, Les Davidson and I arrived at RAF Stanbridge. Steve and I as singlies went into the block and Les, being a "scalie", moved into quarters on the scalie patch.

Okay, here is where we really begin to get into forces slang, mostly RAF but some joint service. I shall explain it as we go along, but pay attention as there will be a test at the end.

Way before I joined the Air Force there were different pay scales depending on your marital status, whether you had children, etc. Married personnel were on Scale E so became known as "Scale E's" or "scalies". This had all changed by the time I signed on the dotted line but the nickname stuck. Married personnel were known as "scalies", their children were known as "scalie brats", their married quarters were on an estate known as the "scalie patch", if you went around to visit scalies at home it was known as "scalie bashing" and so on.

Les, who had married his wife Liz by then, was a scalie and Steve and I being unmarried, were "singlies", so we lived in the block.

Our barrack block was one long building split into four wings, two downstairs two upstairs, with the ablutions and TV room in the central end of each corridor. Each wing was given over to one of the four watches that operated in the Commcen, so that everyone in your wing was going to bed, getting up and going to work at the same time, to lessen the disturbance to those around you. I can't remember the name of our block but one of the two WRAF blocks was called Maxwell House, which always amused me as that is the name of a brand of instant coffee.

Steve and I were on the same watch so were assigned to the D Watch wing, which was up the stairs and turn right. There were the toilets and then our room, first on the right.

We moved into a 4-man room. The other occupants already there were Steve Pitkin and Paul Birtles. A 4-man room was a big improvement over the 24-four man room we were in at Cosford. We each had a built-in double wardrobe and an overhead locker where you could keep things like holdalls and suitcases.

I grabbed the bed in the corner, where the head of my bed butted up against the wall between us and the toilets. The other three beds all had their heads again the corridor wall and faced the windows; Steve was left with the one in the middle.

Next day we put on our No 1 uniforms and officially "arrived" at the camp. Got a blue card from General Office and went around all the sections like the Medical Centre, the Dentists and Stores, so they could register our presence on camp. And then finally we went to the Commcen to announce our presence.

The Commcen building was a very strange design in my opinion. Down at ground level you had the Telephone Exchange (the PBX as it is known), the incinerator, a few other things and this was protected by a brick wall around the building, the height of the ground floor. The actual

Commcen was built *above* this, exposed, with just metal walls. So while the relatively unimportant stuff was protected downstairs, the important Commcen just had metal walls for protection. You could have sat in the road that ran past the camp and taken out the Commcen with half a dozen Rocket Propelled Grenades. Didn't make any sense to me at all.

***

Anyway, as I said the manning at the Commcen was split into four shifts or watches. Steve and I were on "D" watch. When you join a watch you're given an operating number and you use this to sign everything you do. Using your own initials can confuse others, as some people like myself use a different name for signing things. I answer to the name of Tony but I sign and initial all official forms as Antony Rattigan or AR. This would be confusing to others who weren't aware of that. Or there could be several people with the same initials. So, operating numbers are used instead. My operating number was D6, I remember.

The DSM of D watch was WO George Entwhistle. A funny bloke, he used to bring his dog onto nights with him. He would tell us he was taking it for a walk and disappear down the Sgt's Mess until it closed, then come back and get his head down for the night. RHIP I suppose. (Rank Hath Its Privileges.) But all in all he was relatively harmless as a shift WO. His wife was a Warrant Officer too. She ran the Airman's Mess, so they must have been coining it in between the two of them.

The Commcen was a big, scary place. There was something like around forty people on a shift. As you walked through the doors into the Traffic Hall the room stretched away to your left, probably about twenty yards long. Ahead of you sat "The Man in Charge". (Every comms unit around the world had this position – he might be called the Duty Comms Controller\DCC, the Duty Signals Officer\DSO and so on. At Stanbridge he was called the Duty Signals Master\DSM.) He sat behind a desk, on a raised dais, like the Mekon in the Dan Dare comics, so he could survey the entire room.

Behind the DSM dais were some meeting rooms and on the other side of those was Systems, a room as long as ours, where the technicians managed the circuits from the UK to our overseas stations.

I was very grateful that Steve had not only been posted to Stanbridge but was on the same shift as me. It helped having a friendly face around on your first posting out of training. We hung around together in our off time as well and he and Les were the only ones from Tel 12 that I stayed in touch with over the years.

The long room of the Traffic Hall was split into long banks of equipment for various purposes. Looking down the length of the hall from the DSM's dais, the right hand wall was lined with banks of tape printing equipment, where the incoming signals were received.

These were the infamous "tapes" that we had learnt about at Cosford and for which we had had to learn the blasted Murray code. Fortunately these did not have the holes punched completely through them. The tapes you normally see in movies and suchlike have the holes punched completely through and are known as "chadded". The ones that are only partially punched through and have the flap still attached are known as "chadless" as they have produced no chads. (Chads being the little circle of paper that is cut out when the tape is perforated.) I mention all this because, luckily for us newbies, the chadless tapes have the entire contents of the message printed along the bottom of the tape, so one's (in my case) limited knowledge of the Murray code was not a hindrance.

Besides, as the Murray code drifted away in your memory, you soon learned to recognise the important characters that you needed to know when handling tapes such as the precedence, whether it was classified/unclassified, the bit that told you who it was from, beginning of the text of the message, end of the text and the end of the whole signal. In normal practice as long as you could spot those you were fine.

Down the centre of the room and on the left hand side were rows of TASS and TARE transmit banks. At the time, the military Defence Communication Network (DCN) consisted of Telegraph Automatic Routing Equipment (TARE) in which perforated paper tapes are fed into a transmit unit and received at a teleprinter or reperforating equipment at the other end. This is on a single line, point-to-point circuit.

Alternately, there was the Telegraph Automatic Switching System (TASS) which operated like Telex in that you can dial up *any* station in the UK that had TASS equipment and once you had established contact, transmit the message to them. Actually though under normal circumstances we would only transmit to the 76 stations that we were responsible for.

Over in the corner, to the right of the DSM's position was the Local Traffic Office (LTO) where messages to and from RAF Stanbridge were dealt with and also signal traffic from the services to the civilian Telex network were handled. There was also a corridor leading to the offices where the daisies worked. Day staff were known as "Daisies" and shift workers known as "Shifties".

Stanbridge was a major relay centre for the Defence Communication Network (DCN) and via the TARE network we were directly connected to two other major relays, Boddington and Whitehall. They in turn had their own 70 odd TASS stations that they were each responsible for and each of the three of us would be the interface between the TARE network and the RAF TASS stations. So the system operated like this – any Commcen anywhere would input a signal into the DCN destined for one of Stanbridge's minor stations. It would make its way into the TARE network and end up at Stanbridge where we would send it via TASS to said station. Then any replies would come to us via TASS and we would transmit it into the TARE network for onward relay. The same thing happened at Boddington and Whitehall and a dozen other major relay centres in the DCN.

We would know that the signal was destined for one of Stanbridge's responsibilities as we had the Routing Indicator (RI) of RBDP. (This was a group of letters that told man and machines where the signal was to be sent.) Every subordinate station of Stanbridge had the RI of RBDPxx, so we knew it was one of ours. So if a signal had the RI of RBDPAJ for example, the system knew to send it to us for onward transmission. Other relays had their own RI's (RBDA, RBDO, etc.) and responsibilities.

Now this sounds all well and good, and indeed it was a good system but what I need to point out to you is that while Boddington and Whitehall did this by computer, we at Stanbridge had to do it all MANUALLY. Meaning we logged in the signal at the receive banks, someone took it over to a transmit position, someone else then had to dial up a station, take the tape, put it into the transmitter and send it.

There were several drawbacks to having to do manually what other stations did by computer. For example, the signals came in over the receive banks NON-STOP during the day. There was no way that you could book in a signal and then take it to the appropriate transmit station. You had to put the tape into a spring (literally a coiled, metal spring attached to the receive bank) and when it was full, one of the guys standing behind you on "distribution" would take the paper tapes and then distribute them to the right TASS bank.

After a time, you would graduate from "receive" to "distribution" then later on to TASS transmit and then up to TARE transmit. *You were in the big time then! Playing with the Big Boys!*

As newbies, Steve and I we were stuck on the receive banks until we learnt the system and where every station was. It was gruelling at first, as you had to spend the whole shift on your feet, except for tea-breaks. You got used to it after a while though.

To complicate the manual side of things was the fact, if you received a message for two or more stations you couldn't just send it to one and then try to remember to take the tape over to the transmit position of the other station and make sure it was sent to them. It's not practical; too many signals would go missing, unsent. So what you had to do was give it to the Tape Copy position. That operator would then make a separate tape for each station that it was destined for. Then the individual tapes would be distributed to the appropriate transmit station. This as you imagine can get quite complicated but I used to enjoy that job as it called for a bit of skill and technical expertise.

But what really made that Tape Copy system a pain was that every Thursday night they used to send out updates to the book that told us where every unit\sub-unit in the British Forces was (routing amendments they were known as). This one particular signal was about six teleprinter pages long (each page being about A4 size) which gave a tape length of around twenty feet or more. And this had to go to 76 attached stations. So 76 individual tapes had to be made and distributed to 76 stations to await transmission (some of the stations were closed overnight). For that reason everyone used to dread being on nights on a Thursday.

***

Another downside to being a MANUAL major relay is that if Boddington or Whitehall ever went down, we had to cover the traffic for them. Meaning the DCN would re-route all the signals traffic for them and their subsidiaries to us. You think it was busy on a normal day at Stanbridge wait until you have a BODOUT or a WHITEOUT, the place would go crazy. Even though Stanbridge could control things by limiting the precedence of traffic that it would accept, (Immediate, Priority, Routine) the place would suddenly turn into a paper factory!

There would be tapes coming out of the walls, up through the floor, down from the ceiling – not really, but that's what it looked like. Even the guys on distribution couldn't cope and they had to roll out special containers to store the tapes in until they could distribute them. It was organised chaos.

I always used to complain that we were handling signals of too low a precedence, we should have restricted it to only the important stuff, but I guess the people in charge were too worried about their assessments and didn't want it to look as if their watch couldn't cope. It was counter-productive as when the downed relay centre came back online we just ended up re-inputting all the signals back to them, so it was pointless.

I did learn something useful about myself though during those times. At first I would try and keep up with the rush, working harder and faster. Then I would reach a stage where I would get angry with myself because I was failing to get on top of the problem. Then like a switch being thrown in my head, I would just suddenly realise that it was beyond my (or anyone's) capabilities to keep up with that massive workload and I would start to find it amusing. I would laugh to myself and just carry on working at a steady pace, no longer busting a gut trying to cope. I would become calm and relaxed, in a playful mood even. (*I'm not quite sure what that says about me but there ya go.*)

***

Our shift pattern was mornings (0800-1200) and evenings (1630-2300), then afternoons (1200-1630) and nights (2300-0800). After the night shifts we had a sleep day and then a day off (essentially, we worked a two on, two off shift pattern).

I didn't see much of Les as he was on a different watch, until we were experienced enough (*or they wanted to get rid of us, not sure which*) to be put onto the Boost system. Being a 24 hour Commcen there would naturally be periods in the evenings, nights and during weekends where it was relatively quiet and needed less manpower. Conversely, during busy times you sometimes needed more people than you actually had on shift. So they created the Boost system, whereby a pool of operators from each watch would augment the Commcen staff during the daytime, on every shift. This was a great idea, it meant you didn't have to do any nights or weekends for the month you were on it.

You were either on early or late Boost. Early Boost meant you did the morning shift with the watch but starting later (0900-1200) and then came back for the evening shift at 1630 and worked until things had quietened down around six or seven o'clock and they let you off. If the DSM was a mean s*d sometimes you didn't get off until the shift ended at 2300, but that was rare.

Or you could be on the late Boost where you worked the afternoon shift from 1200-1630. I think they used to switch you about from week to week so you didn't get bored. (*I can't swear to all these Boost timings but that's as best as I can remember it. Not even Steve or Les can clarify it, but even though I may be wrong, after all these years it doesn't really matter.*)

Working with different watches allowed you to get to know people outside of your own group. You wouldn't normally see people from some of the watches over the NAAFI, for example, but you could meet them at work. I saw Les again and got friendly with a few people such Mick Smith and Jane West, both of whom I met again in Cyprus.

***

For some of us though it wasn't all pushing tapes. Stanbridge had a "Tactical Comms Cell" or Tac Cell as it was more commonly known. Every so often they used to open it up for Comms Exercises and run a Morse circuit from there to various ships around the UK.

I don't know if it was because he was an SAC and I was only an LAC but every time they opened it up for business, Steve got put in there when we were on shift. The only times I ever got a crack at it was when he was away on leave. As I said, Morse wasn't my strong point and no matter how many hours you spend listening to machine generated Morse tapes, it's a totally different ball-game when you're listening to a real person sending

Morse to you manually.

I wasn't too good at it to be honest, sometimes the Cpl had to step in to assist, which they weren't happy about but I told them frankly, 'What do you expect? You never let me near this place to practice unless Steve isn't around. Once in a blue moon you pick me up and drop me in here and expect me to be perfect. Get real.'

But anyway, as it turns out, that was the last time I ever touched a Morse key in anger during the rest of my 22 year career. It's true. Despite spending most of my career on radios, including a couple of postings where you HAD to be Morse trained, I never worked a live Morse circuit again.

***

Of course this was where I began to learn the RAF slang. Because we played with paper tapes all the time, we were known as "Tape Apes" (obvious) or more obscurely "Peanuts". To this day I still don't understand that one.

People who worked in offices and spent most of their time polishing the seats of their pants on office chairs were called "Shinies". Although it didn't apply at Stanbridge as most of us were on our feet all day long, to be fair that name could also be applied to Commcen workers in some postings.

"Gash" meant something or someone that was bad i.e. not up to scratch – a gash meal, a gash operator, etc. "Lemoned" meant getting picked to do something that you would rather have avoided having to do, such as getting lemoned for extra guard duty. When you were chosen or particularly if it had a habit of happening to you, you were the "Duty Lemon".

"Bubbled" was if you thought you had got away with something but then someone tells on you and you get caught out. Such as your boss accidentally gives you a stand-down two nights running but then someone points this out to him, he "bubbles" you, and so on – the list is endless and we shall come across many more as we make our way through my service career. Stay tuned.

Along with the slang there are the RAF sayings. One of my favourites was always, 'Not me Chief, I'm engines.'

It originates with maintaining aircraft. There are those people that look after the body of the aircraft, the airframe, wings, rudders etc. and then there are those who look after the engines. Each has their own area of responsibility. So if you're the pilot and you try to explain to the engine maintainer that you are having problems with the flaps on the wings, he will respond by telling you that it's not his area of responsibility – 'Not me Chief, I'm engines.' But this was such a good saying and useful in so many circumstances it spread throughout the RAF in general.

So when someone tried to bend your ear about something, or engage you in a subject that you weren't really interested in or it wasn't your area of responsibility, you could say to them, 'Not me Chief, I'm engines.' Its meaning was, (*the polite version*) 'It's nothing to do with me, you can't blame me for it. I'm not interested in what you're saying. Please go away and stop bothering me.'

***

This was the first time I came into contact with Technicians or techies for short. Originally they were called Fitters but a few years after I joined, someone high up must have realised that as their ranks actually included the titles, "Junior Technician" and "Chief Technician", it might be a good idea to actually call them Technicians instead.

Back then we rented all our telecoms kit in the UK from the General Post Office (GPO) later to become BT, and they were responsible for the maintenance of it. Therefore the techies at Stanbridge just did the work in systems. It was only on overseas postings that the comms techies came into their own and looked after the teleprinters, radios etc. Hence their motto "You bend 'em, we mend 'em!"

In the opinion of operators, the techies (or "Nailbenders" as they were also known) way of dealing with any technical fault was to, 'Hit it wiv a big 'ammer.' In fact a techie once told me that the difference between a J/T techie and an SAC mechanic was that the mech knew *where* to hit it and the techie knew *how hard*.

***

Now, during this book you are going to read about a lot of times when I spent time in the NAAFI or some other drinking establishment on camp. The NAAFI as I should have explained earlier stands for the Navy, Army and Air Force Institute. It is a civilian organisation that is attached to the military and in return for having exclusive access on military camps, it guarantees that it will provide services in all forces camps, regardless of how remote they may be. That is why NAAFI staff actually went along on the Task Force to relieve the Falkland Islands. Services provided usually include as a minimum a bar, a shop and sometimes a place to buy food. (Generally known as "a sticky bun bar".)

Over the years, that has expanded on the larger camps to selling such items as TV's, video players and even cars. Originally they were a "not for profit" organisation but during my time in the RAF that changed and they became as money-grabbing as every other similar agency.

(Example: after a UK budget where they put up the tax on cigarettes, the NAAFI at the camp in Germany where I was stationed put the price of their cigarettes up. When I queried why they said, 'Because the price of cigarettes has just gone up in the Budget.'

'Err ... no,' I replied. 'The **tax** has gone up. Your cigarettes are sold **tax-free** so it shouldn't make any difference.' But they'd slapped on a few Marks anyway to increase their profit. Damned robbers.)

What you have to remember is that back in the 70's, 80's, nobody could afford cars except the corporals or junior ranks who had done overseas tours where they had bought one Duty Free. With no bus service at Stanbridge it meant a long walk into town. So we had to find our entertainment on camp.

There was no Internet then; mobile phones hadn't been invented yet so there was no watching vids on You Tube. Each block had a TV room but if everyone wanted to watch Coronation Street and you wanted to watch a documentary on BBC 2, then you'd had it. So you went to the NAAFI.

True, the NAAFI had three TV rooms, one for each channel. (Yes, Dear Reader, we only had three TV channels in those days, BBC 1, BBC 2 and ITV) but if there was a big football match or Top of the Pops on then all the rooms would be tuned to that station and try arguing against it. So you went to the bar.

The NAAFI was the social centre of a camp in those days. This was where you met the people from the other watches who you didn't get to meet at work. They had regular discos, they had a "Pigs Bar" which was like the Public Bar and a Lounge for the more refined WRAF's and airmen.

You didn't have to go over there and get drunk every night (*I'm not saying it didn't happen though*) but it got you out of your room and socialising with others. For many of us this was our first posting and that "being away from home for the first time" got to some people. (*Never bothered me personally but there ya go.*)

As much as I like my privacy and would have liked to have had my own room, there was some sense to having multi-occupancy rooms. The other persons you shared a room with automatically became your new family as you worked, ate and slept with them. (In those days you had a sort of "Duty of Care" for your fellow room-mates, making sure they socialised and didn't just mope around in their rooms. Something I doubt you see much of nowadays, when most have single rooms and are stuck in front of their PlayStations, when not on duty.)

You had a ready-made set of companions to mix with until you sorted out your own group of friends. And it was the same on the other camps I was posted to, for many years to come. All roads lead to the NAAFI.

Fortunately I knew Steve and we used to go over together except for our days off, when he went to see his (then) fiancé, now wife, Margaret who was a WRAF at RAF Medmenham. But I soon had other friends to knock around with.

***

One of the other joys of being stationed at Stanbridge was that Leighton Buzzard down the road had a thing called "Tiddly Tuesdays". This was back in the days when pubs closed at lunchtime and didn't open again until the evening. (*I know, sounds positively Neolithic, doesn't it?*)

Leighton Buzzard had a market day on Tuesdays and had permission for the pubs to stay open all day! So it was quite common for those of us not on duty to go down there and "partake of the local ambience" shall we say. In other words – spend the day getting hammered. Well why not? We were youngsters enjoying ourselves. The world belonged to us. (Stands on table and sings *Tomorrow Belongs to Me* from *Cabaret*.)

Sometimes the more daring would do it straight off nights. I remember one occasion where Steve's, mine and Les' days off coincided and we all went down together. I have vague memories of me collapsed under a tree while watching the two of them play mini-golf.

Ah, happy days!

***

I never went to university (in my day only the brightest and the richest kids did) but you could probably tell that from the way this book is written. So Stanbridge was kind of like *my* university days. First time away from home and in charge of your own life outside work, for many people. At Swinderby and Cosford the discipline was quite rigid. Here, we were out on our own, being treated as adults. Supervised in the accommodation but not closely, bull nights were once a month or less, so we could live how we wanted. So nowadays when I hear my juniors talking about their university days, I always equate it to my time at Stanbridge.

***

We weren't allowed to keep pets in our rooms but that didn't stop some of the guys doing it anyway. One fella across the corridor from me kept a pet snake in a glass case. (*Sorry, I know there is a word for it – probably ends in arium – but even Google can't tell me what it is.*)

He named it Basil. Basil the Snake. If I was in his room I would just avoid looking into that corner where it was. But sometimes you would go into his room and be sitting there chatting and he would casually mention that Basil had escaped from his case and was somewhere in the room. VOOOOOOOM!!! I'd be out of that room like a shot! Sorry, don't do snakes.

One of the techies (I can't remember his name but I'm assuming it was Dobson as everyone called him Dobbo) had a hamster in his room. Had a cage with a wheel in it and everything. I'm surprised there was room for it as habitually Dobbo would dismantle his motorbike and take it up to his room to work on it, so when you went in there would be motorbike parts strewn about the place. (*It takes all sorts.*)

***

Have you ever seen the movie *The Exorcist?* Only horror film that has ever scared me. Went to see it in the nearest big town that had a cinema, which was Luton, with friends. We had a Bull Night in the block that night so I cleaned up my bed space (or pit space as we called it) did my block job early and then went to the pictures.

I don't know if you've seen the film but the first indication that something weird is going on is this "scratching" noise coming from the attic. They think it's rats at first. Then it leads on to more frightening stuff. Very scary, really put the wind up me.

So, anyway, I see the movie, come back to camp and get back to the block about 11 o'clock. Get into bed and turn the light out.

Then I hear this weird scratching noise coming from somewhere. After while I sit up and turn the reading lamp above my bed on, but can't see anything out of the ordinary. Light out. Still this scratching noise.

I listen and it seems to be coming from behind me. As I said earlier, my bed head butts up against the wall between my room and the toilets. So I go next door to the toilets to see what's going on in there. Nothing, no one to seen. Back to bed, scratching continues, it's starting to freak me out a bit.

This goes on for a while, me checking the toilets several times but finding nothing. I'm starting to get quite frantic by now. Wondering whether I should lash the legs of my bed together with my braces to make a cross, when Steve Knight, who is now awake, asks me what the problem is.

Trying to sound cool headed while wanting to scream, *'Get the Padre, we're all going to Hell!'* I tell him that there is this strange noise keeping me awake. Steve, the b*stard, lets me suffer for a bit longer then tells me, 'Look in your overhead locker.'

I nervously open it up not knowing what to expect, only to find Dobbo's hamster, in his cage, running around in his blasted wheel, which was what was making the scratching noise.

Dobbo had nowhere to hide it in his room for the inspection the following day, so they had put it my overhead locker, as I had space – but neglected to tell me.

The B*stards!

Didn't get much sleep that night.

***

Every camp that I had been at up till now, including Stanbridge, people told me, 'This isn't the real Air Force.' Well it sure looked like it to me. I began to get the impression that there was a disused airfield somewhere in Lincolnshire, where half a dozen men sat in a hangar, taking it in turns to polish the single, remaining Spitfire that they had, and they were the *real* Air Force.

***

I nearly made a very nasty mistake while I was at Stanbridge. An MOD place called Porton Down was looking for volunteers to undergo "cold trials". We were told that they would deliberately infect us with the common cold and then give us various treatments to find a cure. They were offering something like £5 a day to everyone who signed up. I don't very often catch colds so I nearly did it for the extra cash but just never got around to doing the paperwork.

Many years later I found out that Porton Down was the place where the UK developed its Chemical and Biological weapons but that programme was shut down in the 50's. They now only develop antidotes to these things. (*So they say.*) But it came to light that in the 70's they were testing out nerve agents on the "cold" volunteers without telling the test subjects. There have been numerous court cases about it since then as many are still suffering the after effects today. I could have been one of them. That was a narrow escape.

***

Now then, the next bit you may not believe but that's up to you. I know what I heard at the time and I'm repeating it here, is all I'm saying.

I was at Stanbridge in 1974. The UK was in a political mess at the time, miners were striking, the country had been on a three day week and a general election had just put a minority Labour government in power, with Harold

Wilson as prime minister. Some people feared that anarchy might break out. From a personal point of view, the government had just announced that they were closing our overseas bases in Singapore and Hong Kong. (*A shame because I would have given my eye-teeth to go to either of those places.*)

Anyway, one day a WRAF told me something interesting. She'd heard a rumour that the senior officers in the services had been considering a military coup to remove the Labour government and restore order to the country. The only reason it hadn't happened was that Lord Mountbatten had said no, he wouldn't lead it.

Of course I found this interesting but didn't believe it for a moment. A military coup in Britain? Never happen. A Military Junta running the country? *It just wasn't cricket.*

So I just put it down to wishful thinking on the military's part, too much drunken talk in the Officer's Mess. Much as I would have liked it to happen, there was no chance.

I've mentioned this to several people over the years, even people who were at Stanbridge at the time, but they don't seem to remember it and look at me as if I've lost my marbles.

Even I began to doubt my memory, but then in the last few years (2015-2016) I started to see more and more reports on the Internet that there *nearly* was a coup in 1974. Various sources on the Internet claim that it did nearly happen. The BBC even aired a documentary *The Plot Against Harold Wilson* in 2006 which mentioned the possibility of that coup.

So, I'm convinced that the rumour was actually true and showed how close we came to a military government. You may think the idea is fanciful but if you don't believe me, go to Google and type in MILITARY COUP

UK 1974 and decide for yourself.

***

When I got to my first posting, I looked around me and I saw that most of the corporals on my watch were 10 or 11 year men who had only just got their tapes up when they were posted to Stanbridge. So I accepted that as the norm. (That's how long it took me.) So fair enough, if it takes everyone 10 or 11 years to make corporal, so be it. Promotion is typically slow in my trade but if that's the system then I will live with that.

What annoyed me in years to come was that some men were getting promoted after 6 or 7 years, when they weren't outstanding or especially good operators, so why were they getting promoted so fast? Okay, we had cr*p promotion in Trade Group 11 but I mean, if it is a cr*p system then it should be cr*p for *everyone*. So how come these guys were bucking the system?

Now I'm not naming names or pointing fingers but there were an awful lot of people that were members of the "Buffs" (The Royal Antediluvian Order of Buffaloes – a downmarket version of the Freemasons.) Or alternatively, a lot of people playing sport for the station, seemed to be getting promoted faster than the rest of us and that's not right. Just saying.

***

After WO George Entwhistle retired they sent us a newly minted WO to be our DSM. Let's call him ... er ... Beach, WO Beach. (Not his real name obviously.)

I had a few run-ins with him over the years, both in the UK and later in Cyprus. Here begins the real story of my habit of nearly always getting on the wrong side of the man in charge. He was supposedly the youngest guy to get promoted to Warrant Officer in my trade, at the time. He had dark hair and a moustache and to my mind was the spitting image of the missing Lord Lucan. I always vowed that if I saw him in Leighton Buzzard, I would phone the police and report a Lord Lucan sighting. Perhaps get him nicked and have to spend a couple of hours in the cells trying to prove his innocence, but the opportunity never presented itself.

I'm afraid I wasn't always a great timekeeper in those days. It wasn't my fault, it was down to the Gorilla, which most of us were familiar with. Apparently there is this Gorilla that, after you've been on a night out, comes around to your room, hits you on the head, pees in your mouth and steals all your money! That's why next morning you wake up with a headache, a bad taste in your mouth and an empty wallet. Because of that Gorilla I would occasionally turn up late for work.

I remember one day walking into the traffic hall late and having to cross to the other side to hang my beret and jacket up. (If I had been older and wiser I'd have hidden them and just breezed in as if I was returning from the toilet.)

Anyway, as I crossed the room, past the dais, the DSM, WO Beach, leaned down to me and said, 'You should have been here at 8 o'clock.'

Me, being young and stupid and never able to resist dropping myself in it, replied, 'Why, what happened?'

Of course I got all the dirty jobs for the next week and deservedly so.

***

The Traffic Hall at Stanbridge.

I met one of the corporals from my watch, Tim Rickards, a few years later. He told me that at one annual assessment time, he and the other Cpls had been tasked by WO Beach to assess all the operators on the watch. Apparently they had ALL given me a decent assessment. Beach couldn't understand it. He asked them, 'Why are you giving Rattigan a good assessment? When you give him a job to do, all he does is argue about it.'

(*True, I was a bit of a Barrack Room Lawyer and thought I knew better than the Cpls.*)

'Yes,' they agreed. 'He will argue but you know that he will then go away and the job will get done. You can rely on him.'

Beach had no answer to that.

***

After I'd been at Stanbridge about a year, The Powers That Be decided that it was high time they either replaced or augmented their crack team of Morse specialists who monitored our Cold War enemy to the East. (I don't know if they took the old specialists out and shot them because they "knew too much" or whether they just needed some fresh blood.)

Anyway, they rounded up all us new bods who were Morse trained and sent us to RAF North Luffenham to be tested for suitability. Nearly everyone I knew from Tel 12 seemed to have been roped in. To cut a long story short, most, if not all of us, were found to be suitable and were told that we would be sent to North Luffenham for pre-employment training and then posted to RAF Digby to do our bit for queen and country.

Unlike the others, I had been a bit slack about taking my SAC exams. Some people accused me of deliberately delaying taking them, in the hope that if I remained an

LAC I wouldn't get posted to North Luffenham. Well, I'll tell you here and now, that's not true. Even I could tell that they were quite willing to take me as an LAC otherwise they wouldn't have even bothered interviewing me. The truth was, at that time I wasn't too worried about promotion, I was earning enough for my simple life style and to me it was like learning to drive, 'Yes, I must get around to that one day, but there's no rush.'

Steve Knight and Les Davidson would also be joining me at North Luffenham. They seemed to accept it with equanimity. Indeed it could be used as a way to advance one's career if you were so inclined. You could either remain in your own trade and hope to eventually break back into the normal comms world or you could remuster to that new trade and have advantages in pay and promotion prospects. But it meant forever being trapped in the world of the "sneaky beaky" or "secret squirrel" as it was known, with subsequent limited posting prospects. Les went over to the "Dark Side" and remustered to that trade, eventually ending up as a Sqn Ldr, whereas Steve was able to rejoin the normal world and went on to become a WO.

Personally I found the thought of sitting in the middle of Lincolnshire, listening to Russian Morse all day, depressing. That's not what I'd joined up to do; I wanted a bit more excitement in my career. Sure I could get better promotion and pay but in a trade I didn't want to do. What was the point? I still wouldn't be happy. I'd signed up for nine years and had served nearly two, so I figured I'd spend my remaining seven years trying to escape from Digby but if I didn't succeed, I would leave the RAF when my time was finished.

First we had to have our security clearances. Being in the communications business we had already been what was then called Negatively Vetted (NV) which cleared us up to Secret. ('Is your grannie a communist? No? Then you're in.') But working at Digby would involve the need for us to be Positively Vetted (PV). This involved interviews by (usually) ex-policemen, ('Are you *sure* your grannie isn't a communist? No? Then you're in.') Giving names of referees who were then interviewed in turn, an in-depth look into your background, who you hang out with, what books you read, etc. etc. All of which I passed.

Eventually the movement orders came out, we were all given our posting dates and that was that. I told everyone that my new theme song (*doesn't everyone have a theme song?*) was going to be "Band on the Run" by Wings. The first verse (which I can't quote here for very expensive copyright reasons) talks about being 'sent inside for ever.' That kind of summed up how I felt about my future at Digby.

North Luffenham was a training school and so worked to a regular schedule, set term times and leave only allowed between terms. I still had a couple of weeks leave owing me for that year and I risked losing them if I went to North Luffenham. Based on that I managed to wangle a couple of weeks off to use up my leave, before posting.

I went home to Coventry and tried to forget about what the future would hold for me when I got back but then a strange thing happened. The last night of my leave, I lay awake in bed and I knew, not just hoped but KNEW that I would not be posted to North Luffenham. I don't know how but I was certain, I would have put money on it. Of course I just put it down to wishful thinking but nevertheless couldn't shake the conviction that my posting was cancelled.

I returned to Stanbridge the next day and as I approached the barrack block, *literally* the first person that I met told me, 'Your posting to Luffenham is cancelled.'

'*What?* Why?'

'Don't know.'

I went back to my room. The rest of my watch were on duty so this wing of the block was empty. I spent the afternoon unpacking, lying on my bed, not seeing anyone to speak to. When it was time I went across to the Airman's Mess for tea and once again, the first person I met said, 'You're posted to Cyprus.'

When my watch came off shift they were able to confirm the truth of it but not the details, I had to wait until I was next on shift before I found those out.

Apparently, thanks to my PV, I had been selected for posting to the Joint Intelligence Section Near East, (henceforth known as JISNE) based at RAF Episkopi in Cyprus. So I was right after all.

As an example of the efficiency of the people who manage the RAF, the Personnel Management Centre (PMC) at RAF Innsworth, AFTER they had told me that I was being posted to Cyprus, they sent me a form to fill in stating the three places, in order of preference, where I would like to be posted overseas. (?) So I filled in Cyprus, Cyprus and … Cyprus!

I told one of the "old sweats" (someone who had been in for a while and knew their way around) and he said I shouldn't have done that, as it would boost their stats on how they had managed to accommodate a person's requests regarding postings. When being audited they could point to someone like me and say, 'See. He wanted to go to Cyprus and we sent him.' It keeps their figures up. Too late to change it by then, I had returned the form.

He was right though, I learnt over the years that they did have underhand ways of meeting their targets, while saving the RAF money. For instance, a favourite trick I noticed of theirs was to promote someone to Cpl or Sgt in the last year of their service. You have to be in a rank for two years to qualify for the pension at that rank. So if you promote a guy to Sgt in his last year:

A) He gets thrown out at the end of the year but PMC are able to claim, 'Oh yes, we made up X amount of Sgts this year.

B) Despite being a Sgt when he left, he only gets a Cpl's pension, thus saving the RAF money.

Sneaky, eh?

Anyway, what did I care? I was escaping North Luffenham and going abroad.

So Yah, Boo, Sucks to you, North Luffenham – I'm off to sunny Cyprus!

The Commcen at Stanbridge.

RAF Episkopi

"Kokinelli and Kebabs"

Arrived 10 February 1975 JSIS HQNEAF (JISNE)

In June 1974 the Turkish military invaded Cyprus. They fought against the Cypriot National Guard and a paramilitary organisation known as EOKA-B. The British wisely didn't get involved in the fighting and simply withdrew into their areas of responsibility, their 2 Sovereign Base Areas (SBA's) and gave humanitarian aid and protection to any refugees that made it onto their bases. There was the Western SBA (based around the RAF bases Akrotiri and Episkopi) and the Eastern SBA (based around the army camp of Dhekelia).

The fighting eventually led to the Turks taking over the northern end of the island, known as the "panhandle" (Cyprus is shaped vaguely like a frying pan). A border was drawn up by the UN, known as the Green Line, which ran across the island cutting it in two. It also ran through the capital Nicosia, splitting it in half.

Now then, most of the world seems to consider the Turks as the aggressor here, especially the Greek and the Greek Cypriots. I've seen posters and maps referring to the "Turkish Rape of Cyprus". But if you look at the facts, it actually looks like the Turks are the good guys in this story.

Greece, Turkey and Great Britain signed an agreement

to keep Cyprus an independent country. One day in 1974, the Greek Cypriots decided that they would carry out their long held desire for "Enosis" with Greece. This is a term meaning Unity. They stated that they were now part of Greece and the Hellenic Republic of Cyprus was declared.

The Turks responded, *quite rightly in my opinion*, by sending troops across to protect the Turkish citizens living in Cyprus. They were just honouring the agreement that they signed with the other 2 parties, maintaining Cyprus' independence. It was the Greek Cypriots that broke that deal.

Anyway, enough politics, on with the story.

When all the fighting kicked off, the Brits brought back the families from any off-base married quarters, onto the SBA's. Also the Turkish Cypriots on the island headed for the British bases, along with many British and foreign tourists including, I have read, Edward Woodward who played Callan in the TV series.

After all the shouting was over and the dust had settled, it was deemed still too dangerous for families in Cyprus, so they were sent home. Only those senior officers who had married quarters on-base could keep their families with them.

Once the families had gone and all the soldiers and airmen were moved into the barrack blocks (which must have been a shock to some who had lived in quarters for years, to be back in the block) and began what is known as an "unaccompanied tour". This normally lasts no longer than 9 months. So, at the beginning of next year many were due to come back to the UK and I was part of the wave of troops that would replace them.

When I first got to Cyprus there were still road blocks on the entrance roads to RAF Episkopi, where I worked. Although you could go down to the local town, Limassol, there was a curfew of midnight when you had to be back on camp. Sadly, the Limassol Wine Festival still hadn't been restarted by the time I left. *Sigh! The hardships we endure for our country.*

***

When I got posted to Cyprus, much to my surprise, I wasn't sent to 12 Signals Unit (12 SU), the major RAF comms centre on the island. Instead I was posted into the Joint Service Intelligence Section Near East, shortened down to JISNE for ease. Run by a Group Captain, I was to work in the Commcen there as my PV clearance was high enough to allow me access to Top Secret and above. (*Oh yes, there's an above but I won't be discussing that side of things.*)

This wasn't the last time I would be posted to an obscure unit while most of my fellow communicators ended up in major centres. It was nice to step outside the normal postings that people of my trade usually filled.

***

When I first got to Cyprus, I spent the first couple of weeks living in transit accommodation at Akrotiri and catching the transport to and from Episkopi every day. (I shall use the term we all knew it by and call it Epi from now on.)

When I moved over to Epi, they put me in a room with all the other JISNE guys. We weren't allowed to be in a room with non-JISNE folk, or let them sleep in our room. The theory being that we may talk in our sleep or accidentally mention something from work in front of outsiders.

I saw a family photograph on one of my room-mates

bedside locker of his kids. He was in his mid-20's I'd say and he had 4 kids!

'You must have started young,' I said to him.

'Well, we had one child, a girl,' he said. 'And we decided to try for a boy. Instead we got triplets!'

I laughed my socks off. So much for "planned parenthood" eh?

***

Mind you there wasn't really anyone else to bunk with as all the 12 SU guys were living down at Berengaria. This was where the married quarters (scalie patch) was, down in Limassol, the local big town. As all the families had been evacuated, the houses stood empty and were vulnerable to vandalism and theft, so they had moved the singlies down there to look after the place.

Berengaria was named after the princess that King Richard I, the Lionheart, had married after England had conquered Cyprus in 1191. As Richard's betrothed, she was on her way to the Holy Land to join him on the Crusades when her ship ran aground off the coast of Cyprus. The ruler of the island threatened her so Richard captured the island and then married Berengaria in a chapel in Limassol, according to Wikipedia. (*As he is generally considered by modern historians to have been gay, she must have found their wedding night a bit of a disappointment.*)

***

Episkopi was a large RAF camp, but not a flying base, everyone flew in and out of Akrotiri. The location was lovely, it was on the cliffs and it had a view directly out to sea. All the barrack blocks and office buildings were constructed so they faced this view. It was great getting up in the morning and seeing the sun shining on the sea, as you made your way to work.

Down below us were several beaches but it meant a long hike down the cliffs or a drive. If you drove, the first place you came to down at sea level was Happy Valley. It had a beach but it also contained the sports pitches and the Saddle Club and was covered by lush, green grass. Rumour had it that it was watered by untreated sewage and that if you got scratched while playing sports there, you had to report to the Medical Centre to get a tetanus jab. Never found out if that was true. It was the only place that I can recall that had green grass, unless you went up into the mountains. Everywhere else was just dry, dusty earth or rock, covered with dry, sunburnt scrub. This type of ground we called "the bondu".

Next up was Tunnel Beach. So called because they had dug a tunnel through the cliff to access another beach further along the coast. This was where the bar and restaurant were and the Sailing Club resided there also.

RAF Episkopi camp contained the Headquarters Near East Air Force (HQNEAF). All the important buildings were in a wired-off compound which contained the headquarters, Air Operations, 12 S U and my section, JISNE.

We were in the same building as Air Ops, they were on the ground floor, the 1st floor was offices and JISNE had the entire 2nd floor to ourselves. It was one long building with a single corridor running along each floor with offices off to each side, with the stairs in the middle of the building. If you came into JISNE through the main door, turned right and walked to the end of the corridor, that's where our Commcen was situated.

Just to be clear, although it was an Intelligence unit, I just worked in an ordinary Commcen, handling signals for the section which was joint military with some civilians, namely the Government Communications Officers. Ordinary Commcen work, it was just the contents of the signal traffic that was highly classified.

The Flt Sgt running the Commcen when I arrived was Ken Pavitt (now no longer with us), a daisie Corporal – at one time it was Brian Mitter but I'm not sure if he was there when I arrived or whether he came later – a technician and 4 shifts of a Cpl and an airman on each shift.

***

We were told that as we worked in an Intelligence section, naturally the queen's enemies would take an interest in us and possibly monitor our activities, waiting for us to do something silly so they could blackmail us. They would love to have got embarrassing photos of me in sexually compromising activities. (*To be honest so would I, but as it turns out we were both sadly disappointed.*)

So we were warned about our habits – don't drink too much, don't go down town on your own, don't get mixed up with "those kind of women" that your mother warned you about, don't take sweets from strange men, etc. etc. This reminder to be careful can be best summed up by paraphrasing one of Lord Byron's poems:

> For we'll go no more a roving,
> So late into the night,
> For the KGB are watching,
> And we'll end up in the sh*te.

***

The working pattern on Cyprus had been designed to give everyone long afternoons off in the sun.

The day shift started at 7 am in the morning and lasted until 1 pm, giving you the whole afternoon to yourself.

For the shift workers, you started your cycle with an afternoon shift of 1pm-9 pm.

Next day you worked 7 am-1 pm, and then came back at 9 pm to do the night shift until 7 am next morning. Then you had 2 complete days off, but as you didn't start back until the afternoon, it was effectively 2 ½ days off.

After a short time when had I learnt the ropes, they put me on shift with a Cpl named Mick. It was a 24 hour Commcen and we only had 1 circuit in and out, directly back to the UK. Here's where things got silly. Communications back to the UK were done via satellite, actually through the Skynet network. *Yes, that Skynet!* The one that's going to come to life and try to kill us all! I'm not kidding, the satellite network for British military global communications really was called Skynet back then. It's obviously where James Cameron got the name.

However, the satellite that Cyprus used to talk back to the UK had not been placed in the correct orbit. It was out of position, so at certain times of the year, it dipped over the horizon during the hours of darkness, so Cyprus had to rely on using High Frequency (HF) radio communication to talk to anywhere.

HF radio by its very nature is unreliable as it depends on bouncing the signal off different ionised layers in the atmosphere which can raise, lower or even disappear completely as the day goes on.

Now this may have been all right if you are using voice or Morse to communicate but when you're using encryption (crypto) gear that relies on maintaining synchronisation with each end, it can cause a world of grief. The crypto gear has to talk backwards and forwards all the time, whether you are actually sending signals or not. Lose that synchronisation for just a second and the circuit drops out, so you have to go through the synchronising sequence all over again.

So Mick the Cpl, or I would spend half the night, constantly phoning systems in 12 SU to ask them to contact the techies at the UK end to attempt re-synchronisation. I say "Mick or I" as we used to split the night between us and get our heads down for half the shift. Everyone did it, it was an accepted practice in the section.

***

Everyone serving overseas gets one free flight to the UK during his tour. This is known as Leave UK Free (LUKFREE). Rumour has it that if you spend your entire tour in the country where you're serving, then you don't have to pay any UK tax, so they give you this free flight to make sure you do set foot back home, so you can't get away with it. (*But that's probably just a nasty rumour, our government would never be that sneaky, would they?*)

Anyway, I claimed my flight and after landing at Brize Norton went to visit friends at Stanbridge and then back to Coventry. Rather than bother with a train journey back to Brize, I asked my (then) brother-in-law, Trevor, if he would give me a lift if I paid for his petrol. He agreed. A few days later he got back to me and asked me if I would like to fly there instead. Apparently, he had a mate called Tony, who had his own plane and was always looking for an excuse to take it somewhere to keep his flying hours up. We would all chip in for the petrol and my share would be £10. I agreed, but I doubted if Brize would allow a civvy plane to land at a military airfield. He said Tony would ask.

Amazingly enough, Brize said yes! I was astonished at first but Tony said that initially they said no, but when he told them he was bringing one of their own to catch a plane to Cyprus they changed their mind. I can see why – just imagine the conversation taking place in Brize Operations Centre.

'Sir, I've got a civvy on the phone asking for permission to land at Brize Norton on Wednesday.'

'Tell him to push off, this isn't the local aerodrome, you know. Why does he want to land here anyway?'

'He says he's bringing in someone to catch a plane.'

'Who's he bringing? What's his name?'

'He doesn't know but he says it's one of ours, going out to Cyprus.'

'Blimey, if it's one of ours and he has his own private plane he must be someone pretty important, like an Air Vice-Marshall or something. Better give him permission then.'

'Okay, sir.'

Boy they must have been surprised when I turned up.

So, come the day when I was due to catch my flight, Tony, Trev and I pile into the plane and fly from Baginton Airfield to Brize Norton. What a novelty that was. How many people can say they flew into Brize in a private aircraft? Normally when I flew during my career, I was a passenger in a VC10 or in the hold of a Hercules and couldn't see much but this time, although I sat in the back seat of a 4 seater aircraft, I could see everything. A great experience.

Anyway, we landed and taxied onto the pan in front of the Air Terminal and they even sent out a Ford Transit to pick us up. When we got out of the plane and talked to the Air Movements people, they asked who was catching the Cyprus plane. 'That would be me, LAC Rattigan.'

'Pardon?'

'Me. LAC Rattigan.'

'Oh … right, better come with us then.'

We all got into the Transit and drove to the Air Terminal. I got led off to the checking-in desk and Trev and Tony went off to Air Ops to pay their landing fees. (Or down to the cells to get beaten with rubber hoses for wasting Air Force time.) I don't know, I didn't see them again before my flight.

So, I got on my plane and flew off to Cyprus.

I can just imagine the conversation that took place in Air Ops next day when they had their review or read the log of the activities of the day before.

'So, we had private plane land yesterday? Must have been someone important. Who was it?'

'Er … LAC Rattigan.'

'Pardon?'

'LAC Rattigan, he was catching a plane to Cyprus.'

Long pause … 'Is that some kind of a joke?'

***

Sometimes the places in the world where the UK has military installations have no married quarters or facilities for families. Or the situation might be a bit dodgy politically, such as Cyprus was at the time.

However, we still need servicemen in those locations, so they were sent out unaccompanied, but they only served a 9 month tour instead of the full 2 ½ or 3 years, such as I did. These short tours were known as "Cook's Tours" as in Thomas Cook holidays.

As an added form of compensation, these "Cook's Tourists" were not charged for food and accommodation on the grounds that they had to maintain a home back in the UK. Fair enough. They ate in the mess for free, so came to be known as "Bean stealers".

These Bean stealers were usually the loudest in complaining about the food in the mess, which, let me remind you, was being paid for them by those such as myself who paid for food. Naturally we used to find this annoying.

'This food is rubbish.'

'Shut up and eat your food. What's your problem? After all you're getting it for free.'

'My wife can cook better than this.'

'Oh, so your wife cooks you a full English for breakfast, a roast dinner followed by desert and pie and chips for tea, EVERY DAY does she?'

'Well no but …'

'Just shut up and eat your foot and be grateful to us singlies who are paying for it.'

***

I've never been very ambitious, never had a plan or a schedule about where I'll be in 5 year's time, that sort of thing. So when it came to getting my SAC exams out of the way, I just dawdled along. It wasn't until FS Pavitt grabbed me by the scruff of neck and shook me (figuratively speaking of course) telling me that I had to get my SAC up, that I knuckled down and got a grip. Thanks for that Ken, I needed that.

As we were all TG 11 together, 12 SU used to allow us use of some of their facilities. The Trade Training guys agreed to let me use their Morse tapes to practice with. Between me and you, they had given me the nod that if I played the game and did actually put in some practice time, they would make sure that I passed my SAC exams.

So, I thought, *you want me to play the game? I can do that.*

They were day workers and knocked off at 1 o'clock. To gain access to the Trade Training rooms after that, I had to go to the 12 SU on-duty WO and ask for the keys. So I made a point of doing this regularly so it would be noticed that I was turning up in my own time and putting in plenty of practice. And I genuinely did practice. If I had to be there for an hour or so to make it look convincing, then I might as well do some Morse practice instead of just staring out of the window. The perfing practice I could do in the section on my night shifts.

Needless to say, word got around that I was in there frequently, and come the day, I passed my exams with flying colours. (Well, I passed anyway.)

According to my service record I was promoted to SAC the 1st of January 1976.

***

Twice a year we used to change our uniforms (around April time) from blues into khaki and then (around October) back into blues. Except for the cooks who wore whites during the summertime. (I once heard an army guy ask a cook why his khakis were white. Think about that one for a moment.)

Every time we had to change over the same thing happened. The Station Commander decided that it was time to change and then the weather would change for a week or so and we would have to suffer the consequences of being wrongly dressed. When we went into blues we would suddenly have a heatwave although the weather had been mild up until then. So we would be sweating like mad in long trousers, ties and jackets.

Conversely as soon as we went into khaki, it would get cold and rain for a week. The choice of whether you wore shorts or long trousers during the day was optional.

(Longs were compulsory after 9 pm.) When it was raining I would wear a raincoat and *long* trousers. Some bozos would insist on wearing shorts, so you would have the ridiculous sight of men wearing raincoats with their skinny legs dangling below, as if someone had sown long socks to the front of the raincoat. Honestly, they looked like flashers but even pointing this out to them was not enough to change their dress sense.

The good thing was that we didn't always have to wear issue clothing. We were allowed to buy shirts and shorts from the NAAFI, which were much better tailored and made from lighter material. It also came in handy later, back in the UK, when I was wearing combat gear as we were allowed to wear khaki shirts instead of the hairy, itchy, green ones we were issued.

***

When I first got out to Cyprus, I found that the Brits stationed there tended to call the locals "Gollies". At first I was disgusted and used to say, 'Come on guys, that's demeaning and insulting. After all, we are guests in their country, blah, blah, blah.' After about 6 months though I understood why the Brits didn't much care for the locals.

Generally the Cypriots had no respect for British women and considered them "sl*gs" (*their words, not mine*) as they could be dating one man for a while, then break up and go out with another. If a Cypriot girl went out on a date they had to be chaperoned. Cyprus was about 50 years at least behind us when it came to female emancipation.

The ones I met that worked on camp were ... shall we say ... lazy? Or shall we say ... "Bone Idle?!" Whenever there was work to do, around the block or tidying the camp, whatever, you would say to them, 'When are you going to do this?'

'Tomorrow, tomorrow. Manyana, manyana, we do it manyana.' (I don't know where they picked up the word Manyana from, I thought it was Spanish and they spoke Greek.) Anyway, their answer was always, 'We do it tomorrow.' They knew that for political reasons they would get paid whether they worked or not.

Another example that used to hack me off was Easter. The Greek Cypriots at our end of the island were all Greek Orthodox which is a Christian religion, so they celebrate Easter. But funnily enough, it was never at the same time as the British Easter. As it is a moveable feast, theirs would always be the week before or the week after ours, meaning they got 2 consecutive, long weekends off on full pay. Strange coincidence that, no?

There is a joke about Cypriots which I think perfectly sums up their attitude and work ethic, and here it is:

A serviceman is stationed in Cyprus and he takes his shoes into the local cobblers to get them re-soled. Shortly afterwards, he is posted home and forgets to collect his shoes before he leaves.

A couple of years later he's posted back to Cyprus and as he's packing his stuff he comes across the cobbler's ticket. He thinks, *I'll take it with me and give it a try, you never know your luck!*

After he has arrived in Cyprus and settled into post, he decides to go back to the cobblers and see if there is a chance that his shoes are still there. He turns up at the shop and says to the cobbler, 'Excuse me, I know this sounds strange but I put a pair of shoes in to be re-soled a couple of years ago. I forgot about them and went back to the UK. Now that I'm back in Cyprus, I wondered if there was any chance you still have them or whether they've been thrown out. I just thought I'd come and ask on the off chance. I still have the ticket.'

The cobbler takes the ticket and ambles off into the back of the shop. He comes out a short while later and tells the guy, 'Yes, we still have them.'

'That's great,' says the serviceman. 'Can I have them?'

'They'll be ready Wednesday,' replies the cobbler.

Enough said.

***

One of the reasons I picked the RAF to join and not any other service, was the fact that compared to the other 2, it was fairly new and didn't have any outdated traditions to uphold.

At Epi we always had a Resident Infantry Company (RIC) stationed there to protect us. They lived and worked in their own little bit of Epi called Salamanca Barracks.

One day I was listening to British Forces Broadcasting Service (BFBS) radio and they were broadcasting the handover ceremony of the Barracks, from one RIC to their replacements.

Apparently, according to the traditions of the incoming lot, the tallest man in the regiment, with a moustache, had to carry an axe during the parade. What the Hell is that all about? Do they choose the tallest man that already has a moustache, even if he is only 5 feet tall? Or do they pick the tallest man and order him to grow a moustache? And what is the axe for?

So I'm glad I'm not party to that kind of nonsense, like the navy shouting, 'Man overboard,' at you if you walk on the grass.

***

Life Lesson No 1

During my life, both in and out of the RAF, I have learnt some valuable lessons. I don't just mean learning a new skill or how to behave, but something so fundamental that it changes your attitude to life and how you deal with it.

At 12 SU there was this SAC, I can't remember if he was a Mechanic or an Operator. Let's call him … Billy Bob. This guy was useless at his job, socially inept, not popular although I used to see him hanging around with people, but I think they may just have been his room-mates that felt sorry for him. In short he was what was known as "A Waste of Rations". If you were in a lifeboat, he'd be the first one thrown over the side.

At that time the 12 SU club was outside camp and you had to track about a half a mile through the bondu to get to it. One night Billy Bob got so drunk that he collapsed on the way back to camp and nearly choked on his own vomit. Someone found him and saved his life.

After that, people were saying that he was so useless that he couldn't even *die* properly! (*Hey, I'm just reporting it, I didn't say it.*)

There was a fad of every unit, or section or watch getting their own T-shirts printed with usually a design and a slogan on it. I saw one that had this incredibly, detailed picture of an eagle (I think it was), really impressive design. Remarkable artwork.

'Who drew that?' I asked.

'Oh, that was Billy Bob. Good isn't it?' came the reply.

And that was when I realised something for the first time. No matter how useless or annoying or "A Waste of Space" someone may appear to be, EVERYONE has some talent that makes them special, if you look hard enough. Everyone has at least one ability that entitles them to their place in this world. I've tried to remember that whenever I deal with awkward people.

***

It was the annual inspection of RAF Episkopi by the Air Officer Commanding (AOC). The camp had been through its yearly wash and brush up in preparation for the inspection, and finally the big day arrived. The first official item on the agenda was the parade for the AOC. The airmen would march past and salute him and then be paraded for inspection. The AOC would wander along the lines of troops and ask the occasional airman the same old questions – 'What do you do?' or 'How long have you been here?' or 'Are you enjoying your time in Cyprus?'

Anyway, the meeting and greeting and drinking of coffee in the Station Commander's office was taking far too long, as the sun blazed down on the airmen who were standing, waiting, on the parade ground, everyone sweating uncomfortably in the heat. The beginning of the parade was late. Fifteen minutes late, thirty minutes late, forty-five minutes late.

At long last, the AOC's car turned up and the parade began. The march past went okay and everyone was lined up to be inspected. The AOC, followed by the Station Commander, strode along the lines checking everyone's turn-out and stopping to have the odd word with the waiting airmen.

Finally he stopped in front of one of the troops and asks, 'And how long have you been here, airman?'

'Forty-five minutes, sir,' came the disgruntled reply.

***

On our days off, if we weren't sunbathing down the beach, we would often spend the afternoon in the 12 SU club and then around tea-time, rather than go to the mess we would round up a few people and go for a meal downtown. The favourite place was to go to was Mahmouts, for a kebab.

The first time I went there I was expecting a "Shish Kebab" like you saw in the movies, all the meat and veg skewered on one long rod (or a sword) and then grilled. Well, that was how they cooked it but they served it up on a plate, or they would bring the sticks to your table and slide the "shish" (pork) or liver cubes onto your plate. A "stick" was a metal skewer with around 5 pieces of meat on it.

A kebab at Mahmouts cost a Cypriot £1 for a 5 course meal (roughly equivalent to a British £1.) I'll say that again because even in 1975 it's incredible – a 5 course meal for a £1! The courses consisted of Cypriot sheftalia sausages, shish, liver, a pork chop and finally chicken (I think that's the order they were served in). And to go with that you could have as much salad and yoghurt as you wanted.

And now here's the best bit … Cyprus is known amongst other things for its wine and spirits industry. As well as the wines, all the spirits on sale on the island are made from the grapes grown on Cyprus.

So they take the grapes and make wine and port and whisky and vodka and brandy etc. etc. out of them. Once they've finished making the wine and port and sherry, they are left with the dregs which are not high enough quality to sell, so what they do is to put it in bottles and GIVE IT AWAY FREE TO ALL THE RESTAURANTS on the island.

The restaurants then GIVE IT AWAY FREE TO ALL THE CUSTOMERS dining in those restaurants.

86

This stuff is called Kokinelli, and because it's made of all the mixed-up dregs it's really potent stuff. Until you became accustomed to it, it would really mess with your head. We used to call it "Looney Juice" or "Electric Soup".

And as long as you stayed in Mahmouts, even if you had finished your meal and were just sitting around chatting, they would keep bringing out bottle after bottle. And all this only cost a £1!

Mind you, by the time I finished my tour the price of a kebab in Mahmouts had gone up to £1.25 and the Kokinelli was only free while you were eating. After that they would charge you 25p a bottle. Outrageous. Downright robbery. Shocking, positively shocking!

**

1 April 1976

Not counting training camps and NATO postings, I was posted to 4 RAF camps during my career. 2 of them were handed over to the army *while I was actually serving* on them. Sorry about that. I guess I must be some sort of jinx.

In 1976 the British government decided to cut back on its overseas military presence by limiting us to Cyprus instead of the Near East. They cut HQ Near East Air Force down to HQ RAF Cyprus HQRAFC. The Joint Intelligence Section Near East got reduced to Joint Intelligence Section Cyprus (JISC) and a Lieutenant Colonel took over our section. RAF Episkopi was handed over to the army and became Garrison Episkopi.

12 SU remained at Epi, so for admin purposes the RAF comms staff in JISC Commcen now came under them. Their Squadron Leader was now allowed access to our Commcen but no one else was.

Funny thing about their Sqn Ldr. The CO of 12 SU is traditionally known as "The Mouflon" as that is the name of the mountain goat which appears on the 12 SU unit crest. The Mouflon who was in charge when I arrived in Cyprus, was a right divvy. Now fair enough, we're supposed to salute staff cars that drive around with a flag flying on the bonnet, to indicate the owner of the car is on board. This 12 SU CO expected everyone on his unit to learn what his *private car* looked like and salute it when he drove by. (If any civvy is reading this, there are no military regulations that stipulate this should be done.)

As soon as he got clearance to enter JISC, he was up there like a shot. I answered the door to him and – me being me – pretended I didn't know who he was. (Well he hadn't been MY CO so there was no reason why I should have known him.)

He went into the Ken Pavitt's office and they were in there for some time chatting. When he left, ignoring me on the way out, Ken told me that the Sqn Ldr had said I needed a haircut. What a surprise, and he didn't even have the guts to tell me himself.

Anyway, much later he was replaced by a new CO who went around telling everyone to call him "Rocky" Thompson out of work, and his wife was as friendly and welcoming as he was. They were a great couple, fitted in a treat with the unit and were regular fixtures down the 12 SU club. Such a difference it made to the morale of the unit.

Epi becoming Garrison Episkopi prompted lots of major changes. A lot of RAF personnel left but as well as 12 SU (who I was now a part of), sections like Air

Operations were still run from Epi, but mostly everything else was taken over by the army.

It was decided that JISC would cease to be a 24 hour section. We would no longer communicate directly back to the UK, but rather across the island to 9 Signals Regiment based at Dhekelia, in the Eastern SBA. They would route all our traffic to us and hold onto it when the JISC Commcen was closed.

What happened was they bricked up all the windows in the section and built a large, steel door at the end of the corridor that led down to our Commcen. The shifts went down to one airman per shift.

So it would work like this – the mornings were covered by the shift worker and the daisies.

The afternoon shift would go on at 1 o'clock and everyone else would leave. When the traffic had died down, mid-afternoon, the shift worker would lock up the section, leave the keys in Air Ops and finish the rest of his shift over at 12 SU.

The night shift would report for duty at 12 SU and then approaching midnight, would sign out the keys from Air Ops on the ground floor, let himself into the section and open up for business. (I can't count the number of times I would try the combination on the steel door and panic when it wouldn't open. Eventually I would always get in though.)

Of course one man working on shift by himself in a secure location – especially given that sometimes we had to climb behind the equipment racks and switch cables between live equipment – wouldn't be allowed by H&S inspectors nowadays. Back then no one seemed to care if you got zapped or not. Plenty more SAC's to replace you. Even if I could have alerted someone to my plight, there was no way they could have got through the security in time to save me.

There was one advantage to working on your own though. Obviously with no windows and the hot, Cypriot sun beating down on it all afternoon, the heat really built up in the building. When you came in at night, even though it was near midnight the place was stiflingly hot. It was a real pleasure to turn the air conditioning on full blast, take your shirt off and walk round half-naked, which you couldn't do down at 12 SU.

The section was spooky at night though, when you were in there on your own. As I said, our Commcen was at the end of a corridor which was closed off by a stable-door (the top half could open separately from the bottom). I presume in bygone days people would ring the bell and Commcen staff would open the top half of the door and accept the signal. During my time there no one seemed to bother about this and everyone just walked in and out. We all had security clearances up the Yin Yang, so it didn't really matter.

Anyway, one night I had just opened up the section but not yet turned on the equipment, so it was still deathly quiet. Then I heard footsteps coming down the corridor towards me. I knew it couldn't be Air Ops as they were on the ground floor and I knew from experience that I couldn't hear them.

Heart in mouth, I locked the door, grabbed something heavy and bent down to look through the gap between the top and bottom of the door, AND THERE WAS NO ONE THERE but I could still hear the footsteps, which arrived at my door and then stopped!

After about 5 minutes I mustered the nerve to unlock the door and go outside, well I had to check if we had an intruder, didn't I? Never found anyone, fortunately.

I reckon that as the building was so quiet, I must have been hearing the policeman doing his security check on the *floor below*, and I had heard his footsteps echo as he walked along the corridor beneath mine. At least I hope that's what it was and that's what I told myself every time after that, when I thought about the incident.

Still, after that, even though I was *supposedly* in there on my own, I always kept the Commcen door locked.

***

Another consequence of handing everything over to the army was that all the 12 SU lads came back to live on Epi, as the quarters in Berengaria were taken over by them.

Unfortunately all the WRAF's moved out of the block and went over to Akrotiri. C'est la vie.

I knew one of the 12 SU lads, Mick Smith, from Stanbridge so through him I got to know all the other guys at the unit. I even met my twin brother! One of the J/T's named Jim Pottle was born on the same day as me. I don't mean we had the same birthday, it was actually the same day. We used to say we were twin brothers, although I was the oldest as I was born at 7.30 am and he was born around mid-day. I don't know if you believe in your astrological sign determining your character but he and I were alike in so many ways, sense of humour, taste in women, it was incredible. Needless to say we got on great.

In 1976 The Powers That Be decided it was safe for families to live in Cyprus as long as it was in the on-base quarters. Later that year Jane West, who I had known at Stanbridge, came out to Cyprus. She had married one of the techies at Stanbridge, Steve Smart, and accompanied him on his posting. Unfortunately she had had to leave the RAF to join him as there was no spot for her at 12 SU. So Steve and Jane Smart, lived at Akrotiri and became regular members of the 12 SU social life. Sadly they're no longer together but I'm still in touch with both of them to this day.

***

As I said earlier, the 12 SU club was in a Nissan hut some distance away from camp, and a visit involved a long trek through the bondu to get there. Then someone pulled a stroke and they managed to get a site on camp, 5 minutes' walk away from my block.

This was a godsend as the NAAFI, which up till then had been almost exclusively RAF, had started to be used by the army more and more as they populated the camp. And that always means trouble. It was nice to have a place to go for a drink on camp where you didn't have to keep watching your back.

There was a nice bar, staffed by 12 SU volunteers, and a patio out the back. Occasionally they showed films there. They even got a regular kebab man in. He would sit there by his fire and you could order a full kebab in a chapatti or just a stick. (The Cypriots called it a chapatti but it was actually just Pitta Bread.)

They only charged 50 Cypriot mills, (a shilling or 5p) a stick. They used to cover the pork in lemon juice and salt every time they turned it over on the spit. If you've never tried that, I recommend you do it on your next barbecue. Lemon juice and salt on any pork you're cooking, it's delicious. (*My mouth is watering now just typing about it.*) Or in your chapatti you could have the little Cypriot sausages called "sheftalia".

***

Thanks to the 12 SU club I nearly became a "legend in my own lunchtime".

The club acquired a pool table. It was very popular and people were queuing up to play on it, so they adopted the usual pub rules – when some people are already playing, another person will put a coin on the table to pay for the next game with the winner. They play the game, the winner stays on and the loser walks away or puts down another coin and waits his turn again.

As there were so many people wanting to play, they decided that to be fair, everyone would have to play doubles during the busy periods, to give more people a chance.

Now I turned out to be quite good at pool. I know I'm blowing my own trumpet here but before I joined up I was a member of a Snooker club and played regularly. For 2 years before I joined I played practically every lunchtime and every night, so I was pretty damned good, even though I say so myself. Alas, when I joined the RAF, every time I tried to play snooker in the NAAFI the cues were bent or some of the balls were missing or the cloth on the table was ripped, etc. and I just gave it up. A short time playing on the 12 SU pool table and it all came back to me. Particularly as the table is only about a third of the size of a snooker table.

As we had to play doubles I teamed up with one of the techies, Marty Biddle, if I remember correctly. We were practically unbeatable together and would stay on most of the night. The funny thing was that before that we didn't even really know one another. We just watched each other play in singles, had a few games against each other and decided that we wanted the other to be our doubles partner.

Anyway, 12 SU decided to have a pool tournament. Singles only, straight knockout, you got beat you were out!

I signed up of course and made my way through the

competition. Even Jane entered as she had become quite skilled at pool and made it to the semi-finals before getting knocked out by the guy who I would face in the final. Shame, I would have loved to have met her in the final. (*And then trounced her!*)

So, I made it through to the last game of the competition and was up against this one guy, I can't remember his name so I'll call him Eric, who I had beaten *every, single time* I had ever played against him.

Now, I didn't get cocky and think I had it in the bag, but I had to acknowledge that it did give me a psychological advantage over him.

They made a big night out of the final, moved the pool table out onto the patio where they had flood lights and arranged all the chairs around it. It was to be just the one game, no best of 3 or anything. So we played.

I sank all of my balls and was chasing the black while Eric still had 2 balls to go. It was my shot and I weighed up my choices:

Option 1. I didn't have an easy shot on the black so I could keep pushing it around the table, playing safe, while Eric tried to sink his other balls, BUT he might do that and get a chance to sink the black before I did.

Option 2. From where the black sat, I could try for a double off the cushion into the centre pocket. It would be a really flashy shot if I pulled it off, but what a finish to the game! People would be talking about it for months. And I would go down in history as the 1st winner of the 12 SU Annual Pool Competition.

There was one small snag though … judging from the angle I would have to hit the black … there was the *tiniest, smallest, wee-est* chance that the white would also go into the corner pocket. It was one of those 50/50 things, it might go in or I could get lucky and it would just rattle in the jaws of the pocket, there was no way of telling. That bit would be in the lap of the Gods.

Being cocky, I decided to go for the flashy ending. I lined up the cue ball, took the shot and true to plan the black bounced off the cushion, doubled back to my side of the table and into the centre pocket, without even touching the sides. The crowd roared and leapt to their feet but I put my hands up and said, 'Wait, wait,' and pointed to the white as it slowly rolled down the table and into the corner pocket, which lost me the game.

Of course, I felt like smashing the cue over Eric's head and tipping the pool table over but I calmly put my cue down, walked round the table and shook his hand, noble and dignified in defeat. Eric won the competition, got the prize money and the glory. My prize money was half the amount I would have got for winning. Oh well, it's just a game I suppose. My one small consolation was that *I had lost* the match, Eric hadn't *won it*. So he still hadn't beaten me.

***

Have you ever seen that thing in movies or on YouTube where two men are going to have a fight – one of them starts leaping around, showing how agile and tough he is by doing handstands and press ups and all the Kung Fu poses, then the other guy steps up and knocks him out with a single punch? I saw that happen for real once. It would have been funny except for the fact that it happened in the middle of a somewhat scary incident.

I've never been one for fisticuffs (*I'm a lover, not a fighter*). During my time in the RAF I was never in any fights. I've been hit a couple of times because I "talked" when I should have "listened", but they never went any further and I've never had to throw a punch at anyone.

Sometimes however, when one of your own is about

to get beaten up, you have to stand with your mates, in the hope that a show of strength will deter the opposition. Always worked I'm glad to say.

There was one such time in Cyprus. Before the base got handed over to the army, virtually the only soldiers we had at Episkopi stayed in their own barracks and we never saw them, presumably they had their own NAAFI too. Once RAF Episkopi became Garrison Episkopi, we started seeing more army guys using our facilities, including the NAAFI.

One night the NAAFI disco was on. As there were no women to speak of, only WRAC's but it would be unwise to start hitting on them and our WRAF's now lived over at Akrotiri, we left the army guys to the disco and we frequented the bars on the lower levels.

Suddenly, one of our guys came in and told us that a RAF guy was in the disco and the army were getting uppity. If we didn't get our guy out soon, he was going to get a hammering. So we rounded up a load of RAF guys, piled into the disco and got our guy out without any trouble. There was quite a few of us and it looked like we had deterred the army from doing anything stupid. Guess not.

They followed us down the stairs and out onto the patio area. We stopped and faced them and they stood there taunting us. It was like a scene out of Braveheart, the way the two sides were lined up, waiting for the action to start. A Mexican Standoff. There were about 10-15 on each side, so it could turn into a major scrap.

Suddenly, someone who had been watching too many Bruce Lee movies, leapt out from the army guys into the "No Man's Land" between us and went into his Kung Fu pose. You know the one, knees bent, one arm forward and the other close to his chest, ready to strike!

There was a pause of about 2 seconds then this RAF

lad, a Geordie, stepped forward and SMACK! decked Bruce Lee with one punch. Both sides stood there gobsmacked. The army guys started scratching their heads and looking at each other, 'That wasn't supposed to happen. What do we do now?' And while they waited for someone with a higher IQ to make a decision, the RAF guys slowly backed away and disappeared into the night.

***

Talking about the army and fisticuffs, The Western SBA covered 2 RAF camps, Akrotiri and Episkopi. The nearest big town was Limassol which was about 15 miles away from either of them. So often after we had dined at Mahmout's in Limassol, we would head on into the discos to carry on drinking.

Now, generally RAF bods are not the "scrappy" type. Occasionally there would be punch ups with the local youths who resented us, but very rarely fights amongst ourselves. So in the discos as they were mainly populated with guys and gals from the 2 RAF camps, there wasn't much trouble.

When Epi became Garrison Episkopi, the army lads would pile into the discos in Limassol and spend all their money getting drunk on the cheapest drinks they could (usually Brandy Sours with Cypriot brandy). Perhaps they were more day workers than us 12 SU guys who were mainly shift workers, but they used to flood the discos at the weekends, which is when the trouble would start. The army lads would fight anyone, RAF or locals, and when there was no one else to fight, they would pick on each other. (And the army officers we had in JISC were proud of that. Claimed that it showed "good fighting spirit". Idiots.)

So we shifties, to whom one day is the same as the

next, would confine ourselves to going downtown during the week. The place was quieter than at weekends and as it was full of RAF guys there was very little trouble.

Sometimes, one would stay the rest of the night in the disco. (Once you're drinking and the windows are shut, you lose all sense of time.) It was a weird feeling to stagger out of a disco thinking it was 2 or 3 o'clock in the morning and find that it was daylight outside. This became known as a "Dawn Patrol".

One of the lads went home on leave and mentioned a Dawn Patrol in front of his parents and his dad asked, 'You don't still do Dawn Patrols, do you?'

'No Dad, it's er ... oh, never mind.'

***

One day I went down the bar after morning shift. It was standard practice, afternoon in the bar, sleep later until it was time to go to work for nights at 9 o'clock. When it came time to go to work that night, I regretted that afternoon's visit. I wasn't drunk, that had worn off, but I had a bad head. It was a Friday and I knew that we would be getting all the end of week intelligence summaries and these things go on for page after page, average length about 6 pages, and the traffic goes on into the "wee small hours" so I knew it was going to be an unpleasant night.

So I thought maybe I could forestall some of the grief by going straight to JISC instead of 12 SU and opening the circuit early. To be honest, there was never any real work for the JISC operator to do on shift at 12 SU. He could never be guaranteed to be there – if JISC Commcen was busy for example – so he could never be given a "proper" job, so he ended up just filling in. Rather than sit around playing cards until midnight, I figured I'd open up early.

So I went into Air Ops and signed out the keys to the section. When I got upstairs, I phoned 12 SU and told them what I was doing. Then I phoned systems and requested they contact 9 Sigs and ask them to open the circuit early. Now all these things like getting the keys from Ops and opening the circuit were all actions that have to be logged by various people, so they were all on record, as was the time they occurred. We opened the circuit and I spent the night receiving traffic.

I'm not sure when, but I think it was when we returned to work after our 2 days off, I was informed by FS Pavitt that WO Beach wasn't happy with me. (Yes, that WO Beach from Stanbridge. He also got posted to Cyprus and ended up in charge of the equivalent 12 SU shift to mine.) He reckoned that I should have contacted him and asked for his permission first. (Okay, maybe he had a point.) But apart from that slip in etiquette, I didn't see that I had done any harm. No one could accuse me of skiving, as I said it was a matter of record that I had been in the section, the circuit was open so therefore I was working, and if 9 Sigs had been asked I'm sure they would have confirmed that there was a regular Friday night, heavy traffic load. SO I HAD BEEN WORKING!

Ken Pavitt said Beach wanted to see me. I went down to 12 SU and entered his office. I knew I was in trouble so I played it by the rules and stood to attention in front of the desk where he was sitting and I stared at the wall above his head.

He tore me off a strip, 'You should have done this, you shouldn't have done that, etc.' when he finished he sat there looking up at me, waiting for a response. I continued to stare silently at the wall above his head.

By this time I was getting a little peeved. As I said, I wasn't skiving and I could prove that I'd been working that night. My only fault was not asking him first.

So when he asked me, 'Well, aren't you going to say anything?' the Devil in me made me reply, 'You made a statement, sir, you didn't ask a question.'

True, and factually correct but that didn't mean that I won. He demanded I tell him what happened, so I related the story to him. I told him if he didn't believe any of it we could contact the relevant people and they could prove I was telling the truth.

This kind of flummoxed him, as really I was guilty of nothing but that breach of etiquette, which put me in the right. However, he was a Warrant Officer, so that put me in the wrong. He eventually sent me away with a warning to watch my step.

I think it was the next day, Ken Pavitt came to me and said, 'The Warrant still isn't happy with you and he wants you to go down and apologise to him.'

I told him the same thing that I'd said to a few people by then, that if I had to apologise for going to work and doing my job, then I think it would be time to quit that job. He prevailed on me to go down and do it, so we could all move on with our lives, so I went down to 12 SU and into Beach's office. By this time I was as angry about it as Beach was.

'FS Pavitt tells me that I should come down and apologise to you sir, so here I am. I realise that I offended you and it won't happen again.' You notice that I didn't *actually* say sorry to him (I have my pride too) but even I wasn't too dumb to realise that the ice was getting thinner and thinner and it was going to crack shortly, so I should head for safer ground.

He gave me the, 'Let this be a lesson to you,' speech or some such and sent me on my way. After that I stayed out of his path as best I could for the rest of my tour. I was learning the lesson about 'let sleeping dogs lie.'

Mind you, I used to enjoy winding him up when I got

the opportunity to come out on top.

First I must give a quick recap on how signals were handled in my day. I'm not giving anything classified away, as this purely relates to the speed with which they are handled and nothing to do with their security.

As I said earlier in the book, when a person writes out a signal, he decides the precedence i.e. how fast it is to be handled throughout the system, based on the nature of the signal. There were four precedences Routine, Priority, Immediate and Flash! (*A-ah, he'll save every one of us.*)

Anyway, this one time, during the day one of my customers in JISC (the Government Communications Officer Cyprus, actually) had been receiving a lot Flash traffic regarding something that was going on in that part of the world, but not directly relating to Cyprus. So before knocking off for the day he had instructed the JISC Commcen operator (who happened to be me) that if any Flash traffic came through relating *to that particular subject*, it could wait until morning, he did not want to be called out as there was nothing he could do about it. In due course JISC shut down for the day and I went off shift.

That evening, I came back on shift and was working in the 12 SU Commcen when WO Beach called me into his office, telling me that the Commcen at 9 Sigs was on the phone and wished to speak to the JISC operator.

Now then, I should point out that under certain circumstances someone can delay the receipt of a signal by giving the other end "Permission To Hold" (PTH) that signal until a more opportune time. Of course it's usually only officers and Warrant Officers that have the clout to do that sort of thing.

In WO Beach's office I picked up the phone. 'JISC operator here.'

'We've got a Flash signal for you. Can you open up

the circuit and we'll send it to you.'

'Is it the same subject matter that we've been receiving signals about, all day?' I asked.

'Yes,' they confirmed.

'In that case hold onto it until we open up at the normal time.'

'Are you sure?'

'Yes. My customer has instructed me that he's not interested in these signals. He doesn't want to be bothered with them out of hours, so it will just sit in his in-tray until morning.'

'Fair enough, we'll see you at midnight. Bye.'

'Bye.'

I hung up the phone and looked at the WO. The blood had drained from his face and he was gobsmacked. 'You're … you're just an SAC, you can't give Permission To Hold on a Flash!'

I repeated what I'd said on the phone about GCOC's instructions.

'But … but!'

'It's only going to sit there until morning, so what's the point?'

He finally had to concede the sense of my actions and what was more galling for him, he had no say whatsoever over the JISC Commcen, so he couldn't even *order me* to open up and receive the signal, so he had to give in. Oh did I have a smirk on my face when I went back into the ordinary Commcen. Petty of me I know but we have to take our victories where we can.

***

As I was now part of the 12 SU crowd, they began taking more of an interest in me and what I did up in the JISC Commcen. I told them, truthfully, that it was just an ordinary terminal Commcen, and we just did a normal Commcen job but the signals traffic had a higher security level and we only had 2 customers – JISC and GCOC.

Of course they never really believed me, so I sometimes played on their suspicions about what I did. I don't mean I pretended to be secret agent or anything, but I suggested that we did more than just watch the "other side".

As well as communications people at 12 SU we had other trades such as Admin clerks and suppliers. I remember 2 suppliers, Clive and Bobbie. One time Clive pointed out a WRAF in the bar and said he knew her from his last camp.

Apparently they were both at RAF XXXX and she dated a bloke, who I shall call Mickey Mouse. He had an old, clapped out car, can't remember what make, let's say it was a Hillman Avenger. It was broken down and permanently parked outside Clive's block and he could see into the car from his room. After the NAAFI had finished, Mickey Mouse and said WRAF would often climb into the back of his car and make out. Naturally Clive, being a gentleman, drew his curtains.

One time I was talking to that WRAF and just for a laugh I said, 'I was reading your file the other day, quite interesting.'

'You've got a file on me?'

'We've got files on everybody – we're an Intelligence section. What do you think we do? We have to be sure you're not the type to sell secrets to the enemy.'

'I don't believe you. Okay then, what did it say?'

'Erm … let me see … oh yes, when you were at RAF XXXX you went out with a bloke called Mickey Mouse. And you used to use the back seat of his car to get "familiar" with each other. A Hillman Avenger wasn't it?'

You should have seen the expression on her face.

I let this run for a couple of weeks and interestingly during that period I had several WRAF's sidle up to me and furtively ask, 'Have you seen my file? What does it say in it?'

'I'm sorry, I haven't read everybody's. I don't have open access to them, I just grab a look when I can. I haven't seen yours,' I would explain.

I may be wicked but I'm not malicious, so after a few weeks I 'fessed up and told everyone that we didn't have files on anybody – as far as I was aware – and I was making it up based on some gossip I'd heard. That seemed to appease them, although I noticed that people were a bit circumspect about what they said around me, for a while.

***

During my time in Cyprus the RIC, who were there to defend us, was for a time the Royal Irish Rangers. Some of their officers were very into the Horse Club, so the soldiers of the company were detailed to clean out the stables and look after the horses.

They use to exercise the horses by riding them up and down the beach. One day one of these idiots was riding the horse along the beach right where my mates and I were sunbathing. Every time he went past he sprayed us with sand.

One of my friends, I think it was Mick Smith, looked up, saw the soldier was on his own and said, 'Oh look, it's the Lone Ranger.' (*Ha, Ha!*)

***

During this period of my life I was just an aimless young

airman, who didn't care too much about his future. I was earning enough money to fund the lifestyle I enjoyed, I was living abroad in Cyprus with its bars, restaurants and beaches, so why should I worry?

I must admit I was a bit careless about responsibility during that period of my life. I would often be late to work, but fortunately it wasn't the end of the world as there was the other shift person to relieve the night shift. But I still felt guilty about it and I swear I didn't do it deliberately.

But when we went over to a single person on a shift, it meant that if I slept in at the weekend, the night shift had to wait until I turned up before they could go to bed. In my defence, I didn't just blow it off and say, 'Yeah, so what?' On the contrary, I was fully apologetic and would agree with whatever they thought was fair, to make it up to them, usually letting them do the same to me, or coming in early to relieve them on shift, whatever it took to pay my dues.

Basically I was bit unreliable. I even remember sleeping in for nights once! I've got a feeling that this was the second time I was charged in my career. I told you I got charged at Cosford at the AOC's parade and I'm sure I got charged a second time during my career but I honestly don't remember where or when. It would make sense that it was this time in Cyprus, when I was still a bit flaky and hadn't learned to take responsibility for myself. I don't remember doing Jankers so maybe I just did extra shifts in the Commcen on my days off.

Eventually though I gave myself a serious talking to, bought a second alarm clock and solved that problem. Never been late again for anything since (unless of course it was beyond my control).

***

Eventually Ken Pavitt finished his tour and went home. In his place we got Flight Sergeant Danno. (*By the way, these phony names are all private jokes, I don't expect you to get them.*)

He was okay as a FS but he was a sports fanatic who spent most of his spare time playing Squash. To him, anyone who spent less time playing sport than he did, was a slacker.

Now I've never been much of a one for organised sport, particularly team games. I preferred to get my exercise walking through the bondu, in the hills around Epi. It's a good way to keep fit, up and down hills, and to get a tan, take your shirt off and walk around in the sun. It beats just laying on a beach down in Happy Valley, you get bored with that eventually.

However, despite my not liking sport, there was one time when my watch compadres at 12 SU were desperate for men to help make up the team at some football competition, so I let them talk me into playing for them. I did my usual trick of running up and down the wing, praying that the ball didn't come my way. But I did my bit by being there.

Come assessment time that year, our Danno writes in my annual assessment – and this is a direct quote as I applied to the RAF and under the Freedom of Information Act was given photocopies of all my F6442's (annual assessment form) and this is what he wrote that year:

'He has no interests in sports, participating or as a spectator.
'He spends most of his off duty time in the Unit club ...'

(*Don't beat about the bush Flight Sergeant – say what you really think!*)

Now okay, fair enough, it was true BUT he could have phrased in a slightly less career damaging way, such as, 'This man is not the sporty type, he prefers to enjoy the social aspects of the unit more.' Or some such.

But that year God was smiling on me because when it came time to see the next person up the reporting chain, the Flt Lt, he read Danno's remark then said to me, 'Well that's not true. I've seen you play football for the unit. I'll change that.'

'*Thank you, thank you, thank you,*' I shouted inwardly. See, there are some good officers.

Just not that many.

***

During my tour I began to hear about this place I never knew existed, 38 Group, Tactical Communications Wing. It sounded a magical place. Made up of telegraphists and techies, everyone wore combats and carried guns and behaved like soldiers. They operated radios out of the backs of Land Rovers and went on exercise to exotic locations all the time. It sounded fantastic!! I wanted some of that, so when it came time to nominate my 3 choices for posting, I put that as my first choice.

Someone in PMC must have been looking the other way that day, and I actually got my posting of choice. Yes, I was shocked too. So there I was, heading for TCW at RAF Brize Norton.

***

Any group of people working in the same occupation will eventually develop their own slang, as shorthand to refer to situations and occurrences unique to their environment. In the Forces, many of them are borrowed from the local languages of the country that a serviceman finds himself in – 'Plonk' for example comes from mispronouncing 'Blanc' for white wine, in France during the 1st World War, 'Dhobi' is Indian for washing and 'Dhobi dust' was invented to mean washing powder, 'Bint' is Arabic for girl/female and so on.

Some are contractions of several words. The most important date in an overseas tour (whether you want to leave or not) is when does it end and when do I go home? So that date is your "Goes home" date, or your "GAZOMIE date". No matter how pleasant an overseas tour is, it is always welcome to go back home and see your family and friends and get back to the life you're familiar with. Some people are eager to go and make up a chart to count down the days until they fly, called a "Chuff Chart" and each day is eagerly ticked off the calendar. Many people have leaving do's which are known as "GAZOMIE do's".

Of course when your GAZOMIE date approaches there are certain things you must do to prepare. Will all my stuff fit into my suitcases? So a couple of weeks before, you would have a "Practice Pack", often to find out that, 'No, it won't all fit in my suitcases.' So then you have to start asking yourself the hard questions. Do I really need this bazouki? What about this Hookah pipe? How about this Greek wall-hanging depicting ancient, sexual rituals? So you have to start giving stuff away to get within your weight restrictions.

You ask around the block, 'Does anyone want this?' Everybody likes a freebie (see there's another bit of slang) so invariably someone says, 'GIZZIT here, I'll have it.' (Give it here, I'll have it.) So, people leaving the country is always a good time for getting GIZZITS and it came to be used for anything you got free, regardless of the source. "Buckshee" is another word for getting something for free.

***

One of the things I used to hate about Station Warrant Officers (SWO's) is that they had complete tunnel vision about how the RAF worked and wouldn't accept that it wasn't all about them and their little empires. They simply couldn't understand the fact that things went on outside their areas of responsibility and therefore they could not control.

On August 3 1977 the spiritual leader of the Greek Cypriots and President of the Republic of Cyprus, President Archbishop Makarios died. The Greek half of Cyprus (where our bases were) went into mourning for three days and everything shut down. No shops, no bars, cinemas, etc. were open. And that included barbers.

I was just about to leave Cyprus at the end of my tour and go on two weeks disembarkation leave when this happened. Admittedly, I was in need of a haircut but as everywhere had shut up shop, I couldn't get one, so I thought I'd get it whilst on leave, before reporting to my new unit. The SWO at Akrotiri saw things differently though.

Ever since Episkopi had been handed over to the army, we were mostly administered from Akrotiri with just a small General Duties office at Episkopi, headed by a Flight Sergeant, to handle day to day stuff. So I had to begin my clearance procedure at Akrotiri.

On the day of my flight home, which was on a Monday so I couldn't have done it the day before, I had to travel to Akrotiri (some fifteen miles away, about half an hour's drive) begin clearing there, travel back to Episkopi to have my security debrief by the head of the Intelligence section, clear from Episkopi, pick up my gear and then travel BACK to Akrotiri, finish clearing there, then catch my flight at 1 o'clock, which meant checking in around an hour before that. Bit of a rush but do-able if there weren't any hiccups.

I picked up my blue card (clearance form) from the General Office at Akrotiri, went to a couple of places for signatures and then arrived at the Guardroom. A quick signature by them and I could have been on my way but no – the SWO saw me, took my card and led me into his office.

'Your hair is a disgrace. I'm not signing your card until you get it cut.'

'But sir, I haven't been able to get a haircut. It's not my fault; all the barbers were closed last week because of Makarios dying. Besides, I don't have time, my flight is at 1 o'clock and I still have things to do at Episkopi. I have an appointment at 11 o'clock for a debriefing from the head of the Intelligence section and I can't miss that.'

(*Now this is where the man first begins to show signs of insanity, in my opinion. After my last statement he then goes on to say ...*) 'Well, he'll have to wait.'

'Sir, he is a Lieutenant Colonel. He's not going to wait around for any old SAC. Also it's my security debriefing, if I don't have it they probably won't even let me off the island!'

'Nevertheless, I insist you have a haircut before you leave Cyprus.'

(*Now at this point he had clearly gone over the edge of reason. Fair enough, if I was going straight to my next camp I could understand he didn't want me showing up looking scruffy as it would reflect on him and his camp, but I was going on two weeks disembarkation leave – which everyone gets when they return to the UK, so he couldn't deny that he knew about it – so if I turn up at the next camp after two weeks, looking smart ((and short haired)) where's the problem?*)

At this point I gave up on any pretence of deferring to one's superiors, even when they're being ridiculous, and just plain told him the truth.

'Well in that case, sir, I'm afraid that you're going to have to call Air Movements and tell them that I won't be on that flight, because it is physically impossible for me to go and queue up for a haircut, then get back to Episkopi to do the things there, then get back to Akrotiri to catch my plane, by 1 o'clock. It just can't be done.' It was about 10 o'clock by this time.

(*I thought B*gger It! If I'm going to get into trouble for missing my flight, with possible severe consequences, due to the intransigence of one of my superiors, then it's up to my superiors to sort it out. If the SWO forces an SAC to miss his flight, then the SAC should not have to take the rap for it. Anyway, as I watched his face I could see his planet slowly orbiting nearer and nearer to what the rest of us normal people call "The Real World" as he realised that his bluff had just been called.*)

'Very well then, airman. But I want you to get a haircut as soon as you get back to the UK!' He signed the blue card and gave it back to me.

'Yes, sir. Of course, sir. The first thing I'll do when I get back, sir,' I grovelled. (*I did realise what a close escape I'd had, so I wasn't going to blow it by giving him any lip. I knew how close to the edge I had come. You don't very often get the opportunity to face down the SWO and live to tell the tale.*)

When I got back to Episkopi the FS in the GD section asked me, 'What did you do to the SWO? He rang up here demanding I charge you.'

I told him the story and as he was a decent chap, he told me, 'I managed to calm him down by saying that there wasn't time to charge you as you were on your way to the plane. I swore that you'd promised to get your haircut as soon as you got back.'

So that's why I think that Station Warrant Officers are small minded individuals who believe their own press about how important they are, and why I've never had any time for them since. I went back to the UK, had two weeks leave (including haircut) and then went to join my new unit, 38 Group Tactical Communications Wing (TCW) at RAF Brize Norton. And guess what? Almost the very first person I met walking to work on my first day was the SWO of RAF Brize Norton, who gave me a b*ll*cking for being improperly dressed! (*What's that they say about Karma?*)

TACTICAL
COMMUNICATIONS
WING

"Lurking within tent"

Arrived 9 August 1977 38 Group, Tactical
Communications Wing, RAF Brize Norton

As far as I remember it was RAF MT that took me from
Stanbridge to Brize Norton to catch my flight to Cyprus.
When I came back on leave from Cyprus I first went to
Stanbridge to visit, so I wasn't aware of the complexities
of getting to Brize Norton from Coventry by train.

Brize is half way between Oxford and Swindon, each
is about 15 miles away. My joining instructions had told
me to go to Swindon railway station, so I assumed that
was the nearest station to Brize. From Coventry that is
not an easy trip. I had to change at Crewe (I think it was)
and the trip took around 5 hours. Once you get to
Swindon (I think there was a Movements office there that
dealt with all the families on their way to Brize, for their
overseas flights). They tell you there is no regular public
transport to Brize, just an irregular coach service run by
Carterton Coaches, so inevitably there was a wait for that,
then a half hour journey.

(Although the camp is called RAF Brize Norton, Brize
Norton is actually just a small village near the end of the

runway. The town that has grown up around the camp and where all the married quarters are situated is actually Carterton – or Cartoon Town as it was known.)

Trusting that the RAF knew what they were talking about, I suffered this soul-sapping trip back and forth to Coventry a couple of times during my first year, before someone pointed out to me that Oxford railway station was on the main north/south line and there was a regular bus service to Oxford. The train went Oxford – Reading – Coventry. Took about 45 minutes. Doh!

***

Remember I said that I got a telling off from the SWO, my first day at Brize Norton? Here's what happened. I obviously would have gone round the camp doing my arrival procedure wearing my No 1 Best Blue, as was traditional. This incident happened as I was wearing ordinary No 2 working dress, so it must have been my first *working* day.

Brize is basically one long, straight road from the main gate which then curves at a 90 degree right angle at No 1 Parachute Training School (PTS), and then continues in a straight line until it ends at the accommodation area. Everyone called this road the "main drag". All the other roads leading to the various sections hang off this main drag.

I was "bimbling" (walking along, minding my own business) down the main drag, heading for the Tac Comms Wing hangar, Hangar 66, which was next to the PTS school. I was dressed in blues, wearing my "woolly pully", (you know the one, every military/police/security guard wears the same one, epaulettes, elbow patches and a round-neck). I was of course wearing it the way we had worn it in Cyprus, *with no tie.*

I'd just got to the PTS hangar when the SWO stopped me and told me off for *not wearing a tie*. Confused, I told him that I'd just returned from Cyprus and that was the way we wore it there, I thought it would be the same here at Brize. 'Not here,' he says. 'Here in the UK we wear it with a tie.' Scratching my head, I apologised and went back to the block to get a tie.

Now allow me to have a whinge about the rules regarding woolly pullys and ties because this sums up perfectly in one example how stupid and intractable the military mind is and has long been one of my pet hates. (*Matron! He's out of bed again!*)

When I first joined the RAF, we only wore jackets as working dress. First it was the hairy Battle Dress and then was followed by the hideous "Thunderbird" jackets that zipped up the front. They made us look like Gas Board employees. Jackets were impractical for engineers who worked on the aircraft line for example or climbed up masts, so the RAF adopted the round-necked, woolly pullys for them and allowed them not to wear ties. (Sometimes it was actually dangerous for them to do so.)

Seeing the sense behind the comfort this afforded, someone sensible suggested that the RAF extend this idea to everyone, not just "techies", at least in Cyprus anyway. (This person was probably court-martialled for letting down the side by thinking about the troops.) So we happily wore our woolly pullys and were comfortable *without ties*.

Then I return to the UK to find that someone has insisted that everyone *wears ties* under their woolly pullys.

Now, wearing a tie under your jumper causes an unsightly bulge at the front of the neckline, so some clown in their infinite wisdom decided that a new jumper must be introduced that has a V-neck so *you can see the tie.* So the purpose of the V-neck is to show the tie that the round-neck was introduced to *do away with*. Am I the only one that sees what nonsense this is?

Admittedly it was easier to get a pen out of your shirt breast pocket in the V-neck than the round-neck but this was easily overcome by putting a pen pocket on the sleeve *but they banned that idea*, which was also ridiculous.

This attitude led to all sorts of nonsense. I have actually stood on parade in the TCW hangar, being inspected in combat gear by the Flight Lieutenant, followed by the Flight Sergeant.

They stopped at one of us who had a pen pocket sewn onto the sleeve of his green woolly pully. 'Flight Sergeant, take that man's name for having a pen pocket on his sleeve. They're forbidden,' instructed the Flt Lt.

'Yes sir.' Then the Flt Sgt proceeds to take a pen out of *his own pen pocket sewn onto his sleeve* and writes the man's name down on his clipboard, for later punishment. You couldn't make this stuff up.

(*Author update: while I was still writing this book in 2017 I saw the annual entries for the RAF Photo of the Year contest. One of them was of a WO from the Queens Colour Squadron of the RAF Regiment, the elite RAF squadron who do all the RAF's ceremonial duties. This WO was wearing his No 2 dress, not his best blues, which included his woolly pully. And guess what? He had a pen pocket sewn onto his sleeve! I wonder how many decades it took for that to finally become legal?*) Okay, rant over but stay tuned for more inanities.

***

As I said in the Cyprus chapter, I was part of a block of men who went out to Cyprus to relieve the ones who had spent 9 months unaccompanied and were due to go home. This meant that as we all went out at the same time, we were due back to the UK at the same time.

By a stroke of good luck, 38 Group had decided to move their Tactical Communications Wing (henceforth referred to as just TCW or "the Wing") from RAF Benson to RAF Brize Norton. To enable the move to go more smoothly they ran TCW down to minimum manning, moved to Brize, then built up the manning again. This was happening around the same time we were returning from Cyprus, so they filled up all the empty manning slots where possible with Cyprus returnees.

Which led to much grumbling from the TCW "old sweats" who had come from Benson but was great for us as although we were joining a large unit (which can be daunting for a new boy) we already knew half of the people. I believe I was one of the first to arrive but the others soon joined me so I wasn't the odd guy out for long.

Why TCW was sent to Brize I'll never understand. When TCW flew it was invariably in C130 Hercules aircraft which were based at RAF Lyneham in those days. Previously when the Wing was deploying abroad, the Hercules aircraft would fly to Benson and pick them up. When we were at Brize, although we were on an airfield, every exercise we had to drive over to Lyneham – sometimes involving an overnight stop – and load the aircraft there. The Hercs would never fly to Brize to pick us up. So it begs the question why wasn't TCW simply re-located to Lyneham instead of Brize?

Some of the following happened before I got to Brize, some while I was there but it turns out that the Brize hierarchy didn't like TCW. I guess that it was all about the aircraft squadrons until we arrived. We grew to be a massive unit so they were no longer top dogs. Anyway, to annoy us Brize Norton tried to implement some really stupid rules that TCW had to fight against.

For example: On airfields, vehicles that actually go onto the airfield side of the station have a large yellow stripe painted around them so a pilot sitting in his cockpit can easily spot them. Fair enough. As our hangar faced out onto the pan and we sometimes accessed it from the airfield side instead of the road side, Brize instructed TCW that they must paint yellow stripes on all their vehicles.

Came the reply, 'You are aware that we have to go into woods and disguise ourselves amongst the trees? Have you ever seen a tree in a wood with a yellow stripe around it?'

'Well, you can repaint your vehicles when you have to deploy off-station.'

'But we are front-line troops. If the balloon goes up we won't have time to queue up down at the MT paint bay to paint over the yellow stripes. Besides, are you seriously suggesting that every time we go out we paint our vehicles camouflage and when we come back we paint a yellow stripe on them? Have you any idea of the cost involved?'

So that idea got binned.

Next, the RAF introduced GREEN waterproof jackets to go with combat gear instead of the normal BLUE ones that ordinary RAF personnel wore.

'Can we have a load then because we are the ones who wear combat gear regularly?' asked TCW of Brize Stores.

'No, they will only go to people who work with aircraft because they are anti-static and we can't have them causing sparks and starting a fire. You can only have the blue ones as they are not anti-static.'

Came the reply, 'You are aware that we have to go into the woods and disguise ourselves amongst the trees? When was the last time you saw a blue tree?'

'Still can't have the green ones.'

Consequently we saw "linies", who worked on aircraft, walking around with GREEN jackets on over their BLUE uniforms and ourselves wearing BLUE jackets over GREEN combat gear. So The Powers That Be were quite happy for this sartorial mis-match to go on but God forbid that we should wear pen pockets on our sleeves!

So I and many others simply went down Millets and bought our own GREEN waterproof jackets to wear on exercise.

At Benson TCW staff wore combats all the time as they are more comfortable and you don't have to be overly concerned about getting dirt on them. When TCW went to Brize the station executives told them, 'You will have to wear blues all the time when you're on station.'

'That's ridiculous,' TCW replied. 'Our people are constantly climbing in an out of Land Rovers, dragging camouflage nets around, loading trailers, dealing with generators, etc. Their blue uniforms will soon get ruined.'

Eventually, after much arguing, they reached a compromise whereby TCW personnel were allowed to wear combat gear if they were preparing for an exercise (prepping) or had just come back from an exercise and were breaking everything down and putting it back into storage (de-prepping). The rest of the time we had to wear blues and often the SWO or one of his minions would stop us and make us prove that we could justify our wearing combats.

***

Like I said, I was one of the first ones from Cyprus to report to TCW and it was fairly quiet as most everyone else was away on exercise. I drew my equipment from stores and someone had to show me how to put my "puttees" on correctly.

Back in those days we didn't have the high-ankle boots that they had later. We just had the old Directly Moulded Sole (DMS) boots we had been issued at Swinderby which just covered the ankle. To provide a seal between the trousers and the boots, we wore puttees. This is a strip of brown, felt-like material about a yard long, terminating in a point. From this point stretches a ribbon about 2 feet long. The idea is that you wrap this material around your ankles, pinning your trousers to your boots, ending up with the point on the outside of your ankle, pointing backwards. Then you continued winding the ribbon around your ankle and finally tucked it into itself to hold it in place. Woe betide you if the point wasn't on the outside, pointing backwards! A flogging offence.

(One of the stories you hear over the years that sound good but probably aren't true, was that one CO of an army regiment got up one day with a hangover and put his puttees on back to front. When it was pointed out to him, he insisted that that was the correct way to wear them and from that moment on, each and every soldier in the regiment would wear them that way.)

Another story you hear was why the British military lace their footwear with the laces going straight across the foot instead of in a criss-cross pattern. So the story goes, during the second world war (*World War II – The Sequel! This time it's political*) the Ghurkhas would crawl through the jungles of Burma or wherever, where the undergrowth was so thick you couldn't see anything, sneak up on a sentry or a passing patrol and reaching out a hand, feel their laces. If they were straight across they knew they were Brits. If it wasn't then he was dead meat.

Anyhoo, what TCW did allow was wearing of high-ankle boots if you could source your own. I bought a pair of Doctor Martens and also the cobbler in Carterton would stitch extra leather to the ankles of your standard issue DMS boots to extend them, which I had done, so was able to do away with wearing those hideous puttees.

Instead you could buy these things in the NAAFI called "Trouser Blousers". They were a pair of elasticated garters with a hook at each end. (Or if you were too tight to buy a pair you could use thick, elastic bands.) You fastened them around your leg, above your boot, and then tucked your trouser bottoms into them, so the hem was concealed inside the trouser leg.

I'd no idea where the phrase "blousing" came from until I recently watched *Band of Brothers,* a TV mini-series about a WWII Airborne unit. In one scene the CO of the unit is shouting at one of his men for "blousing" his trousers before he was a fully-fledged paratrooper. So I guess it goes back to American airborne forces in that war.

***

There were various flights and squadrons making up the Wing. I can't remember them all. There was the Field Comms Squadron (FCS) and then various support squadrons like the Base Support Squadron (full of shinies and the bosses), Standards and Training Flight (STF) Mobility Supply Flight (MSF) who issued all the tents and cooking equipment and the General Engineering Flight (GEF) who maintained all our generators.

There was also an army element to the Wing, 244 Signal Sqn. They took up half of the hangar but fortunately our paths rarely crossed on exercises.

FCS was split into 2 flights, Mobile and Navigational Aids Flight (MNF *yes, I know they missed the 'A' out*) and Airhead Comms Flight (ACF). I was allocated to MNF. The flight's roles broke down as follows. MNF worked radios out of the backs of Land Rovers manned by a Cpl and 2 airmen. Our basic role was to support the helicopter squadrons but along with that any smaller tasks such as providing comms for a bombing competition, was done by us. Our exercises were usually no more than a couple of weeks and mostly in Denmark, Norway and Germany. We went out fairly often.

ACF were the long-range guys. They loaded up big cabins full of radio equipment and flew them around the world, on global comms exercises, in such places as Antigua, Ascension, Hong Kong (*I think*) places like that. Their exercises lasted around 6 weeks but on the other hand they didn't go away that often.

There was long standing argument about which was the better flight but to me it boiled down to this, ACF went to some great places, but once you were there, if you shut the door to the radio cabin you were just working in a Commcen again. All the technical stuff was done by the techies and you were just back to being an operator, typing up messages. And in between exercises they had long, looooong periods of sitting in the crew-room, doing nothing.

MNF however were out in the field quite often. When we deployed we were doing all the things we had been trained to do, all the warfarey, soldier stuff. Although there were techies on the exercise, they weren't in every location so we generally did all the radio stuff and putting up aerials, etc. ourselves. We were much more hands-on. Although the exercises were short, they came along more often and as the ultimate aim was to be out there, doing it,

I preferred it.

***

When I first got to TCW they told me that I would be properly trained on the equipment by the Training Flight STF, allocated my own personal weapon, etc. etc. before they would send me out on exercise.

Yeah, right. I was there about a week before they sent me out.

The hangar was still empty, everyone was still away on exercise, when a commitment came up for a team to go to RAF Lossiemouth in Scotland, to handle the comms for a bombing competition.

I was in the office listening to a Cpl discussing this with a Sgt and asking each other who they could send. They needed 2 teams of 3 men.

'I can go and take Steve Flinders but we need another, who's available?' said the Cpl.

It was like those scenes you see in the movies, they both slowly turned round and looked at me and their faces lit up.

Bearing in mind that I had only been there a week or so and had barely learnt how to put on my puttees without tying both my feet together, I said, 'Wait, whoa, I can't go. I don't know anything about how to do the job. I've only just got here, I've never even seen the equipment.'

'Don't worry,' they said. 'You'll just be there to make up the numbers. You'll be fine, we'll look after you.'

So off to bonny Scotland I went with, if memory serves me correctly, Steve Barnes as the Cpl and Steve "Polly" Flinders as the other SAC in my team and another team of a Cpl and 2. An interesting trip, a 2 day drive with Land Rovers and trailers to the north of

123

Scotland. We stopped overnight at a stores depot in Carlisle.

Eventually we arrived at Lossiemouth and set up our kit in the Ops building. We were there to provide comms, pass weather reports and suchlike to/from the target site. And of course the usual thing happened, an officer came into our radio room as we were setting up and started asking me a load of questions about how we were going to operate. Always happens doesn't it? I bluffed my way through it as best I could and then the Cpl stepped in and took over. The other team stayed overnight and then went onto the target site.

Apparently Lossiemouth had been a Royal Naval Air Station originally, so everything was built to navy standards. For example, in the barrack block we stayed in, the doorways were built up to about 6 inches off the floor, so the doorways were like a hatch, rather than a door and you had to lift your feet to step through them. If you didn't look out of the window you would swear you were on a ship. In fact, we were on the first floor, directly beneath us was the laundry room with big, industrial tumble-dryers like you see in a laundrette. When they started up it sounded like the ship was underway. Weird.

I think we were there for 10 days or a fortnight. The exercise took a weekend break so we drove down to the target site to see our fellow TCW guys. There I saw one of the strangest sights I have ever seen in my life. We were driving along this country lane and we came across a field full of inflatable tanks! They were life-size rubber or plastic tanks that could be positioned anywhere and then used as targets. (Nobody actually fired on them.)

The idea was that the RAF Regiment used Rapier missiles to defend airfields. The aircraft from Lossiemouth would make practice attacks on the tanks and the Regiment would detect them, line up their Rapier rig on the aircraft and then photograph them. Thereby proving to both sides, how close the aircraft got before they would have been destroyed.

I heard also that the Regiment guys were using their camouflage nets to fish for salmon in the local river. Naughty!

I guess it was a good exercise to "lose my cherry" on. It was on camp and we were in the warm all the time, so I can't complain. The task was simple enough and I enjoyed it. I think it was also my first ever trip to Scotland.

***

By the way, you will hear repeated references to the RAF Regiment throughout this book, as our paths cross. They are known as "Rock Apes" or just "Rocks" for short. Nobody really seemed to know why they were so called. Most people assumed it was something to do with the Rock Apes of Gibraltar, but when I was researching for this book I was pointed in the direction of this Wikipedia entry:

In the past the nickname "Rock Ape" has been attributed to their traditional role guarding areas of Gibraltar, but this is not so.

The term came into use after an accident in the Western Aden Protectorate in November 1952. Two RAF Regiment officers serving with the Aden Protectorate Levies at Dhala decided to amuse themselves by going out to shoot some of the hamadryas baboons (locally referred to as "rock apes").

The officers drew rifles and split up to hunt the apes.

In the semi-darkness one of the officers fired at a moving object in the distance. When he reached the target he discovered he had shot the other officer.

After emergency treatment Flight Lieutenant XXXX XXXXX survived to return to service a few months later.

When asked by a board of inquiry why he had fired at his friend the officer replied that his target had "looked just like a rock ape" in the half light. The remark soon reverberated around the RAF and it was not long before the term was in general use.

So now we know.

***

When I got back to Brize the others had returned from exercise and the rest of the lads from Cyprus had begun to arrive so I wasn't "Billy No Mates" anymore. Then we got down to seriously learning the job.

I got allocated to a 3 man team, I can't remember who was the Cpl, either Steve Barnes or Pete Richardson. I worked with both of them but I can't remember in which order. We also undertook in-depth training on Nuclear Biological Chemical (NBC) warfare and weapon training.

Normally you would have to go into the gas chamb-sorry, sorry, Respirator Testing Facility as they now call it. They would just hand you a gas mask and shove you in. It was ill-fitting and not properly adjusted and you would cop a lungful of CS gas. Here on the Wing we were given our own respirators and shown how to adjust them to our individual fits.

Also with the SLR training. Normally you are handed

a rifle at the armoury and expected to shoot that on the firing range once a year. For range practice it normally doesn't matter if the sights are off. If you are aiming at the centre of the target and you hit the top left, it doesn't matter as long you repeatedly hit the top left. It means the sights are off but your aim is consistent.

On the Wing however, you are allocated an individual weapon and nobody uses that weapon except you. (*They didn't let you take it home with you though.*) This allows you to go on the range and do what they call "zeroing the sights". If you are aiming too high they will lower the sight forcing you to lower the barrel. If you are firing too much to the right, they will move the sight to the left, forcing you to move the barrel to the left. That way, when you aim at the centre, you will hit the centre. As it is your weapon, no one else will get the chance to take it out of the armoury and mess about with the sights.

The rules state that RAF personnel must fire a weapon once a year. On the Wing it was once every 6 months and on top of that, before every major exercise you went on.

In the RAF, every year an airman/airwoman had to attend an annual Ground Defence Training (GDT) course to refresh their training on Fire and First Aid drills. Also they are required to fire a weapon once a year.

The Wing were particular about their training. When they were at Benson they used to run an annual course called a "Brutus". When they came to Brize the course that station personnel did was called GDT. That wasn't good enough for the Wing, they had to call their course Operational Defence training (ODT). About a year later Brize started calling their course ODT. The Wing couldn't have that so they changed the name of their course back to Brutus to differentiate us from the station.

***

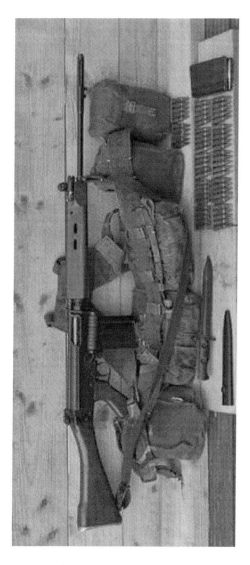

Personal kit you're expected to lug around with you on exercise, although only rarely did we get bullets.

As I said, the idea was that you had to have done a Brutus before you could be deployed but operational needs always overrode that. I arrived in August and it was January before I did a Brutus.

Before I go any further, I want to say something about the guys who ran STF. Now I don't mean to offend anyone that was on it at the time but ... I don't feel that they were the right people to train us. They were just telegraphists, like me! Now fair enough, when it came to Nuclear, Biological and Chemical (NBC) training, there were set down, well documented procedures that they simply had to follow, so it was easy to give a lesson in those, but when it came to warfarey stuff such as attacking or defending a position, then I really think it should have been taught by someone who did it for a living, someone with actual experience or better training. I mean, anyone can do a few courses but that doesn't make you an expert. Why not have someone from the RAF Regiment train us? Or even better, just down the road was Imjin Barracks (formerly RAF Little Rissington). I'm sure that one of their instructors would have loved to get his hands on us RAF types and it would have been more useful. Just saying.

These Brutus' were really brutal (if you'll forgive the pun). The first one I did in January 78. They drove about a dozen of us up to Sherwood Forest in the back of a 4 ton lorry. They dumped us out when we got there, said, 'Split into teams of two and dig yourselves a trench.' And that was it for 5 days. The snow was on the ground up to our knees. The ground was hard (although Sherwood Forest is quite sandy so it wasn't frozen solid). Every day (or night) STF would turn up and teach us something, take us for a map-march, or whatever but apart from that, for 5 days we lived, ate and slept in a hole in the ground in the middle of winter. (*What did they think we were, Hobbits?*)

And they had a nasty habit of attacking us during the night so our rest was interrupted.

I remember waking up one morning and due to lack of space I had slept with my legs bent. When I tried to straighten them it was like red-hot pokers being inserted behind my knee-caps. It was so painful that I knew then that in later life I would have problems with my knees and sure enough, it is now later life and I'm having trouble with my knees.

They took us on a map-march one night. It was through the firebreaks in the wood, the open gaps you get between rows of trees in a managed forest. In normal conditions that would probably have been a slightly tiring walk, somewhere between 5-10 miles long I would guess. But when you are walking through the open spaces which are knee-deep in snow it became a much harder proposition. It's difficult to decide which is more tiring, lifting your legs up every pace to step over the snow, or just ploughing through the deep snow. They are both exhausting and we finally arrived back at our "holes in the ground" to grab a few hours' sleep before daylight.

At the end of the 5 days we filled in our holes, they put us in the back of a lorry and drove us back to Brize.

All in all it was a waste of time in my opinion, as nobody really learnt anything except how cold it was living in a trench in the middle of winter.

The guy I shared a trench with was from the Gen Eng Flight of the Wing. Someone asked him at the end how it had been. 'Horrid. Just horrid,' he replied which made me laugh, hearing this hairy-*rsed engineer using such delicate phrasing to describe his time in the woods.

Now before you kick off and start calling me a Wendy because I'm not tough enough to take it and I need to learn how to live in a cold trench because one day I might have to do it for real … read on.

The next year I had to do Brutus again. As it was annual it fell in January. This time it was for 2 weeks BUT this time they took us to a proper training camp in Sherwood Forest. We lived in a wooden hut, there was a mess to eat in, the hut had proper toilets and showers and we had our lessons in proper classrooms. True, we had to spend a few days in a trench during the second week but that was okay as you knew that you were only a few miles away from a hot meal and a warm bed at the end of it.

I learnt so much more about the things they can't properly teach you standing in the middle of a wood, everyone huddled around the instructor, trying to peer over someone's shoulder to see what's going on. Things like map reading and how to use a compass properly. How to strip and re-assemble a weapon blindfolded, how to fill a magazine with bullets when you are wearing NBC rubber gloves. All the sort of things you can't learn/practice when you are hungry, shivering from cold and exhausted from lack of sleep.

We were also taught about nerve agents that were in use, the various pills and injections that we could take prior to an NBC attack or if we had been contaminated by one. One time we were being shown the pills we may have to take and someone said to me, 'Those pills look a bit large. Do you think you could swallow one?'

I told him, 'I would swallow my bloody respirator haversack if I thought it could save my life!'

Another time they were showing us a film about how the Russians dealt with NBC drills. The Russians at the time dressed their men in one-piece rubber suits and with their long-nosed gas masks looked just like Wombles. The instructor also told us that they gave their men a pill and told them that it would protect them against radiation. 'Ha, ha, ha. Stupid Ruskies!' we all laughed. Then the instructor said, 'What are you laughing at? We give you tablets and tell you they will protect you against nerve agents and you believe us, don't you?' We all looked at each other and went, 'He's got a point. How do we know they will protect us?'

They also taught us something about pyrotechnics, (things that go BANG!) A common one was the trip-flare. This was essentially a white-phosphorous grenade on a stick. You led the trip-wire out and fastened it to a nearby tree, and then removed the safety-pin from the flare. When someone walked into the wire, it went off and lit up the night sky. I became quite a dab hand at setting these up and on a later posting was always the one called on to set them out, come exercise time.

Another favourite was the Thunderflash. Basically this was just a big banger, but I mean BIG. It was supposed to be a harmless substitute for a grenade, but it could still be fairly potent. Back in those days we still wore "tin-hats" instead of the Kevlar helmets that we were issued in later years. Not literally tin of course but made of metal and not a great deal different from what the British "Tommie" wore in WWII. I have seen somebody light a Thunderflash and put it under a tin-hat lying on the ground which was blown about 20 feet up into the air, so they needed to be handled with care.

I nearly had my head blown off by one of these Thunderflashes. During our fortnight at the Sherwood Forest camp, a group of TA soldiers came up for their weekend camp. Our instructors arranged for them to attack us, as we were out one night.

They loaded us into a 4 tonner, drove us around a bit and parked up so we could disembark. There was no pretence at a surprise, they simply told us, 'Walk down this track and somewhere along the way, you'll be ambushed.' So we did and we were!

We went about 200 yards and then we left the cover of the wood. Once we were all clear of the trees they opened fire on us. Rifles started blatting off all around us as Thunderflashes were thrown in our direction. It was quite exciting, Thunderflashes exploding, muzzle flashes, light-sabres scything through the darkness (okay, I made that last bit up) but it was brilliant nevertheless.

We all dived for cover as you should do, and I had this small mound of earth in front of me, only about head height, as I lay there, returning fire. One of the attackers threw a Thunderflash which fortunately landed just the other side of the mound of earth and it went off. If it hadn't been for the mound there's no telling what damage it would have done, but as it was I was *literally* stunned. I didn't know where I was or what was happening. I just stood up in the midst of the battle, looking around me. I must have stood there for about 5 seconds before my wits began to return and I got down on the ground again.

All this only took a few minutes before the order was given to up sticks and leg it to the rendezvous point, which was a clump of trees out past the ambush zone. Apart from nearly losing my head it was all great fun. So the point I'm making is that rather than just give someone a hard time and call it teaching, you can actually put someone through the necessary training but in a way that they will learn something and even have fun, which was the difference between my first Brutus and my second.

I had to do another Brutus before I left the Wing, also in winter, so I used to joke that I was only trained for Arctic warfare and if they ever sent me to a desert country I wouldn't have a clue what to do.

***

Initially there was a bit of an "us" and "them" attitude between the crowd arriving from Cyprus like myself, "Charlie" Thompson, Mick Finlay, Dave Stewart, "Happy" Halliday, etc. – the TCW "old sweats" who had come from Benson, Steve "Polly" Flinders, Ian "Tiny" Buchanan, Pete Broster, Al Pimblett, Billy Fish – and the other new guys who had just joined the Wing from elsewhere, Pete McWilliams, Johnny Mac (can't remember his full name), Ian Bretherton, John Gardner, Paul Walters, etc. (*Apologies to anyone I've forgotten.*)

After a few Brutus' and exercises together though, that sorted itself out and we became one unit.

One of the things that bound us together was we either had, or soon developed (as a survival instinct, I suppose) similar senses of humour. (Not identical, but similar.) I met some of the funniest people I have ever met in my life, on the Wing. I suppose it's a British thing, making jokes when things are bad, reminiscent of being able to laugh during the blitz. When you're on a bad exercise, and believe me some of them were grim, you try and joke about things to make it more bearable.

Ian Buchanan was a big lad, broad as well as tall, with ginger hair and moustache. (*I promised to mention him as he is a Facebook friend.*) Being tall he naturally got called "Tiny". (He was also called "The Honey Monster". He didn't like that – but to everyone with an unfortunate nickname I say, 'Sorry but nicknames are there for *our* amusement, not yours, so you'll just have to live with it.')

Anyway, we were on exercise, somewhere in Germany one time and we had a techie from Motor Transport come on the exercise with us. A group of us were gathered in a tent, huddled around a paraffin stove, trying to keep warm, when one of our sergeants came into the tent and announced, 'There's an MT fitter outside.'

Tiny's reply was, 'What do you want us to do, fill him up?'

(*That joke works better if you say it out loud.*) Okay, it wasn't hilarious but it made me laugh and that's good enough.

Charlie Thompson was another funny guy. We were both down at RAF ST. Athan in Wales for our driving courses at the same time, so naturally we hung around together in our spare time.

We were in the vending area one day and I wanted something out of the machine. I was sorting through my change but I didn't have the right coins so I said to him, 'Do you have 2p?'

'No,' he said. 'It's my own hair.'

(*Think about it ... c'mon, think about it ... there you go, now you've got it.*)

A common joke on the Wing was to look into a tent, see someone there and say, 'What are you doing in there?'

To which the standard answer was, 'I'm just lurking within tent.' *Hence the subtitle of this chapter.*

Pete Broster was another character. Sadly he is no longer with us, died of Cancer, not during the time I was there but later in his career. He was very popular on the Wing and was missed by many. It was characters like him who made the Wing more interesting.

Pete died long after I had left the Wing but sadly one of the corporals did die while I was still serving on it. I have asked a few people who were there at the same time as me and I'm ashamed to say that none of us can remember his name. So much for a man's legacy living on after him.

Anyway, I knew this chap, had been on one or two exercises with him, he was a decent bloke, drank a few whiskies, only smoked the occasional cigar and played squash regularly. Dropped dead at 34 of a heart attack. So when I ask myself, 'Should I drink that extra pint? Should I smoke that next cigarette?' I answer, 'Why not? Healthy living is no guarantee of a long life and you never know when it will end, so make the most of it while you can.'

Quite often the worse the exercise got, wet or miserable conditions, sometimes being under army control and not our own bosses, the funnier we made it and I have had some rough exercises but they were the funniest times I've spent in my life. Two or three weeks of just endless joking and mucking about. As I said, you try and make the best of a bad situation, *well at least most of us did.*

I remember being on a particularly lousy exercise, and one of our number kept persistently complaining and grumbling. This guy, John XXXXXX wouldn't stop. Now, I can be loud and opinionated, and if someone has a go at me I'll argue back, but I'm not normally confrontational. I don't start arguments, preferring to bite my lip and keep quiet for the sake of keeping a smooth working relationship within the group.

But finally I couldn't take any more of his incessant whingeing, so I was forced to blurt out, 'For the love of God, John, will you *just–stop–moaning!* Some of us are trying to enjoy this exercise but your continual bitching is ruining it for everyone else.'

He took his whingeing down a notch or two but I never heard him say a good word about the RAF or TCW again. Eventually he bought himself out of the RAF and went on his way, leaving us in peace.

And guess what? About 6 months later I heard that he was missing the RAF and had joined his local RAF Volunteer Reserve. I just don't understand some people.

Suave Telegraphist about town. What a dork!

Like all large groups of people, you soon find your level and sort out the guys who you prefer to hang around with. I spent a lot of time with Polly Flinders at first as we were on the same team but I also had the great good fortune to have been put into a 2 man room with Paul Ruck, an MNF techie.

Initially we were both a bit stand-offish as he was a techie and I was an operator (on the Wing we tended to be a bit 'cliquey' and stick to our own kind to socialise with) but Paul and I soon found out how similar our senses of humour were (we could finish each other's jokes) and we got on like a house on fire.

I know I keep banging on about "sense of humour" but you've no idea how important it really was. If you have a day job in an office and you don't like the bloke next to you, then no problem, you go home at night and don't have to see him or think about him until the next day. When you were in a job like ours where you go on exercise and might have to spend the next 3 weeks seeing someone *every waking moment*, it's important to get along with them. The easiest way to do that is share a SOH.

Paul and I really got on well and I sorely missed him when he got posted away. This was in the days before video games became freely available. I had purchased a 14 inch Black and White portable TV. I often would come back to my room and find Paul and his mates sat on my bed, watching my TV but that's okay, we all worked on a share and share alike basis.

I'm a technophile (this was when there wasn't much techno around. Digital watches and hand-held calculators hadn't been invented yet. Games like "Pong" were around but only in arcades and cafes, there was nothing for the home market). One day I saw an advert for a Tank game that you could plug into your TV. The only problem was that you had to assemble it yourself. Never been good with a soldering iron myself, despite being trained how to use one at Cosford, so I asked Paul if he would build it for me if I brought it. He agreed so I sent away for it. He put it together for me and we spent hours playing this simple video game where 2 tanks crawled around these obstacles, shooting at each other. It was certainly one of the first TV games in our block, if not the camp.

***

Dave Stewart, one of us from Cyprus, got pally with Pete McWilliams and they used to hang around together. They were the same physical type, tall, thin, Scottish. I used to think of them as "Two tall, too tall, Scotsmen." I used to joke that if they stood on the sports pitch and held hands they would look like a Rugby goalpost.

I got on great with Pete (we had a shared love of *The Hitchhikers Guide to the Galaxy*) and later when I got permission to live out in a rented bungalow, I asked him to take the other room and split the rent. Paul Ruck had been posted away by then, otherwise he would have been my first choice.

Initially Pete was in on the deal and then just before I was due to go away on exercise he had to drop out. I frantically looked around for someone to take his place (they didn't have to just be available, they had to be a decent bloke who I could bear to share a house with). Finally found one of the techies on my flight, Phil Gilham. As I was going away on exercise, unfortunately I had to just dump it in his lap to sort out the handover and get the keys from the rental agency. No worries though. We were all young men but some of the Wing I still considered as "boys" whereas people like Phil and I were "grown-ups".

Besides being a decent bloke, Phil was dating the daughter of the landlord of a local pub. Well, you never know when that sort of thing might come in handy, do you?

It was great living out. Freedom! Able to live like a human being at last. Not have someone breathing down your neck all the time. One day when I was still living in the block I got a phone call at work from the block sergeant. He'd done his informal block inspection and he was ringing to tell me that I hadn't made my bed that morning. I mean, it was a Duvet for Pete's sake! All it needed was a quick tug on the corner to straighten it but no, he had to contact me and tell me off. A Cpl in the office with me at the time asked what was up. I remember saying to him, 'I'm 26 and people are ringing me up to tell me I haven't made my bed. What sort of life is this?'

We could eat what we liked, when we wanted. Both Phil and I were sensible and bought food and cooked for ourselves, it wasn't just takeaways and beer. (Well, there was a bit of beer.)

I was going out with a WRAF at the time and it meant we didn't have to sneak into each other's blocks anymore. It cut down on my NAAFI visits as well. As I said before, you tend to go over the NAAFI/down the pub to avoid staring at the same 4 walls all the time, but I found that when I had my own place I was perfectly happy to sit at home and watch telly with a drink in my hand. Much more civilised and cheaper too!

So I lived like that for my final year on the Wing, until I got posted.

***

Lurking within tent.

Every station, wing, squadron and unit in the RAF has its own official crest. TCW's was a lightening flash with a bird on top. (Of the winged variety.) Being a communications outfit one would naturally assume that the bird would be a carrier pigeon, but no. It was a "Rock Dove" which is a breed of the humble pigeon. (*But we all knew that, didn't we?*)

It had an inscription underneath UBIQUE LOQUIMUR which I think is Latin for, 'Not me Chief, I'm engines.' I'm just kidding, actually it translates as "WE SPEAK EVERYWHERE". (*See, Google really is your friend.*)

Along with the official crests, some units had their unofficial ones. TCW's was a mushroom on top of a lightning flash. TCW were known as the "Mushroom Men" as in they were "kept in the dark and fed on sh*t" just like mushrooms. Before going on exercise many people would cut out the mushroom crest from orange, day-glo, sticky-backed plastic and when visiting another camp or unit, would stick the crest up in obvious places, such as above a squadron bar or on the camp sign at the main gate. This was known as "zapping" and despite the moans from the hierarchy was undertaken by every visiting unit I ever came across, it wasn't just us.

The station executives on a camp would particularly complain if someone zapped an aircraft but you know, I'm sure their people did the same when they came to Brize Norton.

***

I remember after one exercise we arrived back at Brize about 8 o'clock in the evening when everything had shut down. With a couple of other guys I was tasked with going up to Operations and requesting that the Duty

Armourer be called in, as we had weapons and they had to be returned to the armoury.

I swear the following conversation is true. Ops called the Duty Armourer in and after about 15 minutes he turned up and collected the armoury keys from them.

'Okay, let's go,' I said to him.

'Wait a minute,' said the Ops corporal. 'You've got to sign for him.'

I'd never heard of signing for *a person* before, unless you were a prison guard perhaps, so I thought I'd misunderstood him. 'Do you mean I have to sign for the armoury keys?'

'No. You have to sign for HIM,' he said, pointing to the armourer.

I couldn't resist it. 'What if I lose him? How much is a new one going to cost me?'

'Just sign.'

After we had handed the weapons in and escorted the armourer back to Ops to return the keys, I asked if I could have my deposit back, but they didn't appreciate the joke.

***

Every Friday afternoon if you were unlucky to be hanging around in Hangar 66, they made you sweep the hangar floor. As it was a normal working day we were supposed to be there until 5 o'clock, but to encourage us to sweep up they used to promise us that if we did it, they would see about letting us off early.

We'd sweep the floor but they never did let us get away early, so eventually we decided that getting stood down early was just an Urban Myth that the seniors put around and it had never actually happened in the history of the Wing.

143

***

I used to hate Station exercises. Wing exercises I enjoyed, TACEVALS even were okay as they lasted 3 or 4 days but 1 day Station exercises used to leave me cold.

You see, TCW were front line troops, which meant that if the balloon went up, we would pack up and go to Germany, Denmark or wherever we were needed. So when an exercise of any description was called we had to report to the armoury, pick up our weapons, get the radios fitted into our wagons while we collected up our tents and generators and so on, then deploy to somewhere like Little Rissington, just down the road.

On 1 Day Station Exercises however, we had to do all of the above but we would only deploy as far as the other side of the airfield or up by the Airman's Mess. Nevertheless we had to set up our tents, put the aerials up, get the radios working, etc.

When the exercise was called off, the clerks for example, would just lock up General Office and go home, Stores would just lock up and go home. We, on the other hand, had to pack everything up, take it back to the Hangar (mercifully they would usually let us leave the unpacking of Land Rovers and trailers until the following morning) queue up at the armoury to hand our weapons in THEN go home. So our exercises would inevitably last 2 or 3 hours longer than everyone else's and by the time we got to the mess, it was usually shut.

***

One of the things that cropped up regularly was TACEVALs. This is a TACtical EVALuation of an entity such as a station or a unit, or you can have them for individual squadrons and wings. A team of Umpires would descend on the victim and call a TACEVAL. Then the unit involved would go onto a war footing and they would, over the course of the next few days, be judged on how well they carried out their war role. It would involve pretend air-raids, casualties, intruders, etc. all designed to test how well you could deal with these distractions and yet still function normally. Usually on a station it just meant guarding the entrances and every section carried on as normal doing its job. In the case of mobile units such as ourselves it meant deploying, sometimes to another country.

As well as being involved in Brize's TACEVALs and our own, we also got roped into those of the helicopters and Harrier squadrons, so we could find ourselves doing 3 or 4 TACEVALs per year.

One of the "joys" of TCW was the annual TACEVAL just before Christmas. Every year we would arrange our Christmas party, buy tickets, wives and girlfriends would buy new dresses and then the brass would call a TACEVAL and we would all go to Germany for a week.

We were managed from Strike Command at RAF High Wycombe and THEY would call a TACEVAL mid-December, purely so these office wallahs could all go on a Christmas Duty-Free booze run to Germany. We would arrive at our exercise location and the place would be swarming with people from Strike Command we had never seen before, who had crawled out of the woodwork to get in on the booze run.

Okay, we also took the opportunity to stock up but as we did these trips regularly, most had a stock of Christmas booze tucked away anyway. What The Powers That Be didn't realise (*or didn't care*) was that our Christmas party was always screwed up. I think the first time we were able to re-arrange it to another date, but the second time we had to cancel the place we had arranged and just have it in "The Bird in the Hand", the bar in squadron headquarters, and after that we always arranged to have it in our headquarters as we lost too much money by cancelling it each time. So we never got the chance to have a nice, Christmas do in a posh hotel, like everyone else did.

Merry Christmas, you Strike Command T*ssers!

***

I was on TCW back in the late 70's so in my day the RAF still had working Vulcans in service. True they only did displays by then (until they bombed Port Stanley in the Falklands) but they still had a squadron, based at Scampton if memory serves me correctly.

One day, we received a call in the MNF office asking if the Vulcan squadron could borrow a portable VHF radio from us for an air display they were attending. They wanted a man on the ground to be able to talk to them as they approached for their flypast.

Permission was given by the bosses and the Vulcan people said, 'Great! We'll send someone down in the next day or two to pick it up.' Our tech stores were warned to have one ready for collection.

The MNF office looked out onto the pan (the large concrete area where planes are parked while they load and unload passengers) and beyond that the runway, so we could watch the planes as they landed and took off. Next day a few of us were in the office and someone said, 'Oh look. There's a Vulcan coming in to land.' We all crowded up against the windows and watched it land and follow the taxiway to the pan. Then, engines still running, a hatch opened on the bottom and a crewman climbed down and ran over to our hangar.

'Hello, I'm from Scampton. I've come to pick up a

146

radio.'

'Er yeah,' said someone. We'd all been warned to watch out for someone coming but we had expected them to send a Land Rover. 'Follow me.' They took him to the tech store, he signed for the radio, ran back out to the aircraft which then taxied to the runway and took off. We were all gobsmacked. 'Did that just happen?'

Heaven knows how much fuel they burnt while they were waiting for him and how much it cost. I often wonder if they tasked that Vulcan specifically to pick up the radio or did they just happen to be passing?

***

The TCW seniors always tried to make exercises sound more exciting and interesting by giving us a load of flannel about what we could expect.

On one NATO exercise on Salisbury Plain the Sgt warned us that the Dutch Special Boat Service were the attacking force. *The Boat service? In the middle of Salisbury Plain?*

I told him, 'That would explain those blokes I saw rowing past in canoes, a while back.' Which got me a dirty look and I'm sure a black mark on my copy book.

***

One of the (few) good things about being an enlisted man as opposed to an officer, was that while they had to pay for their uniforms, we got ours for free. They may be ill-fitting, cheap and shoddily made, hard to get replacements for … but they were free!

Which leads into one of the RAF sayings I was always fond of. When times were hard and you were having a bad day, such as your Land Rover being stuck in the mud on Salisbury Plain, or you're stranded in some foreign land because your plane home had broken down, or you were just plain fed up sweeping the hangar floor for the millionth time, the more cynical wags amongst us might be tempted to proclaim to his colleagues:

'All this and free boots too. What more could anyone ask for?'

Believe me, the occasion to use such a phrase came up *a lot* on TCW. Hence the title of this book.

***

A lot of people are scared of dentists. Not me. I've had some horrendous times sitting in dentist's chairs, there's nothing they can do to me that will frighten me, anymore.

Not that they were bad dentists, in fact I was told that one of them, a Wg Cdr, had been the queen's dentist, so obviously he knew how to be gentle. Another one, a female, if a tooth nerve started to play up while she was working, she would rub your temples until the pain went away. (Seriously. It was delightful.) I just seem to have deep-rooted gnashers that are hard to deal with, should they need to come out. In fact one time I just went in for a check-up, ended up in hospital and receiving medical treatment for 3 months afterwards.

It was a Wednesday afternoon, I remember. TCW were putting on a display over the weekend and then I was away the following Monday on exercise for a week. I was scheduled for a check-up so I toddled along to the Dental Centre.

The female dentist looked in my mouth and decided that my wisdom teeth on both sides of my lower jaw should come out, and she decided to do it there and then. So she pumped me full of drugs and tried to pull them out. As I said, my tooth roots go down as far as somewhere around my knees, and she couldn't pull them out. So she starts drilling to break them up, then tries pulling again.

I'm in bit of pain by this time, so she injects me with more pain-killers. More drilling, more injections. Then she jabs me in the mouth with what felt like a large screwdriver. I scream and I'm hanging from the ceiling by my fingers and toes when she asks, 'Does that still hurt?'

'*Just a little ... yes.*' I manage to croak.

'Oh well, I can't give you any more pain-killers. We'll have to put in a temporary filling and send you off to Wroughton to get them out.' (Wroughton was the nearest RAF hospital to Brize Norton.) So I went back to the block to get my wash kit and then they put me in an ambulance and took me away to Wroughton.

They operated on me next day, under general anaesthetic. But I knew something was going to go wrong, earlier. A male nurse came in and gave the fellow in the bed opposite me his pre-op jab. This makes your body dehydrate slightly (so you're not drooling everywhere, I suppose) and makes you drowsy. About 20 minutes later they came in and gave me mine. In the left buttock.

Then 10 minutes later they came to collect me for my op. 'Just a minute,' I said. 'You gave him his jab half an hour ago, you should be taking him, not me. My jab probably won't have taken effect yet.'

'No, no, we know what we're doing. You're up next.' Well, what can you do? So I shut up.

The operation went okay. They released me on the Friday and they gave me a 2 day sick note – which meant I didn't have to do the display at the weekend, which was a bonus – but I went away on exercise on the Monday with the others. It was in a forest somewhere with a

149

helicopter squadron.

Anyway, after a couple of days, the spot where they had given me my pre-op jab in the backside had swelled up into an abscess, and as the week went by it got bigger until it finally burst. Luckily the squadron had a medic with them and he took a look and patched it up. He told me I should get it looked at, as soon as I got back to Brize. Which I did.

I didn't even bother getting changed or showered. As soon as I dropped off my personal kit, I limped down to the Med Centre and asked to see the nurse. I just thought it would be a case of cleaning it up properly, which we couldn't do in the field, then sticking a gauze pad on it.

She took me into a treatment room and said, 'Sit down.'

'I can't,' I replied, 'That's the problem.' I explained what was wrong so she told me to drop my trousers and lay on the examination bed. I did that, then as I'm lying there the Medical Secretary walked into the room. She's only a damned clerk, so she didn't have the right to barge in on people's intimate examinations, she's not medical personnel! She was just being nosy.

Anyway, she left and the nurse and I got down to it (so to speak). I thought she would just start cleaning it up but she says, 'I'm going to get the doctor. He should see this.'

So she drags a doctor in and I have to go through the story again and how the abscess is the result of a jab they gave me in the hospital, blah, blah, blah. The doctor was furious (not with me). You see, when they give you that pre-op jab in the backside, what they are meant to do is imagine a line drawn down the buttock and one across, to divide it into 4 segments. Then they are supposed to stick the needle in the UPPER/OUTER segment, near the hip bone. They had jabbed me in the LOWER/INNER segment, right next to the bum-crack, and then to add insult to injury they had used a dirty needle.

He demanded to know who had done it, but to me he was just some nameless J/T in a white coat, I couldn't identify him. He gave the nurse instructions on how to treat me and then he went off to make some enquiries.

The nurse drained the pus off and then told me that with abscesses the important thing is to make sure that all the pus is drained off before the wound closes. To ensure this, they put a "wick" into the wound, like a candlewick, to make sure it doesn't heal up.

She soaked the wick in (what I assumed to be) a saline solution, while she took the old dressings off. Then she had to poke the wick into the hole with a pair of tweezers and it was *really painful* but I behaved like a man and gritted my teeth. Unfortunately, for the next three months I had to have my dressing changed EVERY day and a new wick inserted, even when I was away on exercise in Cyprus!

As I said, it really hurt when she put the wick in, I thought I was just being a wimp but one time I said to whichever nurse was doing the business that day, 'Why does it hurt so much? You're only soaking it in a saline solution or something, aren't you?'

'Oh no,' she replied. 'This stuff is the medical equivalent of industrial strength bleach.'

I never considered myself a wimp, after that.

After the abscess had healed up properly, I had to see the doctor again for him to sign off on it and he said to me, 'You know, I was going to take a picture of your backside and send it off to the nursing journal, as an example of HOW NOT to give an injection.'

So, my bum could have been famous!

Let this be a lesson to you, kiddies, brush every day and floss regularly, or you'll end up with your bum in a magazine, like I nearly did.

***

During my time at Brize Norton I did a parachute jump. Although we were at Brize where the jump training for the Paras took place, it was impossible to get a military training course, jumping out of a Hercules along with a "stick" of other parachutists. They only did that with actual Paras. What you could apply for was a Sport Parachuting course, where you jumped out of a small aircraft, still on a static line but eventually leading up to free-falling. These were very hard to get on and I amongst others, applied for one of these but frankly it was one of those "only if your name comes out of a hat" situations.

Dave Stewart managed to be chosen for one but as he had just been selected for aircrew training, which would involve him having to do a parachute jump to qualify, in an incredibly generous act IMHO, he offered to withdraw from the Sport Para course and offered me as a replacement. Rather than go through the selection again, and as I was there on camp, had already completed the paperwork and had the medical, 1 Para School accepted me as a replacement.

Unfortunately I screwed up my first jump and sprained my ankle badly. They put it in plaster for 6 weeks, that's how bad it was. It was my own fault, I'm not blaming the instructors. They keep hammering it into you, 'Keep your feet together when you land,' but I made the mistake of "stepping down" as they call it, when you are inches away from the floor you automatically reach down with one foot, as if you're stepping off a stool. So you take all the force of the landing on one foot. I sprained my ankle and a girl on the course broke her leg.

Dave Stewart was mortified, as he felt responsible for me being on the course and consequently me being injured, which was nonsense of course and I told him so.

I have a picture of me standing on crutches, with my leg in plaster. In the background you can see my day-glo orange jumpsuit that I wore on the course.

Which reminds me of the time later that I bumped into a guy called Roger at Brize that I knew from Cyprus. He had been my trade but being the sporty type he wanted to remuster (change trades) to be a Physical Training Instructor (PTI). Trainee PTI's had to do a parachute jump to qualify (I don't know why, it's not as if we build the gyms *that high* off the ground) and had come to Brize to do his jump training.

Anyway, a couple of days later I was walking to work down the main drag in my combat gear when I saw Roger and his course mates heading in the same direction. They were all wearing the same day-glo suits that I had worn on my parachute course. Roger started showing off in front of his course mates by taking the p*ss out of me, saying I looked like a tree etc. and they joined in. So to get my own back I asked them, 'You do know why you have to wear those bright orange suits, don't you?'

'No,' they replied.

'It's for when the jump goes wrong. It makes finding the bodies so much easier,' I told them.

I guess they hadn't done their first jump yet as they all went mysteriously quiet and no one made any more fun of me after that. (Well they started it!)

***

Dave Stewart, (again! Don't worry, this chapter isn't all about him. I just guess he had a more interesting life than me) actually flew Concorde! Yes, a mere SAC got to handle the controls of Concorde. Dave told me this story, and as I'd known him since Cyprus and never found his word to be anything but trustworthy, I believed him.

Before Concorde entered service in 1976, it spent some time at RAF Brize Norton doing day and night "circuits and bumps". This is the procedure where they practice take-offs and landings in a continuous loop. They take-off, fly around in a circle (a circuit) then land again on the runway, but instead of slowing to a halt, once they are on the ground but still moving, they gun the engines and head straight down the runway to take-off again (a bump). Concorde had come to Brize to practice doing these circuits and bumps, particularly at night. There weren't many places with a long enough runway to accommodate Concorde which made us an alternate diversion airfield, and they had to practice landing here should it be necessary.

Concorde was exceedingly noisy during take-off. Even though our barrack blocks were near the runway, you would get used to the noise of the VC10's and the Tristar aircraft and could sleep through their take-offs. Concorde taking off used to wake me up when it blasted off as it was an unfamiliar sound and you would sit up in bed, going, 'What the h*ll was that!'

Of course it was okay to annoy us; we were just airman and didn't count.

It came to Brize a few times and whenever it did, the camp had a lottery to pick people from the camp who would get to fly on the plane while it was doing its flying around familiarising itself with the station and its surrounds.

Dave won one of these seats (lucky s*d) and got to fly on Concorde. When they were up in the air the pilot came back to speak to them and, ignoring all the Wing Commanders and what have you, invited Dave up to sit in the cockpit. Dave is pretty tall so it must have been a bit of a squeeze for him. Anyway, as they were sitting there the pilot said to him, 'Okay, take over the controls.' So Dave got his hands on the controls and for a few minutes actually "flew" Concorde. How many people can say they did that, especially a lowly airman? Now that is a story to tell your Grandchildren!

***

Talking about sleeping through VC10's and Tristar aircraft taking off, it was true. After a while at Brize you could quite easily ignore the sound and relegate it to background noise except for one thing ... it used to drown out the sound of my TV.

You'd be sitting there watching a crime story and the detective would be saying, 'The murderer is ....' WHOOSH! Gigantic roar as a plane takes off. Every time. I used to swear that the Air Traffic Controller would hold the plane at the end of the runway, engines throbbing and keep one eye on the TV. As the detective was about to name the killer, the Controller would give the go ahead to the aircraft and he would take off, ruining the dénouement.

Another thing was following a series on TV. At the time Video Recorders were coming on the market, but were too hideously expensive for a lowly-paid airman like myself. So I would faithfully follow a series, say 5 episodes of a 6 part series, and without fail I would always be away on exercise when the last part was on.

I eventually got a Video Recorder but I had to get a NATO posting to do that.

***

Why should Britain tremble?

There was something about being on TCW, living the life we did and doing the job we did that really matured you, made you feel a man of the world. When you compared yourselves to the rest of Brize you felt yourselves head and shoulders above them. Take someone in General Office for example, sooner or later he would get an overseas posting but until then, he probably never left Brize and thought Oxford was "the real world".

I remember walking into the NAAFI one evening behind two guys and one of them was saying, 'I was at a disco in Oxford last night.'

I thought to myself, *last night I was at a disco in Denmark!*

Completely different worlds.

***

TCW was a good place to get your driving license if you didn't have one. Being a mobile unit the more drivers you had the better, obviously. If you were lucky you could even get a HGV license but that never happened to me.

I eventually got a driving course but this all happened before I did, so I never got chance to drive one.

The Wing had one or two ½ Ton or Short Wheel Base (SWB) Land Rovers, as they were known, but the usual vehicle was the ¾ Ton or Long Wheel Base (LWB) Land Rover. These had to be larger as before each exercise they were FFR'd which means Fitted For Radio. The techies would fit radios into the back and we would operate from there when we were on exercise.

Occasionally, depending on your role on the Ex, they would fit teleprinters as well as radios into the rear of the wagon. This was known as a Radio TeleType or RATT fit. Most of us disliked doing those exercises as the bulky teleprinters took up a lot of room and made it difficult to move around in there.

Then Land Rover developed a 1 Ton Land Rover, which was like a small truck and the Wing got their hands on a couple of them. Like the other Land Rovers they had a soft, tarpaulin top which could be removed if necessary.

Some bright spark had the idea that if we fitted a hard top to the 1 Ton Rover, we could fit teleprinters into the back and have them permanently fitted for RATT. So away they went to a body firm somewhere and were converted to hard tops.

They should have suspected something was wrong when the drivers tasked to return the vehicles to Brize were complaining that the paint that had been used in the cabs of the hard tops was making their eyes sting.

Nevertheless, pressing on they proceeded to fit teleprinters into the back of the 1 Ton Land Rovers. Unfortunately, when they took these vehicles for a test drive it was found that with all the extra weight up top, the vehicles were now unstable and were likely to topple over if they went round a corner too fast. They removed the teleprinters and instead of converting them back to soft tops, they were just left to rot in the MT yard and we never got to use them anymore. Sigh!

***

Mind you, this is what happens when you let people have ideas. One that made me laugh was the TACAN trailer. This is a device known as a Tactical Aid to Navigation that MNF were responsible for, a kind of homing beacon. It was about the size of a beer barrel standing on a tripod, around 8 feet tall. The idea was you took it out into the field and aircraft or helicopters were able to home in on it and follow it to your location. So you could use it to set up an emergency airfield for example.

The trouble was that the actual TACAN plus the controls, coupled with the ancillary equipment and the generator, took up so much space that you had to load it into a 4 ton lorry, to lug it all around.

Well this tied up a 4 tonner and TCW would have preferred something that could be hitched to the back of a Land Rover. So they called up the boffins from the Defence Research Establishment, who came along with their pipes, elbow patches, tape measures and slide rules (this was the 70's remember) took all sorts of photographs and measurements of the TACAN gear, and then went away.

Many months later they turned up at Hangar 66 and proudly showed us this trailer that they had designed and created. Actually it was pretty low to the ground so a "skid" was probably a more accurate description.

They loaded all the TACAN gear onto it and it was all fine except for one detail … all together, the weight of the TACAN gear and the skid was so heavy that only a 4 tonner could pull it! So it still couldn't be pulled by a Land Rover and it still tied up a 4 ton lorry.

So the boffins slunk away and we never saw them or their trailer again.

***

One thing that really used to annoy me was RAF bureaucracy and the way it ground slowly. When I first arrived at Brize Norton, my ID card was falling apart. This was in the days before the ID card (RAF Form 1250) was the credit card type. My F1250 was old-style which was a piece of card with your photo attached, laminated for protection. The lamination was splitting and my picture was in danger of falling out. (Or being replaced.) So Gen Office sent me along to the P1 section, who dealt with that sort of thing, where it was taken off me and I was issued with a temporary ID card made of cardboard and the forms were sent off for a new one.

A year later I was still waiting for my new card to be issued. It was in the hands of the Provost and Security Services at RAF Rudloe Manor. I kept going back to P1 and asking where it was and they said these things take time. (Seriously, a year?)

Of course I was going on exercises to other countries and I was having to show this piece of paper to gate guards to try to gain access to foreign airbases. Suspicious or what? If I hadn't been with some of the TCW lads who could vouch for me, I would probably still be languishing in some foreign military jail.

I went back every few months to complain to the clerks. I told one of them, 'People are refusing to accept that this is a real ID card.'

Do you know what the idiot said to me? 'Well, they've got to accept it, it's an official document.'

'You try telling that to a 6 foot, Dutch marine with a machine gun!' I replied. Bunch of clowns. They still wouldn't take any action, I just couldn't get them to accept that maybe, just maybe, P&SS at Rudloe had lost my forms. But no.

Anyway, months later, just to try and stir some sh*t up to get someone higher up to look into my case, I even put in a General Application. A Gen App, as it is known, is when you want to request something on an official basis from the RAF. For example, 'I would like to apply for aircrew,' 'I would like to change trade to be an aircraft engineer,' 'I would like to apply for a change of posting to Scotland on compassionate grounds.' That sort of thing. They always make you grovel when you apply as the first lines of the request are already pre-printed on the form, 'Dear Sir, I have the honour to request …'

So I put one in saying, 'Dear Sir, I have the honour to request that I may be allowed to have a F1250 ID card, the same as the rest of the Air Force.' I got called into the Flt Commanders office and told not to be silly and it went in the bin.

Finally, *finally*, someone listened to my case and made P1 fill out a new set of forms, take a new picture and send them off to Rudloe Manor.

After 18 months, (*18 months!*) I eventually got a new F1250 to replace my *temporary* ID card. I got called down to the P1 section to collect and sign for it. I was in 7th Heaven. And then a week later I got called down to the P1 section AGAIN to sign for my new ID card that had just turned up! After 18 months without one I now had 2 of them. (Who knew ID cards were like buses? You wait for ages and then 2 turn up at once.)

I pondered what to do. It would be handy to have 2 ID cards in case I lost one (a chargeable offence) but then I vaguely remembered reading or hearing somewhere that it was also an offence to have 2 ID cards. I weighed it up and decided it wasn't worth the risk so I handed one of them in.

Bloody shinies! A waste of rations, some of them.

***

It always amazes me when some people are unable to use logic to sort out a problem. It seems that anything requiring them to actually "think" is beyond their terms of reference. I'll give you an example. (*I know this is a silly story but it's one that has stuck in my mind over the years, so I'll tell it here.*)

A few of us went on exercise, unusually to another RAF camp, not out in the woods. One night me and a colleague having missed tea, went into the NAAFI looking for something to eat. Fortunately they had a place that did hot food. Nothing fancy, sausage and chips, egg and chips, pie and chips, that sort of thing.

I wasn't very hungry so I just asked for a sausage sandwich. 'We only do what's on the menu,' I was told, by the woman behind the counter.

My mate said he wasn't very hungry either, so he said he'd just have a plate of chips. 'We only do what's on the menu,' she repeated.

My colleague looked at me and I at him, waiting to see who would do the honours. He left it up to me.

'Okay then,' I said. 'I would like sausage and chips *and two slices of bread*, please.'

'Oh yes, we can do that,' she says and off she toddled to fix it.

I got my sausage sandwich and he got his plate of chips. (*I mean come on, it's not rocket science is it?*)

***

Of course, being in the services I did my fair share of hob-nobbing with royalty. Well, sort of.

While I was on TCW, Prince Charles took over as Commanding Officer of the Parachute Regiment. Fair play to him, he decided that if he was going to be their new CO, then he should undertake the same parachute training as them and do the requisite number of jumps to qualify.

No 1 Parachute Training School was the next hangar along from us, also facing onto the pan. Charles did his training with the rest of the paras on his course and then for several days they all filed out onto the pan and climbed into a waiting Hercules aircraft, for them to do their jumps at RAF Weston-on-the-Green, around 20 miles away from Brize.

When they did their jump, the ordinary paras would pile into a bus and drive back to Brize whereas Charles would jump into a waiting Wessex helicopter and be flown back to land on the pan outside our hangar. It made sense from the security aspect. In a helicopter he was secure but if everyone knew that he would be in a bus, coming back from Weston, he would be easy to ambush.

All of us hanging around in the MNF office would flood outside the hangar to watch this going on. We had sense enough to not shout at him, as that would have got us in deep do-do.

The next time I had a brush with royalty was with his sister, Anne.

We had just arrived back at RAF Lyneham after flying back from Cyprus. We were all dusty and sweaty before we got on the plane and had spent 10 hours in the back of a Hercules, so weren't the smartest of airmen.

We got through customs at Lyneham and were just about to get our Land Rovers and trailers and leave, when we were told to go into the departure lounge and wait there, as Princess Anne had just flown in and they didn't want her delicate senses offended by us or blocking up the road with our vehicles.

So we trudged in there, grumbling amongst ourselves because we wanted to go home and whose car should pull up right in front of the departure lounge? Why, Princess Anne's of course. We all lined up along the window and as she left the terminal and got into her car we all waved at her. She ignored us of course but it made us laugh. Trying to hide us and then positioning us right where she couldn't miss us.

***

BELIZE

I don't know how long the British forces had been in Belize, Central America (we've had a relationship with them for hundreds of years) but some time before I joined the Wing, Guatemala, their next door neighbour, had once again been sabre-rattling and demanding that part of Belize belonged to them and they wanted it back. (*This time Google isn't my friend as I can't find the date.*)

So the story goes (I don't know how true it is) that Guatemala had said, 'Right, we're going to invade,' then launched their air force of Cessna's or whatever tin-pot planes they had. The Brits promptly sent up some Harriers to hover on the Belize border and the Guatemalans immediately backed down, saying, 'Okay. Can we talk about this? We'll just go back now. Sorry to have bothered you. You've got our number haven't you? Give us a call, we'll do lunch some time.' And that was that.

Some of the TCW lads were there and they came back with T-shirts that said,

I FOUGHT IN THE BELIZE WAR ALL MORNING

TCW had 2 standing detachments around the world, one in Northern Ireland and one in Belize. Eventually my name came out of the hat and off I went to Belize.

We landed in Canada where I got my passport stamped, although we never left the airport. Then on to Belize. I saw these T-shirts on sale that said "I Survived the Bermuda Triangle". I wanted one of them but I thought I hadn't earned it until someone pointed out that I

HAD flown through the Bermuda Triangle on my way down there and would on my way back, so I bought one.

There were around 6 or so of us there for 6 weeks each, at a time. Some operators and some techies. Airport Camp as it was known, was right next to Belize International Airport and our accommodation was only separated from the runway by some barbed wire and fifty yards of scrub.

We lived in Nissan huts. You know, the semi-circles of corrugated iron dug in to the ground, with a concrete floor. It was double skinned and sometimes you could hear the lizards running between the walls. The place was malarial so we had to use Mosquito nets on the beds and take anti-malaria tablets.

It's the only place I have ever seen Monsoon rainfall. It was just like you see in the films, literally like standing under a shower. Get caught out in the open and you were drenched in seconds. Incredible.

Not being actually part of the camp personnel, our huts were the other side of the football pitches where there were a row of Nissan huts and a shower/toilet block. They put all the "funny ones" over there who they were not quite sure who they were or how to deal with them. Several huts down from us were the SAS guys or "F Troop" as they were known there, but they kept themselves to themselves.

No one knew for certain why the SAS were referred to as F Troop. There were 2 stories, there was a comedy TV series about a troop of US Cavalry soldiers, called F Troop around at the time (I had seen the show myself) so they called themselves that. The other one was that when they flew into Belize Airport, they were on the same plane as an infantry company. As the movements staff gave the soldiers their instructions, where to stand and wait for their luggage and transport, they were dividing everyone up by which troop they were in. 'A Troop over there, B Troop over there, C Troop over there, D Troop over there and E Troop over there.'

The SAS guys roll up. 'Who are you?' ask the movements staff.

The SAS guys, wishing to remain anonymous, replied, 'We're F Troop.'

'We haven't got an F Troop.'

'You have now,' and it stuck.

Being in the same row of huts as them naturally led some people on camp to conclude that we were the same type of people, which never does any harm to your street-cred, does it?

As I said earlier in the chapter, part of TCW's role was to support helicopter operations and that was why we were in Belize. As they flew around the country, we would talk to them by radio and record their progress and position, get any weather reports for them, mainly just keep tabs on them in case they got in trouble and had to land. This is known as the Heli-Safety Net and was what we did in Northern Ireland as well.

The camp was pretty grotty, Nissan huts surrounded by actual jungle. Looked like all those Vietnam war movies you see. There were bars on camp and one just outside the camp gates. The only entertainment provided was BFBS radio piped into every hut. I had the bad luck to be out there the same time as a Scottish Regiment and they requested "Mull of Kintyre" over and over again on the radio. I was heartily sick of it by the time I left.

A lot of the guys went downtown to Belize City. I only went once or twice as most of them used to frequent the knocking shops down there, so I stopped going. Not my cup of tea I'm afraid. I'm of the opinion that if I ever have to pay for it, then it's time for me to hang up my boxing gloves. So I did most of my drinking on camp.

Many people suffered from the "squits" or the "runs" while they were out there. Not me fortunately. I reckon it was down to 2 things. As we supported the helicopters and they might fly late, we were classed as shift-workers and were allowed to draw rations from the mess. This usually consisted of eggs, bread and butter. The army ran the camp and the mess was terrible, I hated eating there, so my intake for the 6 weeks I was there consisted largely of boiled egg sandwiches (which do tend to bind you up).

Secondly, nearly everyone used to drink the local beer as it was cheapest. I however, used to pay a bit more and drink an international brand, Heineken or Carlsberg can't remember which. Okay it was also brewed and bottled in Belize but being an international brand I figured their standards of hygiene would be better. Anyway, it worked and I never had any problems on that score during my detachment. I don't remember being constipated either so maybe the 2 of them balanced each other out and kept me regular.

I did however catch conjunctivitis. It was quite common out there, particularly when you are sharing wash-basins with infected people. The condition wasn't helped by the army Medical Officer banning anyone from wearing sunglasses, even if they were issue, which some of the RAF guys had. Quack!

Being in the Ops room where the heli-tasking was done, it was quite easy to say, 'Excuse me, have you got any flights going out tomorrow that aren't fully loaded? I've got a day off tomorrow, any chance of me tagging along on one of them?'

It meant you had to turn up early, in your Olive Green (OG) uniform and boots instead of the Khakis we normally wore, but so what? I arranged myself a day out in a heli and said to one of the other operators, 'Do you want to come along?'

'Nah, can't be bothered. I'll have a lie in.'

Great, I thought, *I can sit up front all day.*

A Puma helicopter (in fact most RAF helicopters) usually have 2 pilots and an Air Loadmaster who boards everyone on and off the heli, loads/unloads the stores, tells the pilot about the rear view of the heli when they are landing, etc. Here in Belize they only flew with 1 pilot and the loadie.

So I'm waiting outside the Ops building at the required time and the other operator who was going to have a lie-in turns up, which scuppers my plans. Never mind, I got first go.

I sat up the front, in the left-hand seat, next to the pilot of the Puma. (Lovely helicopter, one of my favourites.) They didn't have a helmet for me but they gave me the liner that they wear underneath which has the earphones and the microphone so I could hear everything that was going on.

First of all we flew to an observation post on this hill, overlooking a Guatemalan army camp. We had been briefed on this camp, which was just the other side of the border, when we first arrived. They had shown us pictures, 'Here are the barracks, here is the mess hall, this is the brothel ...' Blimey, they knew how to look after their troops, didn't they? Anyway, we were on top of this hill and I'm sitting there looking straight down into the camp, and I forget that I have my camera in my breast pocket and could have taken photographs but I missed my opportunity. What a dummy! I was kicking myself for ages afterwards.

The next location we went to was a 500 foot hill in the middle of the jungle. (I know it was 500 feet high as that was what it said on the map and that was how they were trying to identify it. The army had a rebro station there, manned by 2 signallers. Rebro station – when you can't get a strong enough signal from A to B, you put a station in the middle to receive it from A and then rebroadcast (rebro) it to site B. That's what was on top of this 500 foot hill. I took them a while to find but eventually they spotted it. The pilot flew over it and had a look. There was literally (and I'm not making this up) a 12 ft by 12 ft tent and a clear space not much bigger than that. That was it, the pilot couldn't see anywhere to land.

'I can't land there, I'll blow their tent away!' he said.

'But you've got to, they need the rations we're dropping off. Otherwise they'll starve.'

'Okay, I'll just touch down the back 2 wheels on the open space and hold it in the hover while you throw the stuff out as fast as you can.'

'Roger.'

I'm not making this up, I could hear their conversation through my headphones and I remember it to this day.

So we gently touched down on the brow of the hill, one of the men frantically holding onto the guy ropes to avoid the tent flying away, while the other one helped the loadie offload their supplies.

Now the reason I keep repeating that the hill was 500 feet high, was that the pilot thought he would take the opportunity to try and scare the Hell out of me. Once he got the word from the loadie, the pilot lifted off from the hill and *dived straight down, nose first*. At one point he looked across at me, expecting to see me gibbering and crying but I just calmly looked back at him. Little did he know that I loved that sort of thing. Obviously I knew that he wasn't going to risk crashing his helicopter just to frighten me, so he wasn't going to do anything stupid or take it too far. Personally I couldn't get enough of being in a heli when they threw it around. (*In those days that was, nowadays I get nervous if I stand on a thick carpet.*)

I've even scrounged a ride in a helicopter once that

they were taking it up on an engine test. 'Are you sure you want to do this?' a Chief Tech asked me as I was climbing into the heli. 'They'll be testing the aircraft to its limits.'

'Bring it on, I love it.'

So when this pilot tried to scare me by dropping down the side of a hill, he was wasting his time.

He seemed disappointed. 'We had an army guy in here yesterday and he nearly sh*t himself when I did that.'

'Not me, I'm Air Force.'

What amazed me was that in those days, they smoked in the cockpit. They even had little ashtrays screwed to the side of the control panel! Oh well, I suppose the last thing you want is a pilot getting twitchy because he is desperate for a cigarette.

The next stop was picking up one of the F Troop guys in the jungle. We were flying around looking for some orange smoke when the loadie spotted it in the distance.

We flew to it and landed in a clearing. I couldn't see anyone at first then I started to notice these eyes staring out at us from the foliage. Downright creepy it was. One of them came out of the jungle and climbed aboard. Then we were off again.

One of the things that people like to bring back as souvenirs from Belize was machetes to hang on the wall (I hope). You could buy them at APC but they were made out of cheap tin. People who had the opportunity to get down country liked to buy real, working machetes, with a thick blade. The pilot wanted to buy one, so we landed in a field outside a town and the pilot, the loadie, the other TCW guy and I walked into town, leaving the SAS guy to guard the helicopter.

I got tasked with buying the cokes while the aircrew did their shopping and when we got back to the heli I gave one to the trooper.

He took it gratefully and then said, 'I'm terribly sorry, I don't have any money to pay you back for this.'

'Err … no bother. Have it on me.'

'Thanks very much, very kind of you.'

One of our other TCW chaps picked up some F Troop guys on another day and during a stop at one of the locations where the chopper had shut down, one of them spotted him smoking a cigarette and came up to him.

'Excuse me, I know it's terribly rude of me but do you think I could possibly scrounge a cigarette from you?'

'Sure. And would your friends like one as well.'

'Yes they would, that's terribly kind of you. Thanks.'

Incredibly polite these Special Forces guys. I guess it just makes the point that *if you are* really tough then you don't have to prove it. Just goes to show that they don't deserve the nick-name "Hooligans from Hereford".

I don't remember much of what happened in the afternoon as I was sitting in the back. Because Belize is a hot country they flew with the doors open and I had good visibility, so I did see one thing that made me laugh.

Back in the UK there are navigational aids and radar and what have you, all over the place. Here in Belize, away from Airport Camp and Belize International there wasn't any. Which meant that navigation had to be done the old fashioned way, by map and compass. The problem being that outside of the towns, Belize is just jungle, criss-crossed by red, dirt roads. This means there's not a lot of landmarks. At some point that afternoon the loadie, who was also acting as the navigator, admitted he wasn't sure where they were. They flew around for a bit and then they spotted a crossroads.

'Fly down to that and we'll read the road signs,' he told the pilot.

So the pilot duly brought the heli down and hovered around 20 feet up while the loadie read the signs and identified where they were on the map. That did give me a giggle that did.

Had a couple of nice jollies while I was out there. The helicopters used to do R&R runs out to some of the Cayes (islands) around Belize, for the army and RAF lads. Fly out in the morning and return in the late afternoon. The heli would fly out, park up and the aircrew would amuse themselves for the day but staying close to the helicopter. In case something cropped up, like a Search and Rescue situation, one of us TCW guys had to accompany them with a back pack radio and stay in contact with APC. So I went along one time. I had to stay with the crew all day but as they hung around a beach restaurant it wasn't much of a hardship. I set up my radio on the beach, slung my aerial into the trees and established comms with APC. After that I sat in the sun for the day, it was just a radio check every couple of hours and then call them when we were leaving to come home. It was a tough job but someone had to do it.

The other time was when myself, a Cpl techie and a J/T techie took a Land Rover and a radio and went away for the weekend, doing *cough* comms trials *cough*. There was a hotel on the coast that was well known for its lobster but when we went there they didn't have any in. We had a good meal anyway and stayed the night.

As I said the roads were red dirt and as we had the canvas on the driving compartment pulled back because of the heat, you got covered in red dust. When you were off the road it was just all jungle. And at one point I was just literally pulling oranges off the trees and eating them.

We were driving down this jungle road in the middle of nowhere and suddenly we came across these low buildings with a Union flag flying outside. Talk about a corner of a foreign field that is forever England! We couldn't believe our eyes. So we stopped and checked it out. Turned out it was a British army jungle training centre, Sibun I think it was called. We went in and said hello, scrounged a drink of water off them and went on our way.

Another thing about Belize is the size of the insects. As we drove down a dusty road, the Cpl and I in the front of the Land Rover, a cricket (or locust more like) landed on the dashboard, between us. No kidding, it must have been about 6 inches long. We screeched to a halt, the Cpl was driving, and we both leapt out and ran round to the back of the Rover.

'Quick, give us the pick-axe handle.'

'What's going on?'

'Never mind, just give us the pick-axe handle!'

This poor lad in the back was probably thinking we were being attacked by bandits or something. Little did he know that 2 of Britain's finest were having a girly fit because some nasty insect had invaded our personal space. We poked it with sticks until it flew away.

When we got back to camp and pulled up outside our hut covered in red dust, looking like we'd spent 6 weeks in the jungle, one of our TCW guys was on his way to the showers. He and some ordinary RAF guys stopped to watch us. Our guy told us later that one of them had said to his mate, 'See, I told you they were part of that lot,' indicating the huts where F Troop lived. Ha!

***

NORTHERN IRELAND

Eventually I had to do our other standing detachment, Northern Ireland. This was in the late 70's so the troubles were still on over there.

For some reason my name never seemed to come out of the hat to go there, so I kept my head down and my mouth shut. It all went wrong for me when one of the married guys got detached there. (I won't name him as it wasn't his fault.) His wife came down to TCW HQ and started complaining that he shouldn't have to go as he was married. They should only send single guys over there as it didn't matter so much if we got killed! (Her opinion not mine.)

Well, naturally this caused a stink in HQ, (not to mention in the crew room). She was told that he would be going, married or not, but all this fuss caused them to take a closer look at the records to see if there were more married guys than single, going there. And it came to light that I had never been. So I was told that I would be going out on the next turnaround.

When the time came, England was experiencing a heat-wave so I consoled myself with the thought I could spend my time topping up my tan. Nope. No such luck. While England sweltered for the next 6 weeks, it rained nearly every day in Ireland.

The job was the same as in Belize, Heli-Safety Net.

There was very little to do there outside of work. I had decided that as it was only 6 weeks long, it wasn't worth the risk to go off camp and see the sights. No Siree Bob. They killed people like me out there! So that only left the NAAFI for socialising or staying in your room reading a book.

Bob Pritchard turned up as the new corporal after I'd been there a while. I knew Bob from Cyprus and we had got along, so at least there was a friendly face. There's not really a lot else to say about the place. Couldn't wait to leave it. I wanted to get back to the girlfriend. My first 2 years on the Wing, I didn't have one, the last year when I did have one I never spent so much time away from

Brize on exercise and detachment.

Like I said, I never left the camp for 6 weeks and yet, as it was officially classed as a war zone and I had spent more than 30 days there, I was entitled to a medal. This was the same medal that they gave to the poor s*ds who had to patrol the streets. So I felt it wasn't right and determined never to claim my medal as it wasn't fair. It was only many years later when my father-in-law, who was ex-military, explained to me that that sort of thing still meant a lot to many people out there in civvy street, and when I was eventually demobbed it might help me to find a job.

So that was Northern Ireland off my bucket list.

***

One of the downsides of being on TCW was the promotion prospects. There you were competing with another 100 or so telegraphist SAC's for good assessments. To stand out you really had to be exceptional – e.g. standing on the roof of the Land Rover during a lightning storm, holding the whip aerial above your head with one hand, while you tapped out Morse code on the key strapped to your leg, with the other hand – or you had to be a "face" and get yourself known by the seniors. And believe me there was some stiff competition for the latter, the place was full of characters.

The truth is that although a place like TCW was great fun and character building, etc. it was deadly for the career. Unless you were outstanding, you got the normal "good" to "very good" assessments, and then you went before the promotion boards where you were up against people who worked in what we called "RAF Sleepy Hollow". A nice, warm Commcen somewhere, where they handled 3 signals a day, had the time to work carefully and make no mistakes, knocked off at 5 o'clock which gave them ample time in the evenings to do committee work and impress their superiors. It was an unfair competition really. I proved it later, my own promotion came about by working at the NATO equivalent of RAF Sleepy Hollow, but more of that later.

Mind you it was nearly as bad for the corporals, although I did consider some of their tactics slightly underhand and distasteful. We used to support the helicopter squadrons on their exercises and I was with one Cpl a couple of times (*I won't name him*) where I saw him approach the exercise commander and ask him if he was satisfied with the service we had provided. If the officer said yes, then the Cpl would ask him to write to TCW and say that he was pleased.

It's one thing to get noticed on your own performance but to go around touting for endorsements seemed "tacky" to me. Still it worked, I believe he eventually got his 3rd stripe, so what do I know?

***

Some people loved to spend as much of their career on the Wing as they could. Steve "Tricky" Tranter for example would be on the Wing, do an overseas tour, come back to the Wing, do an overseas tour, back to the Wing, etc. If he couldn't get directly back then he would sound out people on the Wing who might be willing to swap. For me however I enjoyed the experience but didn't want to spend my remaining RAF career doing it.

I suppose it's a bit like the Special Air Service. It sounds like a great job for a soldier until you read their memoirs, then you see that they spend a lot of their time on such things as manning a forward observation post. You have to sneak into position at the dead of night. You might spend 7-10 days in there, not being able to have a hot meal or even a smoke as the light would give away your position. You can't walk about to stretch your legs and you have to cr*p into a plastic bag. When you are relieved you have to crawl away taking your bag of poop with you. So it's not all smashing through embassy windows and slotting terrorists!

I remember the point at which I had my, 'I've had enough of this,' epiphany. It came one night on an exercise in Denmark, after I'd been on the Wing about 3 years. We were camped in a forest somewhere and I was on guard. I had positioned myself in a bush for concealment and I could see a main road and was watching the headlights of the cars driving by. It was about 10 o'clock and as each car went by I thought to myself, *He could be going home to his wife and kids and a nice, home-cooked meal. That guy could be going down to the local bar for a night out with friends. I wish I was with them but here I am guarding this bush against a non-existent enemy. Time for a change me-thinks.*

Okay, call me "a civilian in uniform" if you wish. The thing is I was fully prepared to get down and dirty if the situation demanded it … but I didn't want to live my life like that. I liked my creature comforts, to be clean, have regular meals, watch TV, go for a drink when I wanted, etc. I'm not knocking the blokes who enjoyed being on the Wing but for me it was just another posting – a job, not a way of life – so I decided that although I wouldn't actively seek to get off TCW, if my turn for a posting came up I wouldn't fight it.

***

Everyone has a favourite exercise from their time on the Wing (unless they are really unlucky). Either you spend a few weeks sunning yourself in some exotic location or (like mine) you don't go anywhere special but you make a load of money from the exercise.

First I need to explain something about Rates. This is what the RAF pays you when you have missed meals, due to being away from camp. It works like this – I as a single man paid the RAF for my food and accommodation. If for service reasons I am away from camp during the day and I miss any meals I have paid for, I am entitled to reclaim the money from the RAF. Likewise if a scalie also misses a meal that he would normally have eaten at home, then he is entitled to claim money, as he has in effect had to pay twice for the same meal.

This is where Rates come in. To reclaim the cost of your meal is a Rate 5 (if memory serves) and there are different Rates for each circumstance (evening meals as opposed to breakfasts). I don't remember them all but they go up to Rate 1 where you will be away from any service support and basically have to fend for yourself, including finding your own accommodation. Although you claim Rate 5 retrospectively, they pay you a Rate 1 in advance, as you have to pay for your hotel bill as well as for food. At the time (late 70's) that amounted to about £30 a day. So if you were going to be away for 7 days then they would shove £210 in your hot, sweaty, little hand.

And to make things even better, if you were an officer you would get paid more as they expect a better class of accommodation. If you had an officer in your party and you stayed in the SAME hotel/bed-and-breakfast as them, then you were allowed to claim the officer's Rate 1.

I knew some people that would take their Rate 1's and then sleep in their Land Rover if it was just an overnight stop-over but honestly, it's free money so why not spend it as it's meant to be used?

Anyway, my best exercise was the one I spent in the north of Scotland where I spent 3 weeks living in a hotel on officer's Rate 1's.

I can tell you all now as it's no longer been a secret since the first Gulf war but I was involved in the testing of Laser-guided bombs back in the 70's.

What happened is that there is a small island called Garvie Island which is used as a bombing range by the UK military. This island is just off the coast of Cape Wrath, on the western tip of Scotland. Cape Wrath is on the road that runs across the absolute top of Scotland, and if you hop on it and drive east you will eventually come to John O'Groats, which is the eastern tip of Scotland.

On this particular exercise a whole load of RAF personnel and a few civvy boffins headed up there for a 3 week exercise to test out these Laser-guided bombs. TCW sent a couple of teams up there and I was on the team that went to Cape Wrath, whereas the other team went to RAF Lossiemouth to be the other end of our link.

I don't remember the name of the town we stayed in, but it was around October time so it was out of season, with no tourists, so when we turned up and took over the town, literally filling up every B&B and hotel in the place, the locals were delighted to see us and our money. Not being nasty when I say that, it was a low point in the year for them so any extra income from us was more than welcome. They loved having us there and made us very welcome.

My team (I'm pretty certain my Cpl was Ron Lander) all stayed in one hotel which we shared with 2 RAF Reservist Met officers. Bingo! £££! Although we had been paid airman's Rate 1's for 3 weeks, we were able to upgrade it to officer's Rate 1's when we got back. I made so much money on that exercise.

The hotel would feed us in the mornings and evenings, do our washing for us and even let us watch their TV. This was during the big ITV strike of 1979. BBC (*the rats*) took the opportunity to just show a load of dross on TV as they had no competition. When people complained they said, 'Oh no, these were the programmes we had scheduled. We can't just change them like that.' Liars. There is soon a change of schedule if someone famous dies, so you didn't fool anybody.

And the Ex was great too. Everyone was operating from the buildings on the cliffs at Cape Wrath, overlooking Garvie Island, where the bombs would be dropped. To get to it you had to drive along the beach and then up through the sand dunes, until you were up on the cliffs. What a great commute!

It was really windy up there on the cliffs, you could lean into the wind at practically a 45 degree angle. There was a cook on the exercise who supplied us with soup and sandwiches during the day. To supplement his budget, he used to go out hunting rabbits with his air rifle and then skin them and hang them up in one of the rooms, for the blood to drain out. I didn't know this and walked into the room one day. Aaaargh! It was like the Texas Chainsaw Massacre in there. I stayed out of there after that and stuck to the Cheese or Corned Beef sandwiches.

The bombing shut down at the weekends so we would take the Land Rover and go sight-seeing to places like John O'Groats. Not a lot of places to go but the scenery was magnificent. We had a great time.

Up at Cape Wrath we were working downstairs in the tower. Our job was to pass weather reports back to Lossiemouth and then inform everyone when the bombers were on their way to Cape Wrath. After the bombs had been dropped we would pass back any observations that the boffins had. We would go upstairs occasionally to the viewing room and sometimes they would let us have a look through the huge binoculars that were there, fixed on stands.

It was weird watching the bombs fall. An aircraft would point a Laser at the target "painting the target" as they call it, then another plane would drop the bomb. You could follow the bomb all the way from the plane to the target. It would be coming down in a straight line and then start to drift due to gravity or whatever, then a fin would move to alter the trajectory back into the Laser path. The bomb would jink left and right to stay on line, until it finally hit the ground. Fascinating to watch.

Still, all good things must come to an end, so after 3 weeks we had to pack up and say goodbye to Scotland. Considerably richer!

***

Another good exercise was the one where we went to Scotland by sleeper train. A number of us were due to go to the North of Scotland on exercise. Some bright spark calculated that with what they would have to pay us in Rate 1's, the cost of the petrol, the wear and tear on the vehicles, it would be cheaper and better for us if we went up by overnight sleeper train. Brilliant! I'll have some of that.

We drove down to a London station, got a carryout in case there wasn't a buffet car on the train, loaded up the Land Rovers and trailers and settled into our sleeping compartments while the train whisked us overnight to Inverness.

We were cramped in our compartments trying to have a drink, so we asked the steward if it was okay to use the empty 1st class carriages. 'Sure,' he said. 'You pay more for a sleeper compartment than you do for a 1st class seat, so you're entitled to go in there.' So we took over a couple of compartments and we were all sitting there in our combat gear, drinking beer in 1st class! That doesn't happen every day.

Same thing happened on the way back. We came from a different Scottish station as it was going over to the winter time-table (Aberdeen maybe?) the only downside this time there was no buffet car on the train, but we had plenty of drink and some of us managed to hop out at one of the stations enroute and buy sandwiches from a platform stall. Apart from that minor niggle it was great fun. I don't remember anyone else doing that on future exercises so we were lucky to be the ones to test it out.

***

Well, all good things must come to an end, as they say and so did my time on the Wing. My security clearance got renewed so I knew a posting to a Top Secret place or a NATO posting was in the offing. Eventually word came through, the following January I was to be posted to HF Radio Zutendaal in Belgium, a NATO posting.

My reaction was the same as everyone else's when they heard it, 'Where on earth is that?'

I was pleased to be going but my girlfriend (Mim, short for Miriam) was unhappy that I would be leaving her but I decided that we had a good thing going, so I asked her to marry me. We rushed things through and got married in the December.

And that was that. A whole new chapter of my life was opening up, a new posting in a foreign country, a new wife. Who knew what the future would hold?

HF Radio
Zutendaal

"Belgian Waffle"

Arrived 5 January 1981 HF Radio Zutendaal

I had a NATO posting once to Belgium. I lived and worked in Belgium but we were a subordinate site to the main headquarters in Maastricht, The Netherlands. (*Never call it Holland, it upsets the Cloggies.*)

Belgium is a strange country. Most, if not all, of the major European battles of World War I and II were fought in Belgium, not to mention the Napoleonic Wars. (For those who don't know Waterloo is in Belgium.) The poor little country has had the Hell kicked out of it throughout history.

It seems to be made up of parts of The Netherlands above it, France below it and a bit of Germany thrown in for good measure. The top half of Belgium is known as Flanders and is populated by the Flemish who speak ... Flemish, which is actually Dutch, just pronounced differently, less guttural.

The bottom half of Belgium is known as Wallonia and the people are called Walloons (I'm not making this up) and they speak French. (*Needless to say the Belgian French were just as arrogant as the "real" French and would ignore you if you spoke to them in English.*)

The Flemish and the Walloons hate each other. Every

official government document and public sign has to be written in both languages.

There is also a bit of German speaking over on the right hand side and down south, around the Ardennes region. Their road signs are in German and French. All very confusing.

The reason I mention all this is that I ended up working in the Flemish bit and living in the French bit. Which meant "spreching da foreign lingo" got a bit awkward at times, so the wife, Mim, and I came to an arrangement. She had learned French at school and I had learned German. Dutch seems to me to be a mixture of German and English and there are enough similarities to be able to at least read things written in Dutch and know days of the week, count to ten, read road signs etc. When we were up north I handled the conversations, asked for directions, dealt with shopkeepers and so on and if we were in the south then she took over.

Alles Klaar, Herr Kommisar?

***

I flew out to give me time to arrange the quarter and Mim would follow me later, when that was sorted. Unfortunately at that time there were not many posts for British servicewomen in NATO. Being where we would be in Belgium, the nearest RAF base was RAF Wildenrath in Germany, which was some hours' drive away, so it wasn't really feasible for me to live in Germany with Mim at Wildenrath and drive several hours to work before shift and then several hours back home again after shift. Between night shifts it would have been horrendous. Mim didn't drive so it would have had to be me living with her and not vice-versa. Reluctantly Mim took the option to leave the RAF as she was now married.

In those days the RAF didn't mind married WRAF's but they did understand the problems that situations like ours could cause a young couple, therefore at any time during their married life the WRAF could ask to be released from her contract and it was allowed, no charge.

Although the RAF does its long-haul trooping themselves to place like Cyprus and Gibraltar, service people going to postings in Central Europe are trooped via civilian charter aircraft. At that time the planes flew from Luton Airport to RAF Gutersloh in the north of Germany and RAF Wildenrath for all points south.

I went into the system and ended up spending a night back at RAF Stanbridge which was now a big Air Movements camp through which the service men and families were processed.

The big signals relay centre at Stanbridge I had worked in was now closed and the building had become a Logistic computer centre (I think). The whole camp had been refurbished for its new role and I have to admit that I didn't recognise *anything!* The buildings had been remodelled inside and there were covered walkways between all the buildings. The mess was totally different, new layout and I never went to the NAAFI bar as I don't usually drink when I'm travelling and we had an early start next day. I managed to work out that I was in the barrack block next to the one I had lived in years before but that was all, the rest of the place looked totally different. Weird feeling.

When I got off the plane at RAF Wildenrath I went to the movements staff and told them I needed transport to a place called Tongeren in Belgium. (At least that's what it said on my joining instructions, which surprised me as I thought I was going to Zutendaal. It turns out that although I would work at Zutendaal, initially I would live at Tongeren which was where our admin offices were.)

They said, 'Wait over there and we'll arrange some transport for you.' I waited over there and it became obvious that someone else was also waiting for transport, so we introduced ourselves. This is where I met Graham Duncan for the first time. Like me he had a wife back in the UK waiting to come out to join him but for the time we lived in the block as Bean stealers we became drinking buddies. (Remember Bean stealers are married personnel who live in single accommodation and pay no rent or food charges on the grounds that they are supporting another household elsewhere, where they would be living were it not for service needs.)

Unfortunately when we moved to Liege to live I didn't see much of him after that, as he worked in the caves at Maastricht and we lived on opposite sides of the city, so our paths rarely crossed. We have reconnected as Facebook friends since though.

We eventually arrived at Tongeren Kaserne (Kaserne = camp or barracks.) Unusually it was in the town of Tongeren. Most if not all of the camps I had ever visited were on the outskirts of a town. Here you could walk out of the camp gates, turn left and be in the town centre within minutes.

The Kaserne was where all the admin headquarters for the different nationalities were situated, along with the restaurant and the international version of the NAAFI. It was a square, multi storey building built around the parade square. The restaurant etc. was on the ground floor, the individual nations had their offices on the first floor and then the rooms where the single guys lived were on the second floor. Each nation had its own bar on the accommodation floor. The British one was called … wait for it … "The Verge Inn". Aah, British humour at its finest. (/Sarc.)

The whole set up was complicated (on the British side

at least). The majority of Brits worked in the caves at Maastricht. These were *literally* caves, hewn out of the limestone rock by monks, (not making that up) just over the Dutch border outside the town of Maastricht. These caves housed a big, international, military headquarters. Most of the Brits who worked there were signals like me as it was also a big signal relay centre.

All the singlies lived at Tongeren regardless of where they worked.

The married people who worked in the caves had to live in the town of Liege, in the French speaking part of Belgium, about 20 miles south of Tongeren. (To get there you had to cross the Flemish/French language border.) As it was a foreign country, the Brits couldn't just build married quarters like they would do in the UK. Instead they had "hirings" which is where the MOD rent out flats and houses from locals and we servicemen live in them but only pay the normal rental charges that we would pay on a married quarter. The RAF paid the difference. Liege is a town of high-rise apartment blocks, and in each block where they rented flats there would usually be a mix of service families and locals. Often four or five Brit families in a block.

Married personnel who worked at Tongeren or like myself at Zutendaal were allowed to find a local place to rent in Tongeren or surrounds and if the RAF approved it, could live there instead of Liege.

This was my first choice but after visiting one or two rentals I decided against it. They had no furniture and in one place they had even taken out all the light fittings. I realised that it might take months to find a suitable place and outfit it and I was keen to set up home with my new wife. I gave up the quest and requested a quarter in Liege. Besides, I hadn't acquired my own transport yet so it would mean making my way to Tongeren Kaserne to catch the service transport each shift, whereas in Liege they dropped off and picked up on your doorstep.

So I got a nice flat, Quai Orban 48, 4020 Liege, overlooking the canal. The river Meuse flowed through Liege and at one point a canal had been split off to run alongside the river, creating an island in the middle. I lived on the canal side, overlooking the island. There were three other Brit families in the block, Steve and Jacquie Hobbs, Steve was army MT at Tongeren, Taff and Jenny (sorry can't remember their last names) and Harry and Val Titley. Harry and Taff worked down the caves. All the rest were locals.

Mim came out to join me and we set up our happy, little home.

It was quite a travelogue to get to work though. I had to be driven to Tongeren by RAF transport where I caught the international transport to Zutendaal. If the RAF transport was delayed it caused all sorts of problems at Zutendaal as the night shift couldn't leave until we got there. Eventually I got a car and that all went away. It was a thirty mile drive up the motorway and then back roads to get to Zutendaal but it was worth it.

***

HF Radio Zutendaal. I was surprised when I was taken there for the first time. About ten miles north of Tongeren, so in the Flemish speaking part, it was an empty airfield. I won't say it was disused, I don't think it had ever been used, there was no Air Traffic Control tower or anything like that. I guess it had been built as a dispersal airfield. Just a runway, surrounded by woods.

The only two buildings were the one where we radio operators worked and one some distance across the airfield where the technicians worked. Our site was a small building surrounded by a wire fence. You had to buzz the intercom to get someone to let you in.

Inside the building there were the toilets, the kitchen, the rest-room, the Ops room and the Warrant's office. The whole idea of HF Radio Zutendaal was that we were the standby in case the caves at Maastricht ever got taken out due to war or some other catastrophe. In which case all the bigwigs would jump in their cars/helicopters and come to us.

So all we had to do was make sure that our communications set up worked, just in case. That was it. That's all we ever did, apart from major exercises. It was money for old rope.

We had two permanent circuits, a voice radio circuit to a place in Germany, on which we did an hourly radio check, and a teleprinter circuit to the caves. When there was no traffic on the teleprinter we sent channel checks to make sure that the circuit was still working.

Apart from that, every day we would open up different circuits to various places and send dummy traffic to test them out. They could be voice or teleprinter but they all worked over the radio. Every day would involve a couple of circuit activations, so we didn't just sit there and read books all day, but once we had proved its viability there wasn't much else to do. Occasionally we would have problems where the weather was affecting the radio frequencies but nobody got really upset if it didn't work as long as we actually made an effort to overcome it.

The place was run by a Dutch Warrant Officer. There were four watches, ours consisted of the Duty Signals Master (DSM) a Belgian Sergeant called Joe Sax. Normally people did a NATO tour for around three to four years but Joe had been at Zutendaal for about sixteen years. It was cushy job and he had a house just down the road.

Next the Assistant DSM was a Dutch sergeant (name gone in the mists of time), a German junior rank Mickey Lichtenburg, an RAF SAC Tony Wilkinson and me. Later we were joined by another Belgian ranker (Freddie something?)

The Asst DSM on another watch was Cpl Rory Berrie who was the top ranking Brit operator at Zutendaal (everyone else was SAC's). A top bloke and it was him that got me my corporal tapes, so thanks for that Rory!

The top Brit at Zutendaal was a techie Flt Sgt Dave Lewington. It was his write up that got me promoted but it was based on what Rory told him. Dave was a nice bloke, easy going. Because we were out of the way and rarely seen at Tongeren, sometimes the hair would grow a bit long and Dave would get a phone call from the RAF WO at Tongeren. Then Dave would gently remind us that, 'If your hair is longer than the Flt Sgt's then it's too long.' Unfortunately I've been informed that Dave has passed away. A sad loss to the Human Race.

The shift pattern was two days, two nights, four days off. At first when I was still using service transport, the trip home and back again between night shifts was a killer. Only got about four hours at home if you were lucky. We only needed four on night shifts so there were plenty of nights off. Unless we were on exercise, we split the night shifts so you only had to work half of one night. Like I said, money for old rope.

And later when I bought a car and was able to go straight from home to work and back again, bypassing Tongeren, it was bliss. Apart from having to wear a uniform to work, it was like having a civvy job, it was great! After a hectic three years on TCW I really appreciated having an easy time.

Of course, being NATO there were lots of perks that went with it. We could buy petrol coupons at something like half price. You would buy a book of them and just hand some of them over when you filled up your car. As they came in set amounts for each coupon if the amount of petrol you used didn't match up to the amount on the coupons, they would give you the cash difference!

The international shop was much better than the NAAFI. Fags and booze were cheaper and they sold American Demi-Johns of Smirnoff vodka! As a vodka drinker I was in Heaven.

Talking about the NAAFI, I never understood why many people would only shop there. The NAAFI shop was located in the same building as the Families Club, in a dodgy part of Liege. Mim and I would occasionally use the club but it meant a drive there, which meant I couldn't drink as the drink-driving laws are very stringent in Belgium. If you have an accident, one whiff of alcohol on your breath and you're straight in the clink.

Now, I can understand buying some things in the NAAFI shop that you couldn't get locally, such as baked beans (the Belgian ones never tasted the same) Colman's Mustard, HP sauce etc. but some people would buy everything there, despite the fact that everything had to be shipped down from Germany. By the time you bought your bread it was likely several days old and often going stale. The wife and I used to shop at the local supermarket "Bon Marche" in the shopping mall behind our block of flats. Everything was fresh and they had this wonderful machine where you chose a loaf, put it in the machine and it would slice it up before your eyes, then slip it into a bag.

They also sold horse and rabbit in the meat section. Above each type of meat was a picture of the animal on sale. I always thought it might be counterproductive to show pictures of Black Beauty and fluffy bunnies above those meats, but it seemed to work.

I always wanted to try eating horse but Mim being a "horse-loving" type would never allow that, so one day that I had to spend at Tongeren (GDT training or summat) I tried to order it in the international restaurant. What they gave me tasted like beef so I'm not sure if I actually did eat horse, but that was my only chance.

***

Not everyone had their own transport and had to rely on others to get to the NAAFI or the Families Club, so people tended to socialise within their block. Booze being so cheap everyone was always inviting the others round to their flat for drinks.

Later on Tricky Tranter from TCW turned up and he lived in my block. Also a corporal who was destined for Zutendaal until it turned out that he was a Telephonist who had been retrained as a Telecommunications Controller (TCC). The management centre at Innsworth had assumed that once all the Telephonist/Teleprinter Operators/Telegraphists had merged into Telecommunications Operators, we could all do each other's jobs. Not so, to work at Zutendaal you had to know Morse code and being an ex-Telephonist, he didn't. So they shoved him off to the caves instead.

***

Back in those days the RAF hadn't started issuing the lightweight blue trousers and short-sleeved shirts yet and the summers in Belgium were roasting sometimes. The other nationalities had fancy, summer uniforms so the RAF allowed those that had them to wear their KD uniform (long trousers of course, not shorts). It made a welcome difference.

Up in Germany they still wore blues all year round so anyone from Tongeren who had cause to go to Germany for any reason had to change into blues for the trip. A bit silly really but there ya go.

***

A bit of philosophy just to break things up. Who gets to name towns and cities? Surely it should be the people who live in them? Take London for example, the French call it Londres, the ancient Romans called it Londinium and the Germans call it "Target for Tonight".

The reason I ask is that I lived in Liege. The French speaking Belgians who lived there called it LIEGE, same as we do. The Flemish lot called it LUIK. And if you drove around the German speaking bits they called it LÜTTICH. So if you don't know that, it must get mighty confusing as you are driving towards it and it is called by different names, depending on which direction you're approaching it.

Surely if the people living there call it LIEGE then everybody should call it LIEGE?

Just wondering.

***

In the RAF we normally got paid on the last working day of the month. One of the things that used to annoy me was that in Belgium the admin staff at Tongeren controlled the pay and for some reason they used to pay us on the 24th of the month.

Now that is all well and good and you soon get used it, after all, getting paid every four weeks is okay no matter what day it is, as long as it is the same day every month.

But for some stupid reason when it came to December

they would suddenly insist on paying us on the last working day of the month, which was probably the 30th or 31st. When we'd complain they'd say, 'What's the problem? We're only doing what the rest of the RAF does. I don't see why you are moaning.' So we had to survive *the most expensive month* of the year for five weeks on four weeks' pay!

I mean come on, you can't just say, 'That's how it should be done,' when you don't do it the rest of the year. I'm sure that they only did it to stop people spending all their money over Christmas and having nothing left for January. Mim and I weren't too badly off but some families with lots of kids really struggled but the admin lot couldn't see what they were doing wrong. Idiots! That's admin clerks for you.

***

There was very little for the wives to do in Liege. Unless they spoke fluent French the only work options were cleaning jobs at the Holiday Inn or if you were lucky, a job at the NAAFI shop.

Mim managed to do both of these for a while but for most of the time there was nothing for the wives to do except meet up at the Families Club where most of the talk was about babies.

Naturally enough, when I came home after a four day shift the wife wanted to go out and do things. So we did. We could travel up the motorway to the Flemish part or over the border into the Netherlands and go to the pictures as, like on the TV, English speaking films and TV programmes were shown in English with Flemish or Dutch subtitles.

We would hop in the car and go driving, visiting places like Waterloo and Brussels but usually we headed south, towards the Ardennes which were more picturesque than northern Belgium. They were only a couple of hours drive from Liege. We visited Spa, Francorchamps, Namur, Dinant Citadel which you could reach by cable-car, and then Malmedy and Bastogne which are famous from The Battle of the Bulge.

This was a last ditch effort by the Germans to break out through the Allied lines during World War II. The Americans sent men towards them and they were surrounded by Germans and cut off so it turned into a siege of Bastogne. They had to survive for weeks with little food or ammunition, in the middle of winter, but managed to hold Bastogne until they were finally relieved by General Patton's Third Army.

Bastogne was the centre of all the roads in that area and was a strategic point, if you took that you could go in any direction. Visiting it was fascinating. Every road into the town had a crippled tank at the side of the road as a reminder. There was also a museum and a monument in the shape of the American five-pointed star. If you went on top of the monument it detailed the units that were in the direction of each point of the star, during the battle.

Another favourite was the waterfalls at Coo. Beautiful scenery and we always took visitors there for a visit when they came over from the UK.

Maastricht was another destination for a pleasant day out. Language wasn't a problem as most of the Dutch spoke fluent English. I remember wandering around a Maastricht museum one day and reading the signs in Dutch and English that d'Artagan (he of the Three Musketeers fame) had died in 1673 on the city walls at the Siege of Maastricht, during the Franco-Dutch war. I had always assumed he was fictional. (*See, my books are educational, you can learn things by reading them.*)

Life Lesson No 2

Despite what the song says that you should believe only 'half of what you see and none of what you hear,' up to this point in my life I had always (*naively*) believed that although the papers could lie through their teeth when printing stories, you could believe what you saw on news clips on TV as you were actually seeing it with your own eyes. Then I saw one instance that made me realise how even a film clip could be misrepresented by careful editing.

Liege is in a basin, surrounded by hills so the TV reception is terrible or non-existent, so you have to rely on cable TV for your entertainment. I rather enjoyed this as it meant we had Belgian/Flemish, Belgian/French, Dutch, German and Luxembourg/French channels to choose from.

The Flemish and Dutch channels showed English speaking programmes in their original language and subtitled them. You would find yourself watching any old rubbish as long as it was in English, which is how come I ended watching such things as Dallas and Dynasty (shudder). But I would also watch the French and German channels although they dubbed everything, it's easy to watch a programmes like "The Avengers" and follow it even if you don't understand what they're saying.

The same with the news channels. If they had a train crash for example, you can figure out what is going on by the pictures and the numbers of casualties on the screen.

One day there was a miners strike in Belgium and the protestors were marching through Brussels to make their voices heard. *As we all know*, when miners and police meet it inevitably turns into a riot, which is what happened.

I was idling flicking through the news channels of all the countries at six o'clock, and saw the same film clip being shown again and again on the news. Five or six policemen in riot gear were beating the Hell out of one miner with their night-sticks, he was rolled into a ball on the ground, trying to protect his vitals. The Germans, the Dutch, the French all showed this clip. It was only when the Belgian news came on that the WHOLE sequence was shown.

What really happened was that one of the miners had grabbed a night-stick from a solitary policeman and was beating him with it as the policeman lay on the ground, curled into a ball. To my eye it could only have resulted in the policeman's death or serious injury if left to continue. Several of his fellow officers rushed up, pulled the miner off him and gave him a good pasting for what he had done to their colleague. Once the whole story was known it put a completely different complexion on the story for me.

Suddenly the headline agenda changes from, 'Look at the Belgian police brutality!' from all the other national new programs to 'Police save colleague from certain death,' on the Belgium news. They were the only ones that told the truth about their policemen while all the others nations deliberately edited the clip to show them in a bad light.

So since then I have quite rightly refused to believe any slant that is given to TV news images as they are equally as tainted as what they say, as they all have an agenda to push.

***

While I was at Zutendaal I was told that one time the top

brass at Maastricht got together for their weekly meeting, the top German soldier walked in and snapped off a crisp, Nazi salute. Lowering his arm as everyone's jaw hit the floor, he said, 'Oops, sorry ... wrong meeting.' (*Who says the Germans don't have a sense of humour?*)

***

We used to have the NATO servicing team come down periodically from AFCENT in the Netherlands to service our equipment. AFCENT = Allied Forces Central. There was also AFNORTH-Norway/Oslo and AFSOUTH-Italy/Naples.

They were led by an British Army Staff Sgt. He used to sit with us operators, drink coffee and chat while his techies worked on the kit.

One time he was bemoaning the fact that he was 29 years old and he was only a Staff Sgt not a Warrant Officer. I know I slowed down my own promotion prospects somewhat by taking time to get my SAC but still – call me churlish if you will – but for some reason, being 29 years old myself and still only an SAC, I found it hard to sympathise with him.

***

I include this next tale not because I was in any way connected with it but a) it took place while I was in Belgium, b) it amuses me and c) it reminds me of that poem about "For the want of a nail the shoe was lost …"

Handling a weapon is a serious matter, someone could get killed, so therefore discipline when carrying weapons is crucial. To enforce the discipline the punishments can be harsh. If someone accidentally fires their rifle, even if it is only a blank round, this is known as a Negligent Discharge (ND) and is a serious offence. Whether it is a live round or a blank training one, punishments can include loss of rank, imprisonment or even discharge from the service.

Unless of course you are an officer who shoots down a friendly aircraft.

On May 25th 1982 an RAF Phantom fighter shot down an RAF Jaguar aircraft during a simulated combat exercise over Germany. Fortunately the Jaguar pilot ejected safely and was unharmed.

Apparently fighter pilots have to do so many flights a year (maybe just the one, I don't know) carrying LIVE weapons just so they don't get blasé about flying an unarmed aircraft and forget when they fly a live armed one.

The subsequent Board of Inquiry determined that the master armament switch in the Phantom had not been taped into the "safe" position. Apparently they use the old service standby black tape for this (also known as "bodge tape" or "black nasty"). The aircraft engineers had neglected to put tape on the switches and once the Phantom pilot had the Jaguar in his sights, his training kicked in and he fired off a live Sidewinder missile.

The pilot of the Phantom and his navigator were court-martialled and found guilty of neglect. They both received **severe reprimands**. (*That really taught 'em didn't it?*)

If it had been you or I, we would still have been inside breaking rocks, *to this day*. One law for the rich …

Just saying.

Life Lesson No 3

Later in my tour we had a young Belgian soldier join our watch. His name was Freddie. We welcomed him and tried to teach him the job but he didn't seem to pick it up and kept making mistakes.

Naturally everyone thought he was a bit of a dummy and he started to get treated like one. If anything complicated came up, it was just easier to do it yourself than try to explain it to him. Anyway, finally the rest of the watch went to Joe Sax and asked him to speak to Freddie and find out what was going on, as we were sick of carrying him. Although we were six on the watch, what with leave, stand downs etc. there were never more than four of us at work at any one time. Therefore you couldn't afford to have anyone not pulling their weight.

Joe spoke to him and Freddie finally confessed. He couldn't speak English very well. As fluent English is the major requirement of working for NATO, he had somehow bluffed his way through and tried to cover it up, as he was afraid he would be sent back to the normal Belgian army.

Once we understood this, everyone cut him some slack. Joe spent extra time explaining things in Flemish to him and he soon picked it up. Over time his English improved and he became a useful member of the watch.

The lesson is, just because someone doesn't grasp something straight away; don't automatically assume that they are stupid. There may be more going on than you realise, so take the time to investigate. Maybe they just need to taught in a different way, or be taught by someone else. There are so many possibilities, so don't just write the person off, without exploring these other avenues.

Eventually, shortly before I got posted home, the promotion board results came out – thanks to Dave Lewington and Rory Berry, I was going to be promoted to corporal on my return to the UK!

Hard to imagine why, as I didn't do any secondary duties. (The RAF loves you to do secondary duties.) I personally was an "8 'til 5 man" as we called it. I would come on shift and work as long as necessary to get the job done but once it was finished, I went home and led my own life. In my career I have worked 18 hour shifts and once worked a 24 hour shift to cover for someone who didn't turn up for the night-shift due to illness, so don't get the idea that I'm lazy. But once I was out that door I was my own man. The RAF however, would like you to then go and sit on a committee somewhere.

After news of my promotion came through, I happened to be standing at the bar in the Liege Families Club one time when someone started spouting off about why I shouldn't have been promoted. He worked at Maastricht and didn't know me to look at, so I just kept quiet and listened with interest.

According to him, I shouldn't have been promoted because, and I quote, 'He hasn't done anything for this club.' Apparently he thought that serving as a committee member was more important than actually being good at your job. At the same time as me, someone who worked in the caves got his corporal tapes because he organised the International Table Tennis League. (*Absolutely true.*)

Now, call me old fashioned if you will, but surely it's more important when promoting men in a fighting force (who, let's be honest, may one day have to fight and die for their country) that they know their job and can do it well. Furthermore that they have the maturity and ability to lead the men that will serve under them. This MUST be more important than their ability to organise a Table Tennis tournament, surely? Not according to the RAF, but to my surprise somehow this time I had slipped through the net and been promoted. Obviously the board wanted to get away for an early lunch and just passed this one through "on the nod".

Anyway, it proved the comment I made earlier in the book that the best chance of getting promoted is if you are at an "RAF Sleepy Hollow". Here I was at a "NATO Sleepy Hollow" and gotten the points and the write-up to get promoted.

***

I can't remember if I asked to go back to Oxfordshire or whether I left it to chance but my next posting came through ... 81 Signals Unit, RAF Bampton Castle. Bampton is a village seven miles away from RAF Brize Norton and Brize is its parent unit, so we were back to Brize!

81 SU BAMPTON

"10:4 Good Buddy"

Arrived 12 December 1983 81 SU Bampton Castle, Strike Command Integrated Communication System (STCICS)

During the time I was on TCW, in the late 70's, The Powers That Be decided that the RAF HF radio network was too piecemeal, there was Flight Watch at Upavon, the Rescue Coordination Centres in Edinburgh and Plymouth and who knows what else. It needed to be rationalised and controlled centrally and therefore Strike Command created STCICS (pronounced Stee-Kicks) and 81 Signals Unit was formed to manage it. It would be responsible for coverage of RAF communications in the High Frequency (HF) 3-30 Megahertz range.

Two identical sites were built at Findhorn (near RAF Kinloss) 81 SU North and Bampton (near RAF Brize Norton) 81 SU South. Each was commanded by a Flt Lt with a WO under him. In overall command was a Sqn Ldr who, for convenience, was located at Bampton but operationally he might just as well have been at Strike Command at High Wycombe.

To confuse things slightly they co-located 81 SU South in the same farmer's field where 2 SU was already situated. Together these 2 units became RAF Bampton Castle. (*We were always being asked by visitors where "the castle" was but none of us ever found one. Just someone at Strike command being fanciful, I guess.*) For the first few years we literally had to drive through the farmyard to enter or leave 81 SU. Brize Norton MT were always complaining about the state of our vehicle but even if you washed it before you set out, once you'd been through the farmyard it was dirty again. Eventually they built us our own road across the other side of the field, with a proper car park, so that problem went away.

Each site had an identical layout with landlines allowing transmit/receive facilities to the SAME 20 or so stations. The logic behind this is that in the event of the failure of one of the sites, the other could instantly take over all operations and our customers could continue their operations unimpeded.

The only difference between the sites was the Flight Watch frequencies that each monitored. At 81 SU South we monitored 4-5 freqs and the North monitored 4-5 different freqs. But should either of the sites go down, for a power outage for example, the opposite site would already have their receivers tuned to those frequencies, so the outage would be only momentarily. We even used the same callsign "ARCHITECT" so unless your aircraft was actually in the middle of call, you would never know the difference.

(*Authors note: None of this is classified by the way. When it comes to aircraft safety and emergency rescue operations everything remains unclassified so as not delay action. Besides all the above is listed in civilian air publications.*)

Flight Watch is the practice of monitoring said HF frequencies where RAF aircraft call you up after take-off and give you their ETA at their destination, number of crew, number of passengers on board and so on, and at the same time might request Met information for their flight path.

Our job was to take the message and the pass it on over the civilian Overseas Fixed Telecommunication System (OFTS) to all interested parties. As well as aircraft we dealt with anyone that called us up, ships, helicopters, vehicles or even a man with a radio strapped on his back. We called each contact a "mobile". We would pass messages down the phone, over the OFTS, over the teleprinter network, whatever it took.

We also had this clever system whereby we could patch a radio frequency down a phone line. The person at the other end would hear the mobile speak, and the operator at 81SU would key the transmitter for them when they replied. This was known as a Phone-Patch.

I almost did a Phone-patch to Buckingham Palace once. The queen was flying out to Canada on a trip and one of her minions wanted to speak to someone in the queen's office.

I rang the switchboard at Buck House, explained who I was and what I wanted but there was no one in the office. Passed this back to the aircraft who said it was imperative that they speak to someone from the office as they needed certain information. I passed that on to the switchboard and said I didn't know if that they meant they had to send out the Household Cavalry to find them but someone had better take the call. I left her my number to get back to me. (*Ha Ha!* I thought. *My name is on a piece of paper at Buck House. I might end up with a Knighthood out of this.*)

As it turned out, later in the day I asked, 'Anyone heard back from Buck House yet?'

'Yes,' came the reply. 'They couldn't find anyone from the queen's office but the plane said they had found out the information anyway.'

Oh dear, I thought. *Damn, it's all gone wrong and they've got my name. I could end up in the Tower!*

All our people, like TCW, were telegraphists, as at that time we were the only ones in our trade who received any radio training. Of course we had *strict* training in radio procedures. RAF pilots however also had to deal with civilian Air Traffic Controllers so along the way began to pick up their bad habits, such things as saying, 'Did you copy my last transmission?' or 'I copied your last' instead of the procedurally correct, 'Did you receive my last message?' Once again, aircraft safety being paramount, we didn't quibble and insist on strictly correct radio procedure, so as not to distract the pilot, and we soon fell into the same habits so that we could facilitate communications by using the same language. Hence the subtitle of this chapter, *"10:4 Good Buddy."* We didn't actually sink so low as to use CB language, just my little joke.

***

The other side of the job was setting up frequencies for those stations connected to us by landline. Like the FW freqs, the idea of having two sites was not only survivability but using a frequency that is working from the south of England and the north of Scotland, can give two totally different results in performance, related to weather conditions, distance from transmitter to recipient, all sorts of things. So if a station got its freq from the south and the north at the same time, they could switch between them to whichever gave them the best result.

On a daily basis our customers would call up both sites and we would "extend" (as we called it) the frequency down the landline to them. We could if requested just extend the receive side if they only wanted to monitor something but not interact with it. If the freq was unsuitable for any reason or if they required extra freqs, then we would play about with a spare receiver until we found a suitable one, tune a receiver on one of our 30 channels, tune a transmitter, attach it to that channel and then extend it down to them.

Our most important and regular customers were Edinburgh and Plymouth Rescue Coordination Centres. They usually operated the main Search And Rescue (SAR) frequency 5,680 Mhz during the day. More about them later.

***

I turned up at the 81 SU Bampton Castle, still an SAC and everyone in charge went, 'What? We were expecting a corporal.'

'Sorry,' I replied, 'but I've been specifically told by General Office at Brize Norton, that I'm not allowed to put my tapes up until I've done the General Service Training course at Hereford.'

So, as they couldn't put an SAC in charge of a watch, I had to hang around on days instead of going on watch, where they needed me. Fortunately, instead of having to learn on the job, the Cpl who was on days, Jim Ford, took me under his wing and showed me the ropes.

'See those long bits of string-like things, coiled up over there?'

'Yep.'

'Those are the ropes.'

'Gotcha.'

He showed me how everything worked in the traffic hall, before I was thrown in at the deep end, which was extremely useful and gave me a head start so I could hit the ground running, when I finally went on shift. Thanks for that Jim.

The Sqn Ldr was miffed about me being an SAC

instead of a Cpl and kept having a go at me about my tapes as if it was my fault, but as I kept telling him Gen Office had said I was not allowed to be a Cpl until I'd done the course.

Funny thing was, ever since I had joined, although we wore rank badges on our jacket sleeves and jumpers, no one was bothered about wearing them on shirts or raincoats, unless you were a supervisory rank. Basically, if you could order anyone around then you had to show the rank badges to prove it. If you were a nobody like me, then you didn't need to prove you were. Simple.

Then for some reason The Powers That Be decided that everyone must wear rank badges on everything. I'd managed fine for eleven years without wearing them on my raincoat but now I was starting to get told off at work about it.

Too be honest, I was trying to hold off until I got my Cpl's tapes but finally I gave in and asked my wife to sew SAC props on my raincoat. (I was useless at sewing.)

THE VERY NEXT DAY I got my tapes up! Typical isn't it?

It happened like this. Jim Ford and I were in the Traffic Hall doing something and the Sqn Ldr came into the room.

'Why haven't you got your tapes up yet, Rattigan?'

'Sorry, sir, it's General Office. They won't let me put them up, in fact they've even threatened to charge me for impersonating an NCO if I do.'

'Well I'm the CO of this unit and I say otherwise. Cpl Ford, do you have any spare rank slides in your locker?'

'Yes sir.'

'Right, you two come with me,' and the Sqn Ldr led us into his office where Jim gave me his spare rank slides, which I put on the epaulettes of my jumper.

'You're now Acting Cpl Rattigan, get on with it,' said

the CO.

So I had walked out of the Traffic Hall as an SAC, and returned five minutes later as a Cpl!

I didn't shout about it, I just went into the room and waited to see if anyone would notice. It took a while but they did. The people on watch couldn't believe their eyes and were doing double-takes.

Of course the worst bit was having to go home and tell my wife she had wasted her time sewing my SAC props on my raincoat the night before. I slipped my raincoat back on just as I entered my quarter and found her in the kitchen.

'I'm sorry love,' I told her, 'the SAC props have got to come off my raincoat, they're no good.'

'Why not?' she asked, indignantly.

I slid my raincoat off, revealing my Cpl's tapes. 'Because I'm a Cpl now.'

***

There were quite a few people at 81 SU that I had met previously in my career, mainly ex-TCW. Pete Tattershaw turned up one day. Pete had been one of my corporals on the Wing. I was put with him on his first exercise as an "experienced SAC" and it turned out to be a horrible one. All things beyond my control I hasten to add but he must have been thinking, *What have they saddled me with?* Never mind, I proved my worth on later exercises and we became good friends.

***

In April of 1984, at long last, the joining instructions for my GST course came through and I was off to sunny, RAF Hereford.

We were an eight man course, all from different trades. When we wore "blues" we marched everywhere but when we wore combats we had to "double" everywhere, which isn't easy when you're wearing webbing and carrying a rifle.

The GST course seemed a bit pointless to me, after all I had spent eleven years learning my job, so a two week course wasn't going to teach me much to add to that. But then I found out something that made me rethink my opinion.

One of the Acting Cpls on my course was talking about how he had been 'so keen' at Swinderby that he had bought carpet cleaner, to clean the carpet around his bed space. We old sweats listened in disbelief.

'What's he talking about?'

'No idea, something about carpets at Swinderby but that can't be true, surely.'

It turned out it was. They now had carpets at Swinderby. What had happened to the old "Brick on a stick?"

'How long have you been in exactly?'

'Four Years.' (He was a bandsman.)

'*What!* And you're making corporal already?'

'Yes.'

I had underpants that had been in the Air Force longer than him!

Well, we old timers had to go away and have a lie down. Corporal at four years – what was the Air Force coming to? Still, I suppose if you were going to sweep up kids from Kindergarten and then promote them almost straight away, you needed a GST course to teach them what the Air Force was really about.

To be fair, I did learn a few useful things on the course that have come in useful over the years.

The motivation for people to follow orders boils down

to two reasons:

<u>Expectation of reward.</u> This doesn't mean immediate reward but the hope that if they play the game and follow the rules, then at some point in the future they will be rewarded in the form of promotions, good postings, etc.

<u>Fear of punishment.</u> The opposite of above. If they get into the bad books of their superiors then they will get marked down at assessment time, which will affect their posting and promotion prospects.

So when you're dealing with a subordinate, you have to figure out which of those two motivators will be the most appropriate to get them to carry out your orders.

Then the other useful tip was – there are three types of leader:

<u>Authoritative</u> – This is the guy who gives orders, doesn't listen to suggestions, always lets everyone know who's in charge.

<u>Consultative</u> – The sort who says, 'Okay guys, we have a situation here. Any suggestions on how we handle it? Let me hear your ideas and then I'll decide on our course of action.'

<u>Passive</u> –'Erm … well guys, we have a situation here. Anyone know what to do? Somebody sort it out, will you?'

Now for 5 points, the question is … which of those leadership types should you be?

Anybody?

That's right. Anyone who is one of those and *only* one

of those, is doing it all wrong. You should be *all of them* but never at the same time. You should switch between them as the situation demands. When things are easy you can say to your troops, 'Okay, you know what needs doing, who wants to do what? Sort out the guard roster yourselves, will you?' Other times you can include them in the decision making process by asking for suggestions. Then you make an authoritative decision on which action to take. Once you've made that decision then everyone should abide by it, the time for discussion is over.

***

They gave us practice in marching a squad of troops. As we were only eight on a course, they combined us with another course to give a reasonable amount of men.

You can control a squad of marching men by standing still and shouting orders to them, but it's very easy to mix up your lefts and rights when you are stationary and they are moving around, particularly if they are coming *towards* you. Personally I opted for the easier choice of marching alongside them. Easier for your spatial awareness.

We marched up and down on a piece of tarmac, might have been an outdoor basketball court or an empty car-park, I can't be sure. There was a wire fence and a hedge running alongside our little patch. But still, it was easy to make mistakes and sometimes we would be ordered to do a "right turn" and find ourselves heading towards the fence. As none of us had been on parade in years there were mistakes like that aplenty.

As it happens, on the other eight man course who was marching with us, there was one guy who my whole course took a dislike to, for some reason. I thought it was just me but no, the rest of them didn't like him either. I won't name him, it wouldn't be fair as he never did us any harm, but he had the same name as an actor who played James Bond in the movies. That's all I'm saying.

So, we decided that when one of *us* was shouting the orders, we would do what we were "meant to do", even if the order was called wrong. So if our guy yelled "turn right" and it would take us into the fence, we would turn left, because we knew that's what he meant.

When this one guy from the other course called the orders, we would do whatever he said, even if meant us piling into the fence, just to embarrass him.

Petty I know, but you have to take your fun where you can.

***

Along with all the classroom stuff and marching we had a few days where we did field exercises on the sports pitches. The idea was that for each exercise, a different one of us would be the team-leader. Everyone would report to him and he would issue the orders.

You know the sort of exercise. They would give us some telegraph poles, some ropes, and other things like buckets (or whatever the task required) and then give us our objective – get a trailer across a river – that sort of thing. Lots of tying poles together and making tripods. (*The standing joke was, when in doubt, make a tripod.*)

We were being observed and marked by our own instructor who was in charge of us for the two week course.

I did my bit as team-leader and it went okay. The purpose of the exercise is not necessarily to complete it, it's just about lateral thinking, taking charge and working together to achieve the objective. I'm one of those people who always think that he knows better than anyone else, so when everyone is standing there, not knowing what to do, I always step forward and try to take charge. (*Yes, this is a failing of mine, I know.*)

So my turn went okay but when one of the others took charge in a later exercise, he was dithering about, not quite knowing what to do, so I stepped up and started offering advice. During the exercise the other members of the team were coming to me and not the team-leader for instructions and to offer suggestions.

Finally the instructor who was marking us stopped the exercise and asked, 'Who's in charge here?'

'He is,' the others said, pointing at the team-leader for that exercise.

'Then why is everyone reporting to him?' he asked, pointing at me.

Oh dear, I thought. *Me and my big mouth have blown it, I've just shown that I can't be a team-player and I have a need to take charge. That's a black mark for me.*

But as it turned out, the instructor confided later that it had actually won me some points as I had done what was necessary by taking charge. So maybe having a big mouth isn't always a bad thing.

***

For the last few days of the course we went out into the field. I of course was experienced at this having been on TCW, so it was second nature for me. One of the others on the course had done field exercises while stationed in Germany, so he had experience too but he'd never done it for a living, so to speak, as I had. Before we went out our instructor, who was familiar with TCW and what they did, told me that he was relying on me to look out for the others, being the most experienced at getting my boots dirty. *Right ... no pressure then.*

It wasn't all that bad and I didn't really need to guide them much. It was the usual living in a trench, doing guard duties, maybe a few patrols, getting attacked by the DI staff, that sort of thing. For once we actually had blank rounds to fire back with, which made a pleasant change from shouting, 'BANG!'

The only time I had a cunning plan was the last night in the field. Next day we would have to march out from our position across this open field, with the possibility of being attacked along the way. I suggested that we gather up our remaining rounds and give them to the guy carrying the Bren gun, and then the rest of us could clean our rifles, to save us doing it at the end. That didn't work out as they still made us clean our rifles before we went back to Hereford.

I fully expected an attack on the last night, so I warned the others not to get too undressed in case we had to suddenly dash out and fend off an attack on our billet. We were sleeping in tents inside a barn. Surprisingly we didn't get attacked but one of our team woke up in the middle of the night, in the dark, didn't know where he was and half asleep started shouting and yelling. Once we had calmed him down that was a good night's sleep ruined.

So when we came to do the march out next day, we were all exhausted after three days of hard work and little sleep. As we were marching out across the open field in an extended line (mercifully we weren't attacked) one of our group at the end of the line, started wandering off in a daze and falling behind, so I went and swapped places with him on the end of the line, so I could keep an eye on him. I'm not trying to sound heroic here but I was just afraid that if we screwed it up they would make us do the march again.

But we finished the course and they released us into

the wild. I went back to the unit a REAL corporal and was able to go onto shift. Yippee!

**

I got put on 'C' watch, with Russ Wilson as the other corporal. Although we hadn't been on at the same time, Russ was also ex-TCW so we had a lot in common and we got on excellently. I enjoyed the more technical aspects of the job and tended to work on them whereas he was good at man-management and the day-to-day running of the shift. Everyone thought we made a good team.

One of the lads on the watch was called Brian Mitter. It turns out he was the son of the Brian Mitter I had known in Cyprus at JISC. You can't help feeling that when you knew someone earlier in your career and years later you're now working alongside his son, that *perhaps* you've been doing the job for too long.

Anyway, I gave Brian the nickname "Trans" (short for Transmitter) and it stuck, with everyone.

**

I don't remember who the Warrant in charge of 81 SU South was when I first arrived, as he left shortly afterwards and was replaced by WO Jack Ransome. I knew him from my Cyprus days. Well, I say knew him, I knew *of him*, he was 12 SU and I was JISC, we were on different watches, and he was a Warrant Officer and I was a lowly SAC. Nevertheless, I knew who he was and that he was a decent bloke. Silver hair, craggy face and gravelly voice, he was a bit of a character and well-known throughout the trade. (Sadly no longer with us.)

Eventually Jack Ransome moved on as the unit WO

and we got a fella called Pete Froome in his place. To be honest, there were a few people that didn't get along with him but I thought he was great. Like me he was very outspoken and some people don't like that.

He seemed to take a shine to me, he would often stop for a chat on his way through the Ops room and regularly asked my opinion on things, like if someone suggested changing things around he would ask me what I thought of it. I just assumed he was canvassing opinions and was asking people from other watches as well but perhaps not.

A few people on my watch even commented on it. 'He seems to like you. Maybe you remind him of his son.' Whatever the reason he seemed to respect me and my opinion. I thought to myself, *can this be true? I'm actually getting on with a Warrant Officer and not automatically in his bad books because my name is Rattigan?*

It looked as if my luck was beginning to turn after all.

Optimists say that every cloud has a silver lining. What they don't tell you is the flip-side of that, that every silver lining has a cloud.

***

WO Froome arranged a deal with his friends on TCW that on their next exercise to Denmark, they would take along one person from 81 SU and one from 2 SU. It was open to volunteers and it seemed that no one at 81 was interested. After 4 years away from the Wing I rather fancied the chance to get my boots dirty again, so I volunteered.

A young J/T from 2 SU, I can't remember his name so I'll call him Scott, also volunteered. Of course we had to attend pre-exercise briefings and before every big exercise TCW had to go on the rifle range, so we did too.

At all these encounters with TCW I could see that Scott was a bit out of his depth and nervous, and as we were both Bampton Castle I felt I should look out for him, so I took him under my wing. I had been on TCW so when they got a bit lairy towards me and Scott as outsiders I could give as good as I got, because I had done their job before them, so they soon backed off. Because we attended all the briefings etc. together, people started referring to him as "my son". We played along and even Scott took to calling me Dad.

Anyway, we went on exercise to Karup Air Force Base in Denmark. This was the first time I came across WO Keith Glazier. I had never worked under him before and I actually got to know him better when we were both demobbed, as we kept meeting at the job centre and even went to a couple of the same job interviews.

Don't know about all of the troops but I stayed at the main centre on the base in tents. We set up a Commcen in a couple of 12 foot by 12 foot tents laced together. Scott was on one of the remote sites so I didn't see him until the R&R at the end of the exercise.

They patched us into the camp phone system so that we could phone back to the UK and one day in the middle of the exercise, I phoned back to 81 SU just for a chat and they told me that Pete Froome had died of a heart attack!

I then had the sad task of telling Keith Glazier and the other SNCO's that WO Froome had died. I mean they all knew him, him being TG 11 also and some of them were probably his friends. A deeply, unpleasant experience giving them the news.

Every silver lining has a cloud.

I know it was selfish of me but I couldn't help thinking, *well, there go my promotion prospects!*

After the exercise had ended we had a couple of days while we packed everything up and had some R&R. I was in a local bar one evening with the rest of the TCW guys (Bodegas they call the bars) when this attractive woman around my age comes up to me and says, 'I want to take Scott home with me but he says I have to ask you first, as you're his Dad.'

I looked across at Scott and he was with another man and a young teenage boy about 14.

'Well, okay, if that's what Scott wants then it's fine by me.' I had a quick word with the lad. 'This looks a bit odd, could be a family of axe murderers but if not you could be in for the night of your life, so go for it! Whatever happens hold onto your ID card. You can get home on that if necessary.'

And off they toddled, Mother and Toy Boy in tow, followed by Husband and Son.

I went back to the bar and a few of the guys were talking to the barman about her. 'Oh she often comes in here and picks up younger men. Her Husband doesn't seem to mind.'

Well, I figured that if she was a regular in the bar, if Scott went missing it wouldn't be too hard to track her down, so no harm done.

Naturally I checked next morning that Scott had got back safely. He told me he had a good time but didn't elaborate. Nor would I expect him to, I brought my son up properly.

***

When I got back to work at 81 SU they told me that Pete Froome must have been having heart problems over the weekend as when he came to work on Monday he made out his will, called a couple of SNCO's in to witness it and within a couple of days he was dead.

It was either heart murmurs or he had premonition, we'll never know but one way or the other he knew it was coming.

***

After Pete Froome died, naturally we had to have a replacement. They sent us a WO from Rudloe Manor (I think) who I shall call Warrant Officer KLEEN, for reasons which will become apparent.

He arrived during my 4 days off, so people had had a chance to meet him and form an opinion of him before I did. Most of them seemed in favour of him. We were warned that he swore like a trooper and had an extremely strong handshake. (He must have read one of those books where they tell you a strong handshake is a sign of a manly personality, or some such.) I met him when I came back to work and he held out his hand to shake mine. I knew he was going to crush it.

There is actually a way to avoid having your hand crushed in a situation like that. You simply tuck your thumb into the palm of your hand and it becomes uncrushable. Try it. It did cross my mind to do this at the time but I thought best not to, just meeting a new WO for the first time and the last thing you want to do is make him think you're trying to give him some kind of a weird Masonic handshake or something. So I braced myself and let him crush my knuckles together. Eddie Izzard had a good routine about that. He reckoned you should scream and fall to the floor, clutching your hand, to embarrass him.

Anyway, after he left I had a bad feeling about him. I

thought there was something odd about him. I told a few people who I trusted but they said, 'No, you're imagining it. He's all right.'

It began like this. Every night shift the watch had to clean up the communal areas, the kitchen, the toilets, the shower room, etc. At first, until everyone got the message, next working day the WO would call the on duty Sgt into his office and b*ll*ck them because the toilets hadn't been cleaned properly. Apparently he would mark some tiny stones with a felt tip to identify them, and then hide them various place in the toilets. When he came on duty he would check the toilets and if the stones were still there, then the toilets hadn't been cleaned properly. And (this is absolutely true) he would check the toilet for skid marks. Woe betide the night shift if he found any. In fact he even changed the watch pattern for the DCC, so that he would remain on duty after a night shift so that he would still be there when the WO inspected the place.

Now you may think I'm making all this up about the toilet mania, just to malign him as we didn't get along. Even I thought that the people who told me these stories were exaggerating. Then one day his farewell present from his last unit turned up and was hung in his office, for all to see.

It was a white, painted board with a black toilet seat attached. Written on that toilet seat in white paint were the words, (these are quoted *exactly* as I remember they were displayed, including the asterisks):

"What, no F**king Skidmarks?"

I kid you not.

So let's just re-cap this situation, shall we? Here is a

Warrant Officer in Trade Group 11 and his claim to fame is that he is noted for checking toilets for skid marks!!

Hence the name I call him in this book, WO Kleen.

***

I love rules and regulations, don't you? Particularly when someone slavishly abides by them to the letter, instead of the spirit, and consequently ties themselves into knots, because of it.

This one always makes me laugh when I think about it.

We had a welfare fund at 81 SU. It was funded by donations from the members of the unit, contributions from various welfare organisations like SSAFA, and some from our parent station, Brize Norton. It went to paying for Sky subscriptions for the 'shifties', various things like kit for the football team and cricket bats, etc. as well as funding social functions.

We were all classed as members of the fund and given a vote at Annual General Meetings. I always went to these, as it gave me an opportunity to meet up with friends who I didn't see much due to our conflicting shift patterns. Unfortunately not everyone thought this way and the AGM's were usually sparsely attended.

Because you needed 2/3rds of the members to vote on any rule changes, it regularly meant that changes to the rules could not be applied. The Powers That Be decided that this was holding everything up, so they said at the next AGM they would vote on changing this rule.

However, in a perfect Catch-22 scenario, not enough people turned up to the meeting. So you had the situation where you wanted to change the rule stating that you had to have 2/3rds of the members to vote on anything, but you couldn't change it because you didn't have 2/3rds of the members there to vote on it. So they couldn't change the rule and the argument went round and round.

'We've got to change it.'

'I know but there aren't enough people to vote on it'.

'But we all agree that it's a silly rule, that's why we are trying to abolish it!'

'Yes, I agree but we can't get rid of it, as there aren't enough people to vote that it is a silly rule and we need to get rid of it.'

'That's why it's a silly rule and we should drop it.'

'But we can't as there aren't enough members to vote on it.'

Finally, the Sqn Ldr, steam coming out of his ears, declared that he was going to take the rule book home, rewrite it, and that would be an end to it, so there.

But we didn't get to vote on the new rule book.

***

Now then, you may not believe this next bit but if so, I don't care. It's all true and those people who were on shift with me at the time know it's true.

As I said, two of our major customers for frequencies were Edinburgh and Plymouth Rescue Coordination Centres. Ourselves and the North would be forever extending 5,680 Mhz to them, so when it happened you didn't give it a second thought. Sometimes they would ask for additional frequencies if they were managing several operations at once.

Often you would assist them without any or little idea of what was going on, occasionally they would mention in passing what the emergency was. It was only when you went home and saw the news that you realised what you had actually been involved in, albeit in a minor way.

I seem to be a bit of a jinx as I was on shift when some

major, famous disasters occurred. Once again I say, you may not believe this but I swear it's all true. Here is a list of them:

23 June 1985 - Got a call from Plymouth Rescue to extend the frequency to them as ATC had lost contact with a Jumbo Jet coming from Canada. It turned out to be Air India Flight 182 which was blown up by a bomb over the Atlantic. When this came on the news later in the day I listened into 5,680 and heard the rescue crews talking about the bodies in the water. I stopped listening at that point. Too gruesome.

3 July 1987 – Read in the papers on the way to work on the shift transport that Richard Branson's balloon had gone into the sea off the coast of Scotland, as he attempted an Atlantic crossing. Listened in to the Nimrod aircraft as they flew over the area, keeping a watch on him until he and his crewmate were rescued.

6 July 1988 – On night shift and watching the TV as it was quiet when pictures started coming through on the news about an oil rig fire in the North Sea. It turns out that this was the Piper Alpha oil rig. A Nimrod aircraft was already on site as that was where the pictures were being streamed from. Early next morning before we went off shift, I received a request (from the RAF side I think) to set up a Phone Patch between Manchester Radio and the captain of the Nimrod so they could do a live interview over the air. I did as requested.

21 December 1988 – On night shift and Edinburgh Rescue asked for 5,680 as contact had been lost with a Jumbo Jet over Scotland. You don't think too much about these things at the time, maybe the radio has packed up. It later turned into a bit of a flap as it wasn't a communication problem; Pan Am Flight 103 had gone down over Lockerbie.

Later I was tasked by Edinburgh to contact a RAF helicopter that was operating around Leeds airport to cease operations and head north, contacting Edinburgh on the way. I managed to get to them via the ATC and they set off. It was only watching the news next day that the full scale of the disaster became apparent.

I used to joke that I was bad luck as these disasters always seemed to happen when I was on shift. If they would pay me £250,000 to stay at home then a lot of lives could be saved.

Of course it wasn't all doom and gloom though. Occasionally 81 SU would get involved with some interesting projects. Richard Branson tried for a second attempt at crossing the Atlantic by balloon. Unfortunately for him there was a rival team that were competing against him and 81 SU were tasked to do the comms for them.

We set everything up and one day the balloon lifted off the ground in Canada and we did radio tests with them. I personally spoke to the balloon in Canada (I'm sure I wasn't the only one though). Alas, Richard Branson's team got the jump on them and took off first so the rival team packed up and went home as Branson took the record for the first Atlantic crossing by hot-air balloon.

Another one was an attempt to reach the North Pole. (I can't remember what was different about this one, maybe they were doing it on roller-skates or something.) They installed a landline from 81 SU South to the team headquarters and the idea was that we would establish the initial radio contact with the team then extend the frequency down the line to their HQ, as we did with our other customers. Once again, I personally did radio checks with the frozen North before they set out but sadly the attempt got cancelled for some reason, so I never got to speak to them actually at the North Pole.

***

If I'm going to tell the truth, the whole truth and nothing but the truth about my time in the RAF, then I'm duty bound to tell the bad bits as well as the good.

This is the happening in my career that I most regret, the bit I'm most ashamed of. The time my "bottle" went and I didn't fight City Hall. When the System put a loaded pistol to my head, cocked the hammer and I backed down.

It happened like this.

The last day of every month, the DCC of the on duty watch had to gather all the stats about how many calls we had received, how many signals sent and received in the Commcen, how many hours each of the circuits had been used by our customers, that sort of thing and then write a report for the admin staff to include in the monthly unit report.

I was on shift that day and running the watch as the Sarge was away on leave or something. Therefore it was my responsibility to compile the report. I had my operators going through the logs and gathering the information so I could collate it into a report, to be handed up the chain.

Then all of a sudden Brize Norton called a Station Exercise. As they were our parent unit then naturally it included us. Everything but normal radio operations was dropped, everyone changed into combat gear, guards were set out and we went into "war mode". I collected all the data from my ops that they had compiled but I didn't look at it, as it was incomplete; I just put it away somewhere safe. Eventually the rest of the unit arrived, some stayed and the rest were sent home to return later and relieve us, as the night shift. So we played soldier all day and then in the evening the exercise finished. The night shift came on to replace us and everything went back to normal.

Of course I hadn't finished the monthly report so I said to the oncoming sergeant, 'Can you finish collecting the data for me, as I haven't had time? I'm not asking you to write the report, I'll do that when I come into tomorrow, just gather the data.' I handed over the info that we did have. Fortunately there was another corporal (Andy Mitchell) standing at the desk with us as I said it and he witnessed it all.

I came onto shift next day and asked for the stats, so I could write the report and was told it had already been handed in. I wasn't happy about this as the Sgt had ignored my request to hold onto the data. He hadn't even written a report, he'd just handed in the raw data! I knew there was going to be a backlash about that and I knew it would land in my lap. But I didn't know the half of it.

Later that day I got called into WO Kleen's office. As I said, I hadn't checked the stats. Unbeknownst to me, one of my operators had written on the sheet containing all the data, 'Welcome to the monthly report from the sh*thole, 81 SU South.' Nobody had picked this up and it had been laid on the Flt Lt's desk. Naturally, he "threw a wobbly" as we call it when someone loses their temper.

WO Kleen was tearing me off a strip but I told him it wasn't my fault. I explained that I had specifically asked the Sgt NOT to forward the info that I had gathered. If he hadn't done that then I would have spotted the obscenity and it wouldn't have made it to the Flt Lt's desk. He didn't believe me but I had a witness. They called in Andy Mitchell and (thankfully) he confirmed everything I had said. So in MY mind, that was it as far as I was concerned. It was up to the Sgt to sort out his own mess.

Now, I would point out that I was a big boy by this time and always adopted the approach that if "I" screw up, I will put my hands up and admit to it. Accept the fact that I made a mistake and treat it as a learning experience – and make sure it NEVER happens again. So it pains me when I'm expected to take the rap for the stupidity and laziness of other people. Firstly the op who wrote the obscenity, then the Sgt who, if he had really collated the results would have actually LOOKED at the info and seen the message. So he either didn't finish collating the data (so he lied when he said he did) or he saw it and decided to pass it on regardless (knowing the trouble it would cause for me).

Needless to say, none of my ops admitted writing said obscenity. I wasn't going to descend to checking handwriting but I was disappointed that no one owned up. Particularly once they saw the trouble it was causing me. Because it didn't end there.

The Flt Lt was still frothing at the mouth and demanding someone's head. (You can't blame him really; someone was slagging off *his* unit.) And *still* the WO tried to pin it on me! But I had a witness to prove that at no point in the proceedings was I actually at fault – my only failing was trusting other people. If anyone's head should roll it should be the Sgt's. This led to a few heated arguments behind closed doors and pointed fingers between the three of us but I stood my ground.

Once it became clear that they couldn't pin this on me, they circled the wagons and appeared to decide that SNCO's should stick together. Any thought of retribution against a guilty party for that offence went away as the WO soothed the Flt Lt and the next thing I knew was the Sgt was going to charge ME with insubordination unless I gave him a written apology!

It was obvious to me that the Sgt had come up with

this as a face saving exercise for himself, so he could walk away congratulating himself on saving his own a**e and winning that one. (I couldn't believe the way the sh*t kept piling up!) I was given a few days to think it over.

Alas, during that period of my time at 81 SU, Mim and I divorced. It was fairly easy as divorces go (I've seen some horror stories). Neither of us was at fault, we'd just grown apart, and therefore the split was amicable and we behaved like adults and she moved out of the house.

We both wanted different things out of the marriage. She wanted a little cottage with a picket fence and roses growing around the door, whereas I wanted a Scalextric and a conjuring set. (When she sold my conjuring set, the magic went out of our relationship.) Hey ho, such is life.

This was all happening during the above events. So although the split was amicable, it was still a pretty grim time for me, going home to an empty house. I looked forward to going to work to escape the miserable solitude, so I could have a laugh with my watch and other friends at work and feel alive again. Now they were trying to take *that* away from me.

It was pretty clear to me that without the backing of the WO on this, I was gonna lose. Even worse, as I suspected, I was going to get stitched up. "Done up like a kipper" as the saying goes. Insubordination is one of those things that is difficult to prove and equally difficult to defend against. It all comes down to a "matter of opinion" by whoever is judging the case. As that would be the very Flt Lt who had been offended and still wanted someone, *anyone*, to pay for it, and this charge would associate me with the crime, I was on a hiding to nothing. I would probably only have got the ritual humiliation of a week's jankers but the prospect of having a lousy time at home, to be followed by having to face a lousy time at work was too much for me to handle at that time. So I buckled.

One thing life has taught me is – choose your battles carefully. When you're young, you'll rise up and fight against every perceived injustice, every time they try and walk all over you, you take to the battlements (*if you're an ornery s*d like me, that is*). But when you get older experience teaches that you only have so much time, money, energy, personal reputation, loyalty from others – and if you squander it by kicking off every time someone is unkind to you, then when you desperately need them because the battle is really important, you find that the armoury is empty and you have no allies left, as they are sick of backing you over silly, meaningless squabbles. I'm not saying don't fight anymore, just be selective about which battles to fight, ones where perhaps your honour or integrity is at stake and more importantly, ones that you have a chance of winning!

As I said, it was obvious that I was going to lose this battle if I chose to fight it, so yes I admit it, I caved in and let City Hall win. I didn't want to give Kleen the satisfaction of seeing me getting charged and having it on my record. Besides, I knew I was in the right, so a few scribbled words on a piece of paper that I didn't really mean, didn't affect me that much. I wrote the sergeant his letter of apology and made it all go away. I let my watch know that I was disappointed with them for not owning up and my having to take the rap for what one of them had done and that was that. End of story.

I had to work with that Sgt for a few shift cycles, sometime later. I made sure that my work was letter perfect, I always addressed him as sergeant (for to call him by his first name would be insubordination, surely?) I made sure he had no excuse to pick me up for anything. He even bought some beers into work as it was over the Christmas period but I refused to drink any, even though he and everyone else did. (I was driving anyway.) I didn't give him an inch – no chance to drop me in trouble again.

Footnote – however, several years later I attended a football tournament at RAF Rheindahlcn for all the Commcens in Germany. I saw the sergeant again. He greeted me warmly and offered me a beer. I thought … why not? There's no point in holding grudges is there? Life's too short. So we drank beer, talked about stuff (without mentioning that incident) and then went our merry ways.

***

One of the young lads at 81 SU was told by the doctors that he had Gout. He was only 18 or 19 years old. I told him that it was probably because they couldn't spell Multiple Sclerosis. His face dropped.

I've never been much of a one for "practical jokes", I prefer snappy comebacks and funny one-liners but there was one time I accidentally did a prank. I mentioned before about operating numbers and why we have them. The Sgt on 'C' watch was C1, I was C2 and Russ Wilson, the other corporal, was C3 (not C3PO), and so on down the list. One evening when we were on shift I was looking at the watch list and I saw that C5 was not allocated to anyone. (Do you remember Sir Clive Sinclair and his little pedalled vehicle called the Sinclair C5?) I pencilled in the name Sinclair next to C5. Just a harmless little joke, which I thought that someone would see through straight away, go, 'Ha ha, very funny,' and rub it out.

Guess again.

The next person who looked at the watch book, exclaimed, 'Have we got a new guy posted in? It's in the book. His name's Sinclair.'

'I don't know anything about it,' said the Sarge and began asking around the watch. 'Anyone heard anything about this Sinclair?'

I'm sitting there watching this, thinking, *It's a joke, surely they can see it's a joke.* But I let it go out of curiosity to see how long it would be before someone twigged.

Next day the Sarge was in with the day staff, quizzing them about who this new guy, Sinclair, was and when he would be posted in. Of course they were just as puzzled as everyone else. I'm sitting there shaking my head in disbelief at everyone's gullibility, and their "It must be true, it's written down!" attitude.

Finally I had to put my hands up and say, 'Sorry, it's just a little joke I made, there is no Sinclair posted in. *Sinclair C5*, get it? I didn't think anyone would take it seriously. I apologise.'

Which just goes to prove I guess that you CAN fool all of the people, some of the time.

***

Some of you may be thinking that the reason I had constant run-ins with WO Kleen was because I wasn't very good at my job and needed to be constantly slapped down to keep me in line. That's not the case.

I was told on several occasions that when various members of senior staff at 81 SU were asked who were best three corporals at the unit, the answer was ALWAYS Tony Rattigan, Pete Tattershaw and the third varied, depending on who you were asking. Myself and Pete were always in there (not in any particular order, I might add). It's not true to think I was a "wild horse" that needed to be tamed.

***

There were two sides to the 81 SU job, the Flight Watch side dealing with mobiles and the Frequency Management side of things. I loved the FM side. Next door to the Traffic Hall was Systems where all the receivers were and the controls for our transmitters, which were actually 70 miles away. (Otherwise every time we transmitted we would blow our receivers.)

I'm a Technophile and love playing about with electronic gadgets, so I made it my business to learn as much about Systems as I could, to make my job in the Traffic Hall easier. And also teach my troops about it. Eventually, apart from actually taking radios apart and fixing them, I could work Systems as well as any of the J/T's that worked in it. In fact, once or twice J/T's wanted to come in late on the night shift as they wanted to attend someone's going away do. It was only allowed if I was on shift to cover until they turned up.

I know I sound as if I'm deliberately bigging myself up but at last I had found my forte. Despite having enjoyed many of the postings I had been on, this at last I felt was the job I had been born to do and I loved it!

What do you do when you have an asset that is good at his job, enjoys being a shift worker, good at man management and popular with his troops? Why, obviously you take him away from all that and shove him into a rotten day job by himself.

Management had decided that it would be a good idea for each of the Teleg Cpls to work in Systems for a month to learn how it worked. And guess who was the first guinea pig? Moi. Me. Now I know I said I enjoyed Systems but that was as part of the whole package. I went into Systems when I was trying to make the FM side work. But this would now be done by whoever would be on shift and I wouldn't be involved in the decision making process, just pushing buttons when asked to. Also they had taken me away from my beloved shift and put me on days which I loathed.

After a while they decided that it was a bad idea putting Teleg Cpl's through Systems, so they dropped the idea. But did I get to go back on shift? NO, they left me to rot on days in Systems. 6 months I spent in there before their next hair-brained idea.

The next idea was to make me the unit Trade Training Instructor and First Aid guy so they sent me off to RAF Newton to learn instructor techniques. Although the system seems to work for the RAF it went against my way of teaching, which is to break the most complex idea down into small, easily digestible pieces and teach those. Then once the student understands the pieces, you show them how they all fit together so they understand the whole. Whatever, I did the course and got the qualification.

Next I went to RAF Halton for the First Aid Instructor course. Now that was interesting because to obtain the certificate we actually had to become St. John's Ambulance qualified in First Aid. Curiously, the St. John's Ambulance qualification only lasts 3 years and then you have to retake it – I suppose in case God has decided to redesign the body in the intervening period.

Also we weren't just learning First Aid, we were learning how to teach it. To that end they taught us how to do makeup for different injuries. So for example you would make up some oatmeal, stick it on someone's arm and then poke some bones into it to simulate a fracture. Applying blueish make up to someone who is running out of oxygen and so on. Great fun.

We split into two teams and in the morning one team would make up and design a disaster scenario and the other team would have to treat them. In the afternoon we swapped over. That was a good laugh.

On the last day those of us who were First Aiders in the morning decided to play a trick on those who would be in the afternoon, we tied all the triangular bandages together in each First Aid kit. The only snag was that after lunch they told us that for our final exercise, a plane had crashed in the wooded hills around Halton and we all had to go and deal with the survivors. They hustled us off and we never got chance to warn the other team about the bandages. So when we got to the site and found the casualties, the other team started pulling out bandages only to find a long string of them. It was like a stage magician doing that "Flags of all Nations" trick. Of course they were baffled as to what was going on, but we were being watched and marked by umpires so we just had to say to them under our breath, 'Never mind, just play along and deal with it.' It was funny though.

The course lasted two weeks and then it was back to 81 SU.

***

I must admit I didn't take to the role of Trade Training Instructor. I produced all the necessary documentation for the new people to learn when they arrived. I took them under my wing and trained them up, so when they went on shift they could hit the ground running. When we had visitors like trainee Air Traffic Controllers I would give them the lecture on how 81 SU worked and how we could be useful to them in their new careers, but frankly those opportunities were few and far between.

I could never get hold on anyone to do any training either. Nobody on shift seemed inclined to deal with the Trade Training guy, I would go into the Traffic Hall and ask the Sgt, 'Mind if I take one of your guys away and show him how Systems works?'

'Oh no, I can't spare anyone. We're far too busy.'

I mentioned this a few times to the Warrant but he just said, 'Well, you're meant to sit next to them on shift and show them how to answer calls.'

I could see he backed the Sgt's who basically just wanted me to act as an extra operator on their shift. That wasn't what I was there for.

I admit, as the TT guy I didn't exactly cover myself in glory and the Warrant kept banging on about me not doing secondary duties, joining committees or whatever. So basically I had gone from being one of the stars of the unit to an inadequate Trade Trainer. What can I say? If my heart isn't in it then I can't give it my best.

***

Being on days meant I was also in charge of all the niff-naff jobs like restocking the Tuck Shop, making sure the unit had enough tea and coffee. We also used to sell pies and pasties for lunch so I had to buy them from the wholesalers. I was given the nick-name "Mr Pie Man" by my old watch. Trans Mitter even drew a caricature of me labelled as such. It was a great cartoon and he didn't mean any offence by it but I couldn't help feeling a sharp stab in the ego. See how the mighty have fallen! I still have the cartoon to this day though.

Eventually the Sqn Ldr got sick of seeing me around on days, he used to come into Pete Tattershaw's office and find me chatting with him and he promised to get me back onto shift because he could see that I was wasted doing a day job. I should be back on shift where my talents would be better employed. He was as good as his word and before long I was back on shift. Not my old one unfortunately but still, on shift.

When it came around to my assessment time, my watch sergeant (Pete Cornwall) was invited to sit in while I had my annual assessment interview with WO Kleen. This was very unusual; it's normally a private affair between the two of you, so I knew that something odd was going on.

He read his assessment of me. I'd been doing a good job back on shift so he couldn't rob me on the numbers, (8 – 7 – 7 on a scale of 1 – 9 but there is an "unwritten rule" that nobody gets 9's so 1 – 8 really) however, it's in the write up that they can sabotage you, if they want to. The numbers only get you before the promotion board; from then on it is the write up that counts.

He read it out his write up and then ended on this "career killing" paragraph.

'This airman does not do any secondary duties. But if he should suddenly start doing secondary duties, I would advise that it be treated with suspicion.'

So I was screwed either way, there was no way I could ever win, if I did secondary duties or not. The WO's comment meant whether I did them or not, *both* options meant I would get marked down for it. Talk about Catch-22. Now tell me honestly if anyone considers that fair treatment? If he *doesn't do it*, punish him. If he *does do it*, punish him. Where's the justice in that?

He *knew* that he had just screwed my career because he then said, 'Now, the promotion board may see things differently but I don't think so, do you?'

What could I say to that? I knew if I spoke my mind it would only make things worse. He was obviously waiting for me to shoot myself in the foot by mouthing off, but fortunately I'm one of those people who when they get angry get very calm and think before they speak, so all I said was, 'Well, I can't win, can I?' He just shook his head.

238

I signed the form to say I'd been interviewed and the Sarge and I left. I now realised that he was there because the WO thought I might take a swing at him.

At that point I lost interest in the RAF. It became just a job instead of a career. I would just turn up, do my job then go home. I had already extended my engagement from 15 to 22 years otherwise after that assessment I wouldn't have stayed in the RAF, as my future prospects had just tanked.

They lost themselves a good man that day, even though I say so myself. Someone further up the chain of command should have read that and said to the WO, 'You can't say this! You're ruining this man's career and that's unacceptable.'

Funnily enough, a few years later I bumped into the Flt Lt who had been the next link up in the chain at 81 SU. We were in the Falklands at the same time but serving on different units and we just met in passing one day. He was on the RAF side and I worked in the Joint Operations Centre, which was mixed military, so he wasn't in my chain of command. I walked into this Ops room and he was sitting there. He recognised me and said, 'Hello.' Then he looked at my corporal's tapes and said, 'How come you aren't a sergeant yet?'

Choosing my words carefully, I replied, 'You tell me sir, you wrote my assessments.'

'Oh,' he said. I doubt if he even remembered what had been done to me, so we muttered the usual, 'Nice to see you, take care, etc.' and went our separate ways. Never saw him again.

Author's note: All of the last section did happen and what I have written is how I remember it, it is what WO Kleen TOLD me he had written. If you track down Pete Cornwall he may remember it as well as it was unusual to be invited to sit in on someone else's assessment interview. On the other hand, he may not remember it as clearly as I do, as it wasn't HIS career that was now a smoking ruin in the bottom of the waste basket. Things like that tend to sear themselves into my memory.

However, since I wrote that, I have managed to get hold of all my assessment forms, Form 6442, for my entire career and what WO Kleen actually wrote is different from what he told me he had written. They often do that, the Reporting Officer tells you one thing and writes another. What he actually wrote was not as bad as what I have repeated above (although still a career killer) but I didn't know that until 30 years later, so I laboured on for the rest of my service believing that he had finished my career. Telling me it was worse than it actually was, was kind of counter-productive, don't you think? Because from that point on I stopped caring about the RAF so it didn't achieve the effect I suppose it was meant to. Instead of working harder, I turned my back on them.

This is what he actually wrote, ACR = Annual Confidential Report (so why was my sergeant invited along?) and RO = Reporting Officer.

'This is my third ACR report on Cpl Rattigan and I am disappointed that he has not shown the will to make a definite overall improvement during the past reporting period. I concur his well deserved 8 for his general proficiency, as he is extremely knowledgeable and efficient. He has a detailed grasp of STCICS operations and he does his utmost to ensure that his primary duties are carried out to an extremely high standard. He willingly helps his operations staff towards learning the complexities of STCICS and then strives for them to attain a high standard. Unfortunately Rattigan shows very little inclination towards the acceptance of secondary duties and the first RO has been most generous by implying that Rattigan's secondary duty is NCO IC First Aid. The fact is I sent him on a first aid course to RAF Halton, so the unit had a first aid instructor for ground defence exercises. He was counselled on the importance of secondary duties towards his 1987 ACR, and I know that the first RO has repeated the exercise again this year. Since his last report Rattigan has divorced and he seems to have come through the trauma exceedingly well. He is always of smart appearance and bearing. In summary, if promotion was based purely on ones efficiency in primary duties, then Rattigan would be an outstanding candidate; but I believe that the standards, traditions and the quality of life within the Service extends past the bounds of primary duties only. Rattigan will be interviewed by me and informed of my comments in this ACR.'

There it is, verbatim. To summarise – Rattigan is a good operator and supervisor but I don't think we should promote him as he doesn't sit on any committees.

Remember the story I told you about when I got promoted in Belgium where one of the others got his promotion letter because he organised the International Ping-Pong tournaments? That's what wrong with the system.

**

I went into work at the beginning of a four day shift cycle and was told that there had been a policeman looking for me the day before, when I was off. No one knew what he wanted. I must admit that I started to get a bit worried. I knew I hadn't done anything wrong but I was concerned that something had happened to someone in my family. Later that day a Chief Inspector turned up at the main gate wanting to talk to me. (What's going on? They don't send Chief Inspectors out to tell people they've lost family.)

I let him in and we found a private room. As soon as we were alone I asked him. 'What's happened? Is it my family? Is someone dead?'

'Oh no,' he said. 'I'm just here to do your PV interview. Didn't they tell you that?'

I nearly fainted with relief. 'No, nobody told me why you wanted to talk to me.'

My Positive Vetting security clearance had lapsed as I hadn't needed it for 81 SU, all the work was never higher than Secret which only required a Negative Vetting. Suddenly, someone, somewhere had decided that it needed re-activating. I still had 5 years left in the RAF, so naturally I thought, *Whoo Hoo*, a nice posting coming up, probably overseas, possibly a NATO job. Bring it on!

We went through all the processes, everyone got interviewed that needed to be interviewed, stones were overturned, backs of sofas checked and eventually I got my PV. Then I sat back and waited for a nice, juicy, foreign posting to come in. Finally it came through.

I was to be posted to RAF Marham in Norfolk to be the Supervisor in the Telephone Exchange.

What ... The ... F**k??

It was long held amongst RAF personnel that postings were decided by the Personnel Management Centre at Innsworth by throwing darts at a dartboard. This seemed to prove the case. This time they had excelled themselves. They'd even wasted the cost of a Positive Vetting (estimated to be around £5,000 at that time) apparently for no other reason than just to get me excited

242

for nothing.

The WO Ground Radio Flight (GRF) at Marham, Pete Jessop (my new Boss) called me at home that weekend and we had a chat. Apparently they were losing their Cpl soon and needed a replacement. (*Lucky Me!*) He'd arranged with 81 SU for me to go to Marham for a week to get acquainted with job, and then I would have something like three weeks to get ready for my posting.

So I got to go to Marham for a week while the current supervisor showed me around and told me about the job. It's like being shown how to fly a plane in a week. They can force feed you all the information they want and show you how the levers work, but none of it sinks in. It's like the conveyor belt on the TV show, The Generation Game, just an endless stream of information floating past your eyes.

RAF Marham is a very hard place to find actually. (This was the days before Satnavs.) It doesn't seem to exist on any maps as a RAF base. It's on top of a hill and you can't spot it from anywhere lower down. Normally MOD camps are pretty well signposted but there were none for Marham. I only found it by spotting one of those really old, country road signs; you know the ones, the white painted arrow with the black writing on it, saying Marham Aerodrome. *Really?*

Anyway, after a week there resisting the temptation to hang myself, I went back to Brize. I then had only a short amount of time to put my stuff into storage, and get the house cleaned up to rent out.

Finally, three weeks later I packed up the car, handed the keys of the house over to the rental agents and set off for Marham.

RAF MARHAM

"Telephones and Dam Busters"

Arrived 17 March 1989

So I went to Marham, settled into my room, and took over the job in charge of the Telephone Exchange. Technically it was the Private Branch Exchange (PBX) and that is how they are known throughout the RAF. And "lucky me" was the PBX Supervisor.

One of the staff was currently AWOL. If memory serves me correctly, he had gone AWOL, they'd bought him back and he'd run off again. Apart from him, I had three civvies working for me, 2 ladies of "mature years" and a male who was an ex-RAF Telephonist. Then I had 2 airmen and 2 WRAF's.

To my surprise when I had visited Marham a month before on my familiarisation visit, I saw that the PBX was equipped with an old Strowager telephone exchange. You know, the one where they plug cables in to answer your call and then connect you with another cable, the one you see in the old black and white movies. This was 1989 and they were *still* using it, I hadn't seen anything like that since the 70's. The BT guy told me that he kept getting requests from a museum for it, should we ever decommission it. There were 2 positions so 2 people could man the board at any one time.

My next one up in the chain of command was the Commcen sergeant, Norman Cudmore. We sort of

244

vaguely knew each other as our paths had crossed in the past, TCW I think it was, so it was helpful to have a friendly face there. I also found out why I was there when I had a PV. WO Jessop was the Crypto custodian, (looked after all the secret codes for the communications systems) Norman was the alternate custodian and I was along as the alternate, alternate custodian. I never did find out if they just took advantage of my PV or whether it was the reason I was posted there in the first place.

We all came under Ground Radio Flight (GRF) who were a good bunch of lads and helped us out when they could. One of them, Sgt Dave Grant, used to sometimes sit on the switchboard during quiet afternoons, to give the ops a break. All in all, one big happy family. But despite all this it seemed that WO Jessop had a bit of a down on the PBX, particularly the civvies.

The switchboard had a thing called "Night Service". I believe it made the call bell ring louder or something, (maybe it kept increasing in volume too, can't remember) in case the operator nodded off during the quiet hours. There was a key provided so if the supervisor didn't trust his ops, he could pull down the toggle switch and lock it in the ON position by removing the key.

There had been some argy-bargy about this apparently, before I was posted in (I imagine about ops missing calls at night) and the WO gave me strict instructions that the Night Service MUST be locked on at the end of the day shift, and the key removed, and he made it pretty clear that he wouldn't be pleased if that didn't happen. Being new I didn't really understand the ins and outs of it all, so I just agreed and did as I was told.

So we got to the end of my first week in PBX. Friday evening one of the civvy ladies came in for the night shift, I'd met her before but hadn't really spoken to her properly. I locked the Night Service on and put the key in

245

my desk drawer. With a sigh of relief I headed off, knowing I could have the weekend away from it all.

Not so. I'm sitting in the Airman's Mess eating my tea when it comes over the tannoy, 'Can the PBX corporal please report to the PBX.' I finished my meal and headed back to the section.

The civvy lady was quite distraught. As she described it to me, that Night Service bell was really upsetting her as she was at "that time of life" and it jangled her nerves when it went off in the early hours. She had complained about it and threatened to quit over it, but no one had even bothered to discuss it with her. So unless I sorted it out she was going to walk out, then and there.

What was I to do? I didn't know how to operate a switchboard and I wasn't sure that I could get hold of any of the other operators. Besides which, I had been told in no uncertain terms that the Night Service WOULD be switched on every night. I was kind of between a rock and a hard place, as they say.

So I said to her, 'Look, I've been ordered by the Warrant to switch the Night Service on and take away the key, so I have to do that.'

Her face fell.

'However, I keep the key in my desk drawer and if you should happen to find it while you are "looking for a pencil" shall we say, then it's not *my fault* is it? Just make sure the key is back in the morning.'

Man Management 101 – Look after your troops first.

So we left it at that and I went off for the weekend.

***

The previous supervisor must have been a bit tardy in his time-keeping. Once I started work in the PBX I used to get calls from the WO just after 8 o'clock, our start time.

Later in the day, regardless of how many times we had spoken during the day, I would get a call from him again, just before knocking off time. Nothing substantial, he 'just wanted to check some detail with me,' or to 'make me aware of something.' It took me several days to figure out what was going on. He was checking that I was actually at work at start time and end time. The other guy obviously had a reputation for turning up late and skiving off early.

Once I realised this, I was determined that I would be there whenever he called, even if I had to stop what I was doing and get back to the PBX for knocking off time, so I could take his call. After a couple of weeks he got the message (or he believed that I had got the message). Either way, he stopped calling except for genuine reasons.

***

I felt pretty lousy being at Marham. I had never even set foot in a PBX before, let alone been in charge of one. When they combined Telephonists, Teleprinter Operators and Telegraphists into one trade – Telecommunications Operators (TCO) or Cpls and above Telecommunications Controllers (TCC) – the people at Innsworth stupidly assumed that we all knew each other's jobs. (Hence my posting.) When they started cross training everyone, they started with the lowest trade, Telephonists. Having been a Teleg all my career, I hadn't been born and brought up in the PBX like the Telephonists, so I didn't know the first thing about them. Because of that, I figured that this posting was a career killer. Even were it not for WO Kleen's bad assessment, the final nail in my coffin would be the PBX at Marham, which was going to send my career down the toilet.

There wasn't much in the way of entertainment at Marham. I had brought a portable TV with me but reception was lousy. One day I tried the radio to see if I could find out what was going on in the local area. There was an exhibition on in the local town, Swaffham, about "The History of the Potato." I nearly topped myself there and then.

I was at a horrible camp, in the middle of nowhere, one of my staff was missing, my career was spiralling downwards due to being given a job I had never done before and likely to spectacularly fail at, my boss seemed to have a down on Trade Group 11 in general and PBX corporals in particular, and the biggest attraction in the neighbourhood was a potato exhibition! Dear God, where had I been sent to? 'Oh death, where is thy sting?'

(*You see, this is why I don't buy lottery tickets.*)

But, as they say, it's always darkest just before the dawn. (*Which is why it's the best time to steal your neighbours milk from their doorstep.*) So before you throw this book down in disgust, thinking it's just one long whinge, let me tell you that eventually things got a lot better. Although the job didn't improve, in time and with a lot of help, I got a handle on it. Once I'd proved myself as hard working and willing to learn, the Warrant and I began to respect each other and (I believe) even ended up liking each other.

***

The MP's bought back my missing airman. His name was Howie, can't remember his last name. Prior to his return, the others in the PBX had filled me in about him. Apparently he had written a book about bomber squadrons during the war and how badly they had been treated by Bomber Command. The RAF didn't like the tone of the book, it made them look bad, so they had a down on him from the start. The book had been published and Howie used to give talks to various groups such as Veterans societies, that sort of thing. He was obviously highly intelligent – a real "switched-on-kiddie" as we used to say.

Along with that there was some talk about him constantly getting messed about, not getting leave, having it cancelled at the last minute, that sort of thing, so Howie had decided he'd had enough and "done a runner" and not for the first time.

I was at work one day when the Sarge brought Howie over after seeing the Warrant, and the three of us went into the restroom for a chat. Howie was a big bloke, he towered over us. If he had decided to "kick off" I don't think me or the Sarge would have got out of there alive. Fortunately though, he was a gentle giant.

He had a habit of standing close to you, so you had to look up to him. (After getting to know him better I don't think it was done deliberately to unnerve you, it was just his way.) I've learnt a few psychological tricks in my time, so I made him sit down while we remained standing. That way he couldn't use his height to intimidate us and we were looking down on him, which gave us the advantage. Then, when he was explaining why he hadn't returned to camp, he had a habit of wandering off the subject (maybe trying to cloud the issue) so I'd shut him down and insist he stuck to the subject. It became obvious to me that he was trying to work his ticket and get out of the RAF. I couldn't believe what an incredible mess I had walked into at Marham.

Personally, I've always believed that if someone has had enough of the mob, let them go. Sure, make them wait 3 months – 6 months just to make sure they really mean it and it wasn't just some drunken decision one night when they were fed up. The RAF will argue that they have spent a lot of money on training this person, but they should counter this with how much damage he will do if he is made to stay when he doesn't want to. Even if he doesn't actually damage the equipment he works on, there is no way to calculate the harm he does to the morale of the people around him. He brings them down with his moaning and at the same time it illustrates to them just how little the RAF cares about its people. Just sayin' ya know?

The Sarge told Howie the truth that he would almost certainly go to the big forces "nick" at Colchester and then probably be kicked out. Then he left the two of us alone. What was I going to say to Howie? We were that short staffed that we really needed this man to make up the numbers and therefore I needed his support. If he was going to head for the hills every time he got upset, it would just make my job that much harder. So I told him this …

'Howie, you don't know me and I don't know you. *I'm* not responsible for the grief you've been getting in the past. On the other hand you've never done *me* any harm and I've got nothing against you, so we start off even.

'There's going to be a lot happening between now and when you leave the RAF, and you might take it into your head to "act up" on the grounds there's nothing worse we can do to you, as you're already going to get kicked out. On the contrary, I can make the rest of your time at Marham pretty miserable by continually charging you for petty misdemeanours and making sure you spend most of your time on jankers.

'However, I would only do that if you drove me to it. I'll make you a deal … if you don't f*ck me about then I won't f*ck you about. Fair enough?'

Thankfully he thought it was fair enough, he took the deal and mostly kept to it. Once or twice he would come in late, after the 08:00 start time. I'd give him a stern look and say, 'Howie, we start at 8 o'clock.' And he would be as good as gold after that, never gave me any problems.

He got sent to Colchester for something like ten days and then came back to us while he waited to be demobbed. Once again, he didn't give me any trouble. I treated him like a grown-up and he acted like a grown-up.

I'll put my hand on my heart and swear that this next bit is true. When it came time for him to leave, as I shook his hand and wished him luck, he said to me, 'You know, if you had been here from the beginning, maybe I wouldn't have had to go AWOL so much.' Wasn't that a nice thing for him to say?

To me that was just another example of "*How Not to Treat Your Staff*". Maybe the last corporal hadn't spent enough time caring about his troops but if so, someone further up the tree should have spotted it and made enquiries to see what was going on. I think that Howie would have been a valuable asset to the RAF if handled properly. Another wasted opportunity.

***

First thing I had to do was get to grips with the job. There was an SAC there, Adie Owen, who had been the previous corporal's No 2. He seemed a good bloke who knew his stuff, so once I had got him to teach me the general stuff of day-to-day running of a PBX – totalling up calls to be charged to people's mess bills, that sort of thing, I left him in charge of that while I got a handle on the main job involved in PBX management.

Now let me explain how things worked back in the late 80's. British Telecom (BT) had the monopoly on all the telephone lines and equipment in the UK. Sure, you could buy a phone or an answering machine for your home line, but God help you if it went wrong or caused problems on the line. They could end up charging you a lot to fix it.

There was no such luxury on MOD sites however; ALL the phones had to be rented from BT along with all the lines. In fact while I was there, I heard of a case where the PBX supervisor at another camp had got some petty cash and gone to Dixons, and bought a load of handsets. These were considerably cheaper than BT's phones and he was swapping those out for the Dixons ones, whenever they broke down. Oh Boy, did the excrement hit the rotary air-cooling device when BT found that out. I believe he was executed, whilst his superiors who had condoned it had to spend time in the public stocks. (*Okay, I'm exaggerating but it was nearly that bad.*)

So every piece of telecoms equipment had to be rented from BT. To make sure that that could be properly accounted, EVERY single piece had to be recorded. Sounds easy, doesn't it?

Imagine you have a phone line into a hangar office. Fine, a phone line (a circuit requiring a circuit reference, so it can be billed) and a handset (also billed). FYI the handsets were only rented not bought, so there was a quarterly charge for them too. Then you decide to have a line out from the office phone to a bell in the hangar, so anyone working there will know the phone is ringing in the office. So that is another circuit with its own circuit number and a bell, which are also individually recorded and billed. Or you might have a phone line from a hangar out to a gate, if it is a secured area, that is 1 circuit and 2 handsets to go onto the register. Now imagine you are looking at a flying station, with 3 operational squadrons.

Try and guess how many of the above there are in all the offices, hangars, flight lines, fuel dumps, ammo dumps, messes, fire sections, dog sections, etc. etc. And *each and every* line, handset, bell and whatever else, has to be individually accounted for so BT can bill the RAF accordingly.

They handed me the station records for Marham in a folder. It contained a fan-folded paper, computer printout, A3 size, approximately 2 inches thick, listing all this equipment and how much we paid for it. The amount was staggering. The quarterly BT bill for Marham came to around £250,000, (*and this was in 1989*). The Warrant said to me when the next quarterly bill came in from BT, he wanted me to go through it and check each bill against the station records and make sure we were not still being charged for circuits we had cancelled.

At first I thought he was just being hard on me, but I soon discovered that like all big, commercial organisations, BT find it easier and cheaper to just let things ride unless the customer complains. I have seen it many times since, changes are requested and the work is done, but unless you monitor it closely the billing carries on as before, presumably on the grounds that it is more cost efficient to leave it as it is, unless the customer points out the mistake.

I had to backtrack through all the previous requests for a "cease" on a circuit to match up the cancelled ones against the bills. Sadly, with some of the circuits I couldn't even identify what they were. Sometimes it would involve a visit to the supposed location of the circuit, to find it was just a piece of wire hanging down the wall in an empty room, where someone had ripped a phone out years before, and we were still paying for it.

Fortunately I had an "ace in the hole". RAF Marham was considered that important that we actually had a BT engineer stationed there full-time, he even had his own office/workshop. So for any circuit rentals that I couldn't find out for certain, he would check his own records (which after all were records of what *actually* was live and what wasn't) to find out the truth. Les Williams had been at Marham for about 15 years by the time I got there, and was only too happy to help with any problems I had with BT and/or the documentation. The good thing about him being there for so long, was that he knew "the history of things" as well as what was on the documentation.

For instance, there might be a rental charge for a phone in the office of the Airmen's mess and one for the servery in the same location. Les could tell me that the one on the servery was actually a spare line that had been moved there FROM the office, (because he was the one that had moved it) so we shouldn't be paying for both. That sort of information was invaluable and he helped me immensely while I was stationed there.

To try and keep track of all these lines and handsets the RAF decided to produce their own piece of computer software to manage it, rather than have to rely on BT. They gave all the PBX's in the land an Olivetti computer, with the promise that soon all we supervisors would be trained on and issued the SADE database. I don't remember what the initials stood for but everyone just called it "Sadie". (More of that later.)

Now this is where I began to come into my own. I had always been interested in computers. I'd done a word processing course at a local college while I was at 81 SU and I had my own Sinclair ZX Spectrum. (Not the one with the rubber keys, the one after that.)

I used my home computer as a tool, not a games machine. I had word processor and spreadsheet programs on it; I even did my home budgeting on a spreadsheet, it wasn't there to play Jet-Set Willy on. (*Jet-Set Willy was a popular computer game back in the 80's and not an occupational disease for fighter pilots.*)

So when they gave me the Olivetti, with word processing and spreadsheet programs, I was ahead of the game and soon used it to computerise everything I could in the PBX.

I'd never had a "real" computer before but some of the GRF guys came over and installed useful programs and showed me how to use them, and I could always call on them for help.

All letters and notices were done on the word processor instead of a typewriter, all the mess bills were put on a spreadsheet, etc. I suddenly became popular for doing posters and invitations to parties and dances, with the clip-art. (*It sounds nothing now but it was a big deal back then.*)

And I showed the others how to use it. Some couldn't really grasp it or weren't interested, so I let them do things in the old way and we'd transfer it to computer later, but for those who were interested I taught them as much as I could. I'm one of those people who believe in sharing the information around. My predecessor was a "Knowledge is Power" kind of man.

Me, I think that the more people that know what is going on, the easier work becomes, because YOU don't have to be there every time something needs doing.

I have spent my life trying NOT to be indispensable. When you are the only man who knows what's going on, it means you're always the one that gets called in when there's a problem, so I do my best to spread the knowledge around. Unfortunately, I wasn't able to avoid being indispensable at Marham. I lost count of the times that I would be back in my room and there'd be a knock at the door. A copper standing there would tell me I was needed back in PBX. Or at the weekend I'd go to Great Yarmouth or somewhere for the day, there were few mobile phones then so I was out of contact, but when I'd get back there'd usually be a note pinned to my door – 'Please contact PBX soonest.'

I used to think back longingly to my days at 81 SU. At least there, if you were having a bad day, say during a troublesome communication exercise, at the end of the shift you could hand the problem over to somebody else. When you came back on shift, either the problem had been solved or it had at least advanced 12 hours towards a solution. Here at Marham, whatever problem you left on your desk at the end of the day, would still be waiting for you when you came back next morning.

***

I have a habit of applying my own meanings to abbreviations and acronyms. The Warrant's office was in the GRF section, which was located in the Air Traffic Control tower, that was painted green, as camouflage. In my mind the WO became "The Wizard of Oz," who lived in the Emerald Tower. So whenever I went to see him I used tell my crew that I was, 'Off to see the Wizard, in the Emerald Tower.'

Silly, I know but it amused me.

***

We had 3 flying squadrons based at Marham, 617 Sqn (the Dam Busters squadron) which flew Tornado aircraft, 27 Sqn who also flew Tornados and 55 Sqn who flew the old Victor bombers, which by now had been repurposed as air-to-air refuelling tankers.

Mostly they were all right and didn't give PBX too

much trouble but what a bunch 617 were. When you rang their squadron headquarters they would answer, '617, the Dam Busters squadron,' like they had actually been on the raid themselves. Bunch of posers. Glorifying themselves on other people's bravery and sacrifice.

One time we were given a brief on the wartime role of the Tornado squadrons. Apparently their main job was airfield denial to the enemy. To achieve this they had a weapons pod attached to the underside of the aircraft, containing multiple small bombs. In action they would fly very low, along the length of an enemy runway, scattering small bombs as they went, which exploded and rendered it unusable as a runway. They were quite proud of this low-level, precision bombing tactic.

When they went into action for real in the first Gulf war, flying so low made them an easy target for the airfield defences and they started to get shot down rather more frequently than they would have liked. This caused them to have a rethink of their tactics and subsequently they carried out their bombing runs from a higher altitude.

I mean, who'd have thought that flying low, over an airfield equipped with anti-aircraft weapons, would result in them getting shot down? Certainly took me by surprise.

***

The NAAFI bar was lousy. The barmaids always used to play the music from the jukebox too loud. Even if you asked them to turn it down, the next time you went in there it was back up again. You literally had to shout to be heard by someone sitting at the same table. I couldn't take it and did most of my drinking in the station bowling alley.

For some reason the camp was swamped with RAF policemen, "Snowdrops" as they are known due to their white, peaked caps. There were suggestions about opening a corporal's club but what would be the point? It would only be filled with RAF coppers, who were all corporals, so it wouldn't be any better than the NAAFI.

The reason I was against that idea is not because I have anything against policemen. (*Well, not civilian ones anyway.*) It's just because of how the RAF has some silly ideas regarding rank structure. RAF policemen and Physical Training Instructors (PTI's) leave training with the rank of Acting Corporal. Though in reality they are only LAC's, nevertheless they have stripes on their arms and can order people around.

This in turn gives them an exaggerated sense of worth and ideas on how to treat subordinates. People like myself, who started out as LAC's, know what it's like to be ordered around and having someone senior giving you a hard time. Hopefully, when you're in a position of authority yourself, you remember this and it tempers your treatment of your juniors, because you know what it's like for them. When you start out as a corporal however, you don't have that experience to guide you and this leads to a, 'I'm a corporal, do as I tell you!' attitude. This is particularly noticeable amongst RAF coppers.

An even worse case I heard of was at one time they had these things called "Super Techs". These guys came in with high qualifications and they passed out of training as actual corporals.

I often thought that we should be like the Israelis in that everyone joins up at the lowest rank, works their way up, and then the officers are chosen from the enlisted men/women. Having a degree does not automatically make you a good officer. Sometime after my stint on the Wing, I was told that one of their new officers had a degree ... *in geology!* Tell me how that qualifies someone to lead a group of electronic communicators?

***

The station was the standard layout from WW II days. Station Headquarters facing the parade ground, the opposite side of which was a building containing the Airmen's mess in one half and the NAAFI in the other.

My room was in one of the newer built blocks, situated behind the guardroom. I thought that at least as the PBX supervisor I could justify having a station telephone extension in my room. Nope, I couldn't even get that. (The old PBX corporal's room which had a phone, had been taken over by one of the GRF guys. I didn't like that block anyway, it was a pre-fab.)

When BT installs a junction box for phone lines, there are a finite number of phones they can attach to that box. Each connection requires a spare "pair" on the box. Unfortunately, there were no spare pairs on the junction box that fed the guardroom (and my block). The only way to justify fitting another junction box was if someone (i.e. me) paid out of his own pocket, to have a standard line installed. Not a PBX extension but a Direct Exchange Line (DEL) such as you would have fitted in your own home. This would have made it necessary for them to fit an extra junction box, thus providing spare pairs. But if I paid for my own phone line then I wouldn't need the station extension, which was the whole point in the first place.

So the only way I could get a "free" phone in my room was for me to fork out £100+. S*d that for a game of soldiers, so I did without.

***

Another thing that nobody warned me about when running your own section was managing WRAF's. Don't misunderstand me; I have nothing but the greatest respect for WRAF's in general. They do the same jobs as us men and as well as us men. Some of the best operators and supervisors I have worked with have been female. It's just that they sometimes have complicated lives and as their boss, it's sometimes unavoidable getting involved.

It's like being a father to teenage girls I guess, but as I never had been, I didn't really know how to handle it.

Most of my time there I had 2 WRAF's working for me. I'd worked with WRAF's before but usually they had spent some time in the Air Force, these 2 were straight out of training. I don't want to embarrass either of them should they read this, as they were both nice girls, so I shall designate them as one being Scots and the other English.

The English girl was already there when I arrived. The "wee Jockette" turned up a couple of weeks later. She was smartly turned out and everything but emotionally she was a mess. As so often happens, it's their first time away from home, they meet someone in training, think they're in love and they want to get married. (*Hey, I'm not being critical, it even happened to me! Young, dumb and full of ... well, you know the rest.*)

She was bawling her eyes out a lot of the time, as she claimed that she just couldn't live without (insert name here) who had been posted to another camp. She wanted to be with him, she couldn't live without him, the world was going to end ... you get the picture.

The chain of command goes *up* as well as down, so I ring the Sarge ... 'Norm, we've got a slight problem.'

The Warrant eventually had a word with her and I think he promised her that if she soldiered on at Marham for a month or so and still couldn't hack it without her beloved, he would do his best to get her cross posted. I'll give him his due, considering he was a techie and probably spent most of his career in an all-male environment, he sure handled her well. I was impressed. So she settled down and within a couple of weeks had forgotten all about (insert name here).

Fast forward a few months and lo and behold – she has fallen in love with a new guy, (insert name here), at Marham and they're going to get married! Anyone with an ounce of common sense (which meant all of PBX) could see that this was doomed from the start. It's really galling when you have to smile and pretend to be happy for them, then stump up for a wedding present, when you'll be surprised if the marriage lasts through the honeymoon.

So they got married. But it doesn't end there. Sometime later, (I'm not sure how long but I was only there a year in total so it can't have been too long), (insert name here) gets detached to the Falkland Islands for 4 months. Our little Scottish lass get lonely, meets someone at the Bop (insert name here) and guess what? She falls in love again!

I got posted away before hubby came home from down south, so I never got to see the fallout, but I bet it was messy. It's the parents I feel sorry for, they spent a fortune on her wedding and it was just money down the drain.

Mind you, I think they had brought her up to be a bit of a Prima Donna. "Mummy's little girl." The Scots WRAF was a Drum Major in a marching band, back home. Won all sorts of prizes in competitions, apparently. One occasion she needed time off to attend a competition. As I said we were strapped for staff and I really *could not* spare her. (I would've let her go if I could have – hey I've even worked shifts for my people so they could get time off.) But this one time we just didn't have enough people. Regretfully, I told her she couldn't be spared.

'Well, you'll just have to ring them up and tell them I can't make it!' she replied.

'Sorry love, I don't have to ring anyone one up and tell them anything. Let me explain to you how the RAF works …'

So amidst all this drama, the English girl was a steady rock, apart from an inability to understand the rules sometimes. One of the surprising things I discovered at Marham is that people like to know staff in the PBX, because they think they can get free calls, so everyone's nice to you. Therefore, if you work in PBX and especially if you're an attractive WRAF, (*Damn, I was so close!*) you can get a lot of favours.

The RAF had taken to issuing dark blue shirts for the techies (*worn without ties, I refer you to an earlier chapter*) instead of the standard, lighter blue ones, the rest of us wore. My PBX girl had taken a fancy to them and wangled a couple out of stores, then started wearing them to work. I had to point out to her that unless she was planning to go on the flight line and fix aircraft, after her shift in PBX, then she wasn't entitled to wear those shirts.

She wasn't happy about that but Them's the Rules!

The biggest SNAFU (*Google it if you don't know what it means*) though was when she started telling us all in PBX about how she was going to RAF Gibraltar for her holidays.

'Oh, yes?' we replied. 'Why? Do you know anyone there?'

'Yes, I've been talking to this guy on my night shifts, who works in the PBX there. We get on really well and he invited me out there for a holiday.'

Something didn't sound quite right and alarm bells began to ring in my head, so I asked, 'This guy you've been chatting to, he's single is he?'

'Well no, but he says he and his wife don't get along.'

I pointed out that perhaps visiting a married man wasn't the best of ideas and maybe he had been lying about the state of his marriage. Possibly he had just pulled of a major coup by persuading someone to fly hundreds of miles to be his "bit on the side", but she was adamant that it was all true and it would be fine.

I resisted the urge to bang my head on the desk. Then I resisted the urge to bang HER head on the desk. Then I thought about it for a while. To be honest I agonised over it for a few days. What to do? Should I tell someone?

I could have just ignored it and let it happen but to be honest, in my opinion we have a "duty of care" for those people serving under us, and if they're too young and naïve to understand when they're being taken advantage of, it's our duty to step in and put a stop to it, or at least warn them.

My choices were to let it happen with probable (nay, certain) consequences to her career. Just smile and wave her goodbye as she flies off into the sun to wreck some guy's marriage (and what about the wife?) OR let the bosses know.

Chain of command ... 'Norm, we've got a slight problem.'

The Warrant came over and gave her a talking to, so for the moment it didn't happen but I can't swear it didn't, after I left. I felt guilty as hell doing it, but at the same time I still feel now that it was the right thing to do.

She didn't accept that I was acting in her best interests and she never really forgave me.

C'est la vie.

Then funnily enough we had a Youth Training Scheme (YTS) girl turn up later, who told everyone to call her "Taff", which fits in with the general theme of this section of the book.

She was 16 going on 25. No one would have believed to look at or talk to her, that she was only 16. (*It's true, I swear, Your Honour!*)

It was a strange situation as although she wore the uniform, she wasn't in the WRAF, so it was a fuzzy area when it came to discipline. Could I tell her what to do or not? Not that that was a bother. She was a great lass and never gave any trouble, fitted in well. But none of us had dealt with YTS trainees before so we didn't know the rules.

She had a bad habit of turning up without a bra on though. On more than one occasion I had to politely tell her to go back to the block and put one on, as she was upsetting all the male members of staff (including me).

***

We eventually got the SADE program for our computer. We had to go to Rudloe Manor for a day's training on it and collect the discs. It's an underground complex near Bath and a long way from Norfolk, so it meant staying in a hotel for 2 nights on the RAF's coin (which is always nice). It used to be where the RAF communications network was managed from. It's closed down now, so I don't know who does it these days. Judging by the way they civilianise everything they can, it's probably run by Talk Talk now, for all I know.

When we got there, me and all the other PBX supervisors that were on the course were shown how to use the software (it was just a database, Access users will be familiar with it nowadays) and then given the installation discs and the data discs they had already populated it with for each, individual station.

Back at Marham, the GRF guys installed the program

for me and we were away. Sadly the info on the data discs was almost useless. Only about a quarter of our station records had been entered and a lot of that was incorrect or out of date, so basically we had to start from scratch. Never mind, at least that way I knew it would be accurate. Each entry had fields for the A end and the B end of each circuit (important, as the A end always pays for the circuit) location, rental cost, equipment attached to circuit, extension numbers, date installed – moved – ceased, all the good stuff.

The good thing about it was you could "Search" by various criteria – all the landlines, all the external phone lines, all the handsets on the station – that sort of thing. So when the Warrant asked for info on how much we paid in rental on internal phone lines, I could give him a detailed answer.

Luckily for me (*Ha!*), I didn't have much of a social life so was quite happy to spend some evenings in the PBX, entering data into SADE. I'm a perfectionist when I'm doing work like that, so I actually enjoyed mastering the program and entering the data so that MY records would be 100% accurate when I'd finished. Personal pride in my work. Unfortunately we received SADE nearer the end than the beginning of my time at Marham, and my one regret is that I never finished bringing it up to date before I left. I got about 90% there but didn't have time to finish it all. I showed Adie how to use it but I didn't want too many people entering data, as I couldn't trust that it was accurate then.

From time to time I would have to phone other PBX supervisors and I discovered there was like a secret society of PBX sups. You'd get to know some of the others and if you had a problem that they couldn't solve, they would often refer you to someone they knew who could. 'Phone Fred Bloggs at Honington, he knows about that sort of thing.'

'Oh you want to know about ordering DEL's? Harry Carry at Odiham is the guy you want to speak to.'

Conversations would sometimes go into SADE, 'Do you know how to do this in SADE?' And we would help each other out with what meagre knowledge we had.

After a while I started getting phone calls from sups who I didn't know, asking for SADE assistance. I'd do what I could to help and then ask, 'Just out of curiosity, why did you phone me?'

'Well, the word is you're a bit of an expert on this system.'

'Oh … okay, thanks. Bye.'

Smug, Cheshire Cat grin, on my end of the phone.

***

Me and my "smart mouth" often get me into trouble or nearly into trouble. Mostly I just mean it as a joke and I'm not being confrontational. For example, I remember one time that I left PBX and went downstairs to the Post Room to pick up the section mail.

The Station Warrant Officer happened to be in there, drafting a signal. I should explain that all NATO signals traffic and the Commcens that send them, operate in Greenwich Mean Time, similar to global air traffic, so that we all know we are working to the same time. Each one hour time zone has its own letter of the alphabet, so for instance BST is Alfa time zone, GMT is Zulu time.

The SWO looked up when I came in and said, 'Ah, you're signals, you'll know what the time is in Zulu time.'

I looked at my watch. This happened during the summer so it was BST, I told him, 'It's 3 o'clock now, sir, and we're an hour ahead of Zulu.'

'So that will be 2 o'clock then?'

'Yes, sir.' (Pause) 'Or 14:00 as we call it in the RAF.'

You should have seen the look he gave me. If I'd been wearing a nylon shirt it would have melted. I gathered my mail and quickly exited stage left. Can't take a joke some people.

***

Just to add to the excitement and really give my morale a boost, at some point a message came through to say that I had been put on the Preliminary Warning Roster (PWR) for the Falkland Islands. This meant that my name had come out of the hat and at some, as yet unspecified, time in the future, I would have to go and do a tour of duty in the Falklands. Lucky old me, the fun just keeps getting better and better.

***

RAF Marham is the nearest airport to Sandringham so the queen flies into it when she visits Sandringham. They don't make a fuss when she arrives (it's not treated as a Royal visit) she just gets in her car and drives off. However protocol dictates that the Station Commander goes out and greets her as she gets off the plane. One time (I was told) communications got mixed up and the Stn Cdr got the message that the queen's plane was landing. He went out to greet it, only to find that she had sent the Corgis ahead on the plane and he was standing there, ready to salute the dogs as they come down the stairs. Like Queen Victoria, he was NOT amused.

***

If you ask any serving or ex-forces personnel they will all be able to quote instances of when they went down to Stores for a new shirt/pair of boots/raincoat/whatever, and were told by the civvy storeman that they couldn't have them as they only had one left on the shelf.

My usual answer was, 'Fine, I'll take that and you can order some more in.'

'But supposing someone else comes in and wants one?' (Someone else? He meant someone of a higher rank.)

'Well, tell him you've got some on order and could he kindly come back next week.'

Never worked though and I would be the one who had to wait until they had some more in.

The worst case of "Last-one-left-itis" I ever came across was at Marham. The RAF had a special form to order items/services from BT. ONLY this form could be used and ONLY the PBX Supervisor could order things from BT. If I recall correctly it was called a Form 799. (I may be wrong but that doesn't affect the story.)

I'd never been in charge of my own section before. Running PBX made me realise that there was a Form Store where you could acquire pads of any form that the station used. Prior to that I thought they just "magically" appeared in the stationery cupboard.

One day I noticed that I only had a few F799 forms left on my pad so I went to the Form Store to pick up some more.

'We've only got one pad left and you can't have that,' I was told.

'Why not?'

'Well, somebody else might need it.'

Now then, I'll repeat something I said a few lines ago that this storeman, if he knew his job, should have known. By virtue of my position as the PBX Supervisor I

WAS THE ONLY PERSON ON THE STATION THAT WAS ENTITLED TO USE THAT FORM! Sure it had to be countersigned by the WO and he or the Sarge could fill it in my absence, but that was only because they were substituting for ME.

So the very idea that denying that form to *literally* the ONLY man on the station who could use that form, on the grounds that 'someone else might need it,' was pure nonsense. I tried explaining this to him but he wouldn't have it. It's ingrained in the nature of storemen, instilled in them from birth, I guess. Anyway, I didn't get my forms (and I needed it as I had some orders coming up.) I had to go away, phone the Sarge, who phoned the Warrant, who phoned … who knows? Eventually I was told to go to the Form Store and pick up the last pad, while some more had been ordered for me. Once again, you couldn't make this stuff up!

**

I may have made WO Jessop sound like a bit of an ogre but all he was doing was asking for the best from his men and I learnt so much from him. Chiefly amongst them was – do the job you're being paid to do, don't be half-*rsed about it.

I said earlier that I'd given up on the RAF but I still had my personal code of ethics. I believe in giving a fair day's work for a fair day's pay. If someone is paying me to do a job then I will do that job to the best of my ability. Although the Warrant wasn't personally paying me, it was some faceless clerk at Innsworth, Jessop was my Boss, and so I owed my loyalty to him.

He was a hard taskmaster. You were expected to know your job (unless like me you had just been parachuted into it) and if you didn't … you'd better damned well find out fast. If he asked you a question in a meeting it was NOT acceptable to say, 'I don't know the answer to that.' But he was fair. It was acceptable to say, 'I'm sorry, I don't have that information but I'll find out and get back to you later.' But by God, you'd better live up to your promise.

I soon learnt to be ultra-prepared for meetings, if you were providing information, it had to be correct, no guesstimates. Drafting proposals for him, you had to cover all the necessary details, cost out all the options, calculate the effect on the station telecoms budget, etc. etc. If you were presenting a request to install a new telephone, for example, you couldn't just say, 'Well, they asked for one.' You had to fully justify *why* they should have one. If you gave a good reason then he would agree to it.

He was hard work to be sure but what a challenge! What a learning curve I had to go through. And I responded to that challenge. I was determined to show everyone that if this was going to finish off my career, I was gonna go down fighting.

I also learnt a lot about office politics and how to handle people. I'd always been interested in psychology, or to put it honestly, "How to get people to do things that I want them to do." So in time, I even learnt how to "work" WO Jessop. He didn't like Les Williams (I don't think it was personal, he just didn't like a civvy having input on military matters) so any proposals that Les made, the Warrant instantly shot them down.

Some of Les' ideas were good though and bore investigation, so occasionally I would put forward one of Les' suggestions as my own, and if the WO agreed they were a good idea and implement them I would casually drop into conversation later that it had actually been Les' idea.

Or on other occasions I'd suggest something to the WO and he'd reject it. I'd let it lie for a few weeks then I'd come back to him and say, 'You know that idea of yours about such-and-such? Well, I've been thinking it over and it might be worth trying after all.'

By this time all he could remember was that we'd discussed it – he wasn't sure whether it was his idea or not, so would often approve it. I often wondered if he deliberately let me get away with these tricks because it showed initiative on my part, or whether I had genuinely fooled him.

But back to my original point – I learnt so much from him about knowing your subject, preparing your brief, finding out the answers in advance, drilling down into the detail and so on. It was a wonderful training ground and I'm grateful to him for that.

He taught me lots of useful tricks as well. When you see something being done and you know a better way to do it, because you learnt it at your last posting, don't say, 'When I was at so-and-so, we did it this way.' Instead say, 'I've just had an idea about how we can do this a better way.' Much smarter, as you get the credit for coming up with the idea.

***

During the course of the year I cultivated my contacts at BT. In the early days in the job I had to rely on them to help me out with lots of new service requests. I knew they would be useful and I'm always friendly to people I have business dealings with, so I had a good rapport with them.

This paid off big time when we had a new Wing Commander take over as OC Engineering Wing. The Warrant took him around the camp, showing him his new empire and bought him to PBX.

Before taking him into our restroom for a chat and a cup of tea, the Warrant said to me, 'The Wing Commander will need a phone in his quarter. Can you find out how long that will take, please?'

'Certainly, sir. Just give me his address and I'll see what I can do.'

As soon as they went into the back room I got straight onto BT customer service and spoke nicely to one of my contacts. When they came out of the back room I was able to say casually to the Wg Cdr, 'BT will be round tomorrow to fit your new phone, sir.' That pleased him no end and made the WO look *really* good. I got a pat on the head and a lump of sugar for that, I can tell you.

Another time I got "Smartie points" was when another Warrant Officer wrote us a very polite memo requesting a new phone for his section. He said he was aware that times were hard but it would be nice if we could bring ourselves to let him have one, blah, blah, blah. He then quoted Dickens' *A Tale of Two Cities*, 'Tis a far, far better thing that I do, than I have ever done,' accrediting it to the character, Charles Darnay.

Of course all such requests had to be passed by my Warrant so I showed it to him. I earned a ton of Smartie points when I pointed out that I'd read the book, and it was actually Sydney Carton who had said that, NOT Charles Darnay. I didn't see the reply but I don't think that section got their new phone.

***

Finally after around a year at Marham my posting to Germany came through. Oh I was so pleased. But then the Warrant dangled a carrot in front of me. I had proved myself to him by this time and he said to me, 'If you stayed here I could almost guarantee you your third.' Stripe that is.

I had a choice, I only had 4 more years left of my 22 year engagement, so I could risk waiting at Marham another year or longer to MAYBE get my sergeant's tapes and then nowhere to go except back to 81 SU for my last tour of duty, OR have a last fling overseas in the land of duty free booze and cars. No contest really. I was on my way out so I might as well make the most of my remaining time. Germany, here I come!

One thing that is really worth mentioning. That year at Marham gave me the self-confidence to believe that I could tackle *any* job that didn't require specialised knowledge or a particular skill. If it just relied on common sense and mastering the routines, just give me time to learn the ropes and chance to get a grip of the job and I would come out on top. I proved this in later postings and in civvy street.

I'd been thrown in at the deep end and came out smelling of roses. I'd proved to myself and everyone else that I could do *any* job. Since then I've approached every new job with the self-confidence that the Marham experience gave me, it even got commented on in later annual assessments.

RAF Gutersloh

"Beer and Bratwursts"

Arrived 25 July 1990

I made my own way out to Gutersloh. I had a crappy old Morris Marina estate car so I packed it up, took a ferry from Harwich to Rotterdam and then drove across country to Gutersloh. It was a long drive and I arrived in the area about 2 o'clock in the morning, so I found a field somewhere, parked up and went to sleep. Got a rude awakening next morning as the farmer picked that day to plough that particular field and the noise of his tractor woke me as he drove it around the field. Typical of my luck.

I had no idea of where the camp was so I had to pull into a petrol station and get directions with my meagre German. 'Entschuldigen Sie bitte, wo is der Flugplatz?' 'Excuse me please, where is the airfield?' Learnt a new German word – 'Ampel' meaning traffic light. I was on the right road and so I had to go through 3 Ampel and I would arrive at the camp.

Gutersloh is an old Luftwaffe camp from the war and is all 3 or 4 storey original buildings. A few new barrack blocks have been built but on the whole the accommodation was the old buildings. Accommodation was a bit sparse as they were in the process of renovating the blocks so every 6 months or so everyone had to move blocks while their own was being refurbished.

I got stuck in the transit accommodation which was on

the ground floor of one of the blocks that hadn't yet been done up. We had to park at the back of the blocks and as I had a car-full of stuff, I didn't fancy lugging it around to the front entrance, so I pulled the car up to the rear of my room and began to throw my gear through the window.

As I did, a bearded, turbaned head popped out of the window and asked, 'Do you want a hand with that?' And that was how I met Bali Flora, a Sikh, who I would be sharing a room with for the next few weeks. Gratefully I accepted and he helped me in with my gear. I handed it in through the window to him and he dumped it in my bed space.

After we had brought all the stuff in, we got to introducing ourselves. Here is where coincidence and "What a small world it is," comes into play. Bali was a Cpl in Logistics, not Stores, he was more than a "Blanket Stacker" as we called the people in stores who handed out shirts and the like. He was in the side of things that arranged fuel and spare parts for the flying squadrons.

When we got to the bit, 'Where are you from?' it turns out that he was from Coventry too! And not only that but we'd even gone to the same school. (*I'm not saying which one as they are the standard questions that websites ask, so I don't want to give away any personal details. Identity theft you know.*) I was a few years older than him but we were there at the same time and as there weren't that many kids wearing a turban at my school, I must have seen him around. Anyway, we became good friends and I'm still in contact with him to this day.

The room we were in was full of the old, free-standing, single wardrobes, so we were able to build walls with them to give ourselves some privacy in our bed spaces. It made it a bit more bearable than being in an open plan room.

We lived there and hung around together until Bali got

a quarter and brought his family out from the UK and I moved into my own room in a barrack block.

***

The Commcen was situated in a large, concrete building called the Combat Operations Centre (COC). There were 2 Sgts and 1 Cpl in the Commcen and 1 Cpl running the PBX. I figured that once they knew I was from a PBX then the current PBX supervisor would ask to go into the Commcen and hand the PBX over to me but no, to my relief he was perfectly happy to remain there.

The Sgt who ran the Commcen was my old mate Rory Berry from Zutendaal, the man who had got me my Cpl's tapes, so obviously I was off to a good start there. The other Sgt was Fiona Evans who worked in the back room of the Commcen, handling all the Crypto and the coding/decoding of any sensitive signals traffic. The Commcen Cpl was Mick Apps and Paul Thornton ran the PBX, which was across the road, in Station Headquarters.

At Marham the Commcen came under Ground Radio Flight (GRF). We still did here at Gutersloh, but we were actually supported by CIS Engineering techies, they fixed our teleprinters and equipment, but for the life of me I can't remember what CIS stood for. Something Information Systems probably. Never mind, not important.

It was quite a busy little Commcen. Apart from the day-to-day traffic you would expect on any normal camp, we had 4 flying squadrons to cater for and we also handled traffic for an army camp on the other side of Gutersloh town.

There were 3 Sqn and 4 Sqn Harriers, 18 Sqn who flew Chinook helicopters and 230 Sqn Puma helicopters. The squadrons always used to turn up at their knocking off time with a bunch of engineering reports and requests back to the UK and they were several pages of numbers and figures, absolutely horrendous to type up. The poor night-shift operator who was there on his own, had to struggle his way through them during the evening.

My role was to be a daisy (day-worker) as although there was enough work to justify 2 Cpl's, a civilian message distribution operator and 4/5 operators on a day shift, the squadrons stopped flying in the evenings so it only required 1 operator to man the Commcen overnight.

**

I hadn't worked in a busy Commcen since the mid 70's back at Stanbridge. Even though most of the places I had been in the meantime had Commcens as part of their duties, apart from Marham, my main focus had been on radio work.

Mick Apps and I had very different approaches to work. He was very much, 'What does the book say?' I was, 'I've done it this way a thousand times.' Mick was one of those I told you about earlier, an ex-Telephonist who had been retrained to be a Telecommunications Operator (which now included teleprinter work) and then promoted to corporal. This happened in lots of places after they remodelled our trade, a newly trained, newly promoted tradesman ended up supervising people who have done the job for years.

Mick's way of dealing with this, I guess, (and this isn't a criticism of him) was to learn the procedural manuals inside out, whereas I relied on my previous experience to make decisions, only checking the books when I wasn't sure. A point which was brought home to me one day by a WRAF that worked in the Commcen with us. She asked me some obscure point of message handling procedure. I told her I would have to check the manuals to find out.

'Mick would know,' she rather sniffily informed me.

'That's the difference between Mick and me,' I replied. 'Give me a radio and a roll of copper wire, send me out to the car park and I can communicate with Cyprus. Mick can't.'

My point being that in a time of war, (particular if you have to abandon the camp and take to the woods – this was Germany during the Cold War, remember) knowing the teleprinter procedure manuals by heart might not be your best weapon if you wish to survive and continue to operate.

***

Fun with phones!

Over the years I had a few laughs with telephones. One of my favourites when I was younger was to answer the phone in the Commcen with, 'Hello, is that Stores?'

Naturally they would say no (unless by some wild coincidence it was Stores).

So I would say, 'Sorry, I've got the wrong number,' and hang up, hopefully leaving the person on the other end baffled, saying to themselves, 'Hang on, didn't I ring him?'

One of the things that caught me out when I first started working in the Commcen at Gutersloh was the camp phone system. It was computerised and you could do all sorts of fancy things with it, for example, if you rang a number and it was engaged you could press a couple of keys (*4 or whatever) and when the line became free, it would automatically ring both ends of the call. However, as you were probably ringing a busy squadron registry or possibly an Ops room, the people at either end may not be the same people who were originally involved.

So you might walk past the phone and it would ring and you would answer it, 'Hello, Commcen.'

'This is 4 Sqn.'

'What can I do for you?'

'Nothing, you rang me.'

'No I didn't, you rang me.'

'No, you rang me.'

'Look here, I was just walking past the phone, it rang and I answered it.'

And it would descend into a shouting match with much cursing and casting doubts on each other's parentage. This happened a few times before someone explained to me how the phone system worked and I learned to turn to the room and ask, 'Has anybody got anything for 4 Sqn?'

***

Because I drove an old Morris Marina I was unable to get left-hand drive headlights for it (where the lights dip to the right instead of the left). I had driven out to Germany by fitting yellow filters to them, which slant the light in the other direction. I had hoped that I could carry on using those but was told by the MT section that the headlamps themselves would have to be changed. This was going to work out expensive, trying to actually track down a pair of left-hand headlights for an old Marina and then get them fitted. (There was no such thing as *eBay* then.) Eventually I accepted the fact that I was going to have to get rid of the car.

I was still going through that "skint" phase after my divorce, so buying another car, even a second-hand one, was out of the question. I knew that eventually I would buy a duty-free one. Most people bought them from a company called Nato Cars, as they knew all the pitfalls and sorted out all the paperwork for you, so I got in touch with them and they agreed to accept my crappy Marina in part exchange against a guaranteed purchase later. So that's what I did, it got it off my hands without me having to go through the bother of trying to sell it in the UK or scrapping it and it gave me some money off the purchase price of a new motor. I wangled some leave, drove it back to the UK and handed it over to them. Sorted!

It did mean though that I was without a car for the next year or so. What with that and only having the weekends free, it rather put a dent in any hope I had of doing much sight-seeing in Germany. In fact I only ever got off camp if Bali or Paul Thornton came to pick me up.

Even though we didn't work alongside each other, I got more pally with Paul from PBX than I did with Mick and would often go scalie-bashing at his place or Bali's. In fact Bali and his family practically adopted me and would often take me along on their day trips out to visit places.

***

As in Belgium, I noticed that there were two types of servicemen. Those that drank in the bars on camp, shopped in the NAAFI shop, watched Coronation Street on BFBS television and lived life as if they were still in the UK, only the currency being different.

And then there were the other sort who frequented the bars off camp, got in with the locals, played for local football teams and in some cases ended up marrying German Frauleins.

I always suggested to new guys in the Commcen that

they try and be like the second lot. It's such a waste to live in a foreign country but to never see it. For many of these it was their first tour of duty overseas. It was my third so I could afford to be a bit blasé about it.

Unfortunately, due to only having weekends free when I just wanted to relax and sleep off my hangovers, and not having transport, I became one of the first kind. The NAAFI wasn't very good although they had Discos several nights a week but there another bar called "The Kegelbahn" which was a bowling alley in the basement of the Airman's Mess. It was the old-fashioned kind where you had to set up the pins by hand, not that I ever played. It was staffed by servicemen volunteers and the atmosphere was more convivial than the NAAFI, no Rock-Apes there.

At that time there were about 3 Deutsch Marks to the pound. In the Kegelbahn beer used to cost about a Mark and you could get these different flavoured shots of "Korn" for 50 Pfennigs. Most people, me included, used to think that spirits in Germany were called "Schnapps". You see them drinking it all the war movies. I used to ask for that in German bars but they didn't seem to know what I was talking about, 'Korn?' they would ask me, so I'd just shrug and say, 'Ja.' (Schnapps does exist, I bought a stone bottle of it on one exercise when I was on the Wing.) But also on TCW I discovered this wonderful drink called "Appel Korn" and it is what it sounds like, Apple flavoured spirit made from corn. It's meant to be drunk as a shot, like tequila, with a beer chaser. At the time we could only get it while on exercise in Germany but now they sell it in the UK.

At Gutersloh I found that they make all sorts of flavoured Korn and there was nothing nicer than swigging down shots of Raspberry or Blackcurrant Korn, followed by a beer. Boy, you could get so drunk on it, so cheaply!

It really was the land of the Duty Free. Booze was so cheap that on Disco nights you could see the WRAF's drinking PINTS of Baileys. I'm not making this up! The bar staff would take a plastic pint pot, fill it with ice cubes and pour Baileys into it until it was full.

You could buy booze in the NAAFI shop to take back to the block, which would do you for a night in front of the telly Having booze in the block wasn't strictly legal but they turned a blind eye to it. A 6 pack of small bottles of beer cost around 3 DM (a pound). Or you could buy a 10 pack of Herforder Pils with a carrying handle, known as a "Herfie Handbag". Which prompted one of the eternal mysteries of life that has puzzled philosophers over the years, namely … 'Why is a 6 pack not enough but a 10 pack too much?'

It was very much a booze driven culture. Each squadron or section had its own bar and every Friday afternoon it would open around 3 o'clock and when you could get away, you would slip over to the bar (ours was in GRF) and have a drink and a chat with people you might not normally see during the week.

There was another bar on camp, forget what it was called but it was run by one of the charities such as the Women's Royal Volunteer Service or some such. You could get food there as well but I didn't frequent that much as it was where the Rock Apes hung out, so it wasn't very popular with the normal airman.

***

(*This next story I know to be true as I was actually at Gutersloh when it happened.*)

The helicopter squadrons at Gutersloh used to go annually on a two week exercise to a training ground called Sennelager, *(probably the worst lager in the world)*.

In the middle of this two week period they traditionally stopped the exercise and held a barbecue to give the guys a break and to keep the families sweet, as they were all invited to come out to the barbecue.

So, all the families were bussed out to the site of the squadron HQ. Unfortunately, one of the wives could not find her husband, (let's call him Cpl Bloggs). 'Oh,' they said, 'he must be out at one of the dispersed sites. We'll get you shipped out there.' The wife was duly driven off to each of the dispersed sites in turn but Cpl Bloggs was not to be found at any of them.

By this time the wife is starting to get worried as indeed are Cpl Bloggs' superiors. They think perhaps he's lying in a ditch somewhere and no one has spotted him, so they check the admin records to see *precisely* where he is supposed to be. To everyone's embarrassment, it turns out that he isn't even on the exercise. He told his wife that he would be away on exercise but in reality he has taken two weeks leave and gone on holiday with his girlfriend! The poor wife was driven away in shame and I would dearly love to have been a fly on the wall at Cpl Bloggs' "Interview without coffee" with his CO.

***

While I was in Germany the first Gulf War started up. (*You know, the legitimate one.*) Also known as Operation Granby by the Brits and Operation Desert Shield/Desert Storm by the Yanks, which was kicking the Iraqi's out of Kuwait.

Being as I was already on the Preliminary Warning Roster to go to the Falklands, I thought that they would simply point that list of people to the Gulf instead and I'd better get my desert boots ready. Apparently though, it takes that long to move all the pieces around the chess board to get everyone in position to man the Falklands that The Powers That Be decided to leave us as we were and grab others to go war in the Gulf.

It ended up with Mick Apps and one of our ops, Matt "Tommy" Tucker, going instead. That was a close escape. Don't get me wrong, I'd have gone if they sent me with no arguing (after all that's what we sign on the dotted line for) but as I said, no sane man actually *wants* to go to war. So if they didn't send me, so much the better.

The Intelligence Cell in the COC had Sky TV installed so they could keep up to date by watching all the news broadcasts. Call yourselves Int guys? We might just as well have put Kate Adie on a retainer and saved some money. Kate Adie was a BBC reporter who always seemed to be in the thick of the action wherever it was taking place.

N.B. My favourite joke of the war. A news journalist was interviewing a British officer (I think RAF but I'm not sure) about the war action. He told them, 'Well there's the Americans over there, The Desert Rats over there, the Iraqi's are facing us, the situation's dangerous, blah, blah, blah. But we're not worried as Kate Adie hasn't shown up yet.'

***

In the run up to the Gulf War, various units started shipping out as they didn't want to miss out on any of the fun. Across the other side of Gutersloh town there was an army garrison. It contained assorted units, amongst them a Field Gun Regiment. These are BIG guns, don't know why it wasn't called an artillery regiment, but it wasn't. This field regiment packed up all their gear and their CO appeared on BFBS TV and radio talking about their deployment. 'Yes, we'll be moving out at 0800 tomorrow, travelling up the A2 to Bremerhaven where we will be loaded onto ships and set sail for the Gulf.'

What a fool!!

In the forces we have various abbreviations to describe different types of security. OPSEC for operational security, COMSEC for communications security, PERSEC for personal security, DEMI-SEC (*no wait, that's something to do with wine, isn't it?*) but anyway, this clown was giving away all the regiment's movement details just for the sake of having his face on TV. As Bugs Bunny would say, 'What a maroon!'

So all Saddam Hussein had to do was order his men, which (if he had any sense) he had previously scattered throughout Europe, to attack this convoy, damage the guns, kill some soldiers and effectively remove one of the pieces from the board. Multiply that by all the regiments, squadrons and naval units that were taking part in the war, then you can even the playing field by crippling your opponent's logistical lines. It is a long held opinion that if you can't afford the tanks, planes and boats that your enemy has, then you focus on training your men into Special Forces with skills in infiltration and sabotage. That is what Saddam should have done to win that particular war.

***

While they were in the Gulf, people started sending back postcards to us at Gutersloh, supposedly showing the local scenery. I say "postcards" but they were actually just pieces of sandpaper with postage stamps stuck on the back. They were out in the desert so what else would the view be but sand?

(*That did make 'oi larf, that did.*)

Anyway, we kicked Saddam out of Kuwait and Mick and Tommy came back safely.

***

Then one day the moment I had been dreading arrived, my movement instructions came through for me to go to the Falkland Islands. Duh, duh, duuuuuuh.

***

The Falkland Islands

"RAF Most Unpleasant"

Arrived 1 July 1991 RAF Mount Pleasant - Joint Communications Unit Falkland Islands (JCUFI)

I landed in the Falkland Islands after 2 x 8 hour trips on a Tristar aircraft. 1 to Ascension Island, followed by 1 from there to the Falklands. A mind and arse numbing flight on which we weren't even allowed to smoke.

Although it was July, with my impeccable timing I had arrived in their winter as they were in the southern hemisphere. Fortunately I had taken a thick coat along.

I was met at the terminal by the guy I was replacing. That was the routine down there. You flew in one day, were met by your predecessor who was the Falklands Old Guy (FOG). You were the Falklands New Guy (FNG). Some sections had plaques made up which were worn around the neck on a chain, which had to be worn on the last week for the FOG and the first week for the FNG. Fortunately my section didn't play those childish games.

Anyway, he would meet you, show you to your pit space, take you to the bar that night, introduce you to your watch and then he would fly out on the return trip of the plane that you came in on. That was in our section. Maybe in others, the more technical, they did a longer handover but for us it was "one in, one out".

Mount Pleasant living accommodation consists of one long, wooden building with a central corridor wide enough to drive a Land Rover from one end to the other. (Presumably this was in case hostilities broke out again and we drew back to the building to defend it, so we could quickly transport arms and injured people from one end to the other quickly.)

The building was split into two halves, the top end was called 12 complex and the bottom half 38 complex. 12 complex was the RAF half, where all the RAF Mount Pleasant personnel, the WRAF quarters, the officer's mess and the Sgt's mess were. The main reception was also there and above the door they had a sign that said,

'This may not be the End of the World but you can certainly see it from here.'

How true those words were.

38 complex was where all the riff-raff lived, the army/navy chaps and RAF personnel like myself who worked for a joint service unit. The women on our watch however, regardless of which service they belonged to, were housed in the WRAF quarters. Which was a good job too. 12 complex was reasonably civilised being run by the RAF. 38 complex was known as, "The Bronx," as it was a bit rough down there. I suppose I could have stood on my rights and demanded that as a RAF Cpl I should be allowed to live in 12 complex, but that didn't seem right as the rest of my watch lived down there and

for morale purposes it was best that we stuck together as a watch.

Each complex had its own mess. The 38 complex one was mediocre as it was run by the army and my fellow male shift workers and I would meet up there before going to work. The RAF mess was better and occasionally we would meet the ladies there and have a nicer meal.

The watch was truly Joint Service, I can't remember how the other watches were made up but on ours it went like this:

Army Sgt (DSO/DSM) male.

RAF Cpl (me – indeterminate gender) as Crypto-Fascist – sorry I mean Crypto Operator, dealing with any encoded signals going in and out. When I wasn't required there I was the shift supervisor in the Commcen.

A navy Killoch (equivalent to a Cpl) male.

A WRAC Lance-Cpl (Women's Royal Army Corps).

An RAF SAC, male.

An army private, male.

A navy guy (I dunno – able seamen or whatever).

A WRAC private.

A navy WREN (Women's Royal Naval Service).

I was also the shift driver. Don't know if I was the only one that had a license but I copped for all the driving jobs. I had to leave early to take the section Land Rover to meet the oncoming shift and then hand the keys over to them, so I got to the mess early. Then in return when we were going on shift, I had to drive them all back to the complex afterwards.

I also had to pick up the meals on the nightshift. Always took a female along with me as they would flutter their eyelids at the cook and he would give us extra rations.

I don't remember the shift pattern but wisely they didn't give us too much time off between shift cycles, just a couple of days I think, otherwise everyone would get into too much trouble.

***

Booze and fags were Duty-Free but at NAAFI prices. So people coming from the UK to the Falklands were banging on about how much cheaper things were, but if like me you had come there from overseas, it was actually more expensive than what I was paying back in Germany.

Not that there was much choice either. For a start, The Powers That Be had decreed that we lower ranks were not allowed spirits. Only the officers and Sgts (who were often only in their 20's) could be trusted to drink spirits and not cause trouble. Whereas people like myself, who was in my mid 30's and a house-owner, couldn't be trusted.

It was a bit of a pointless ban though, as copious amounts of beer followed by a large quantity of wine could get you so drunk you couldn't even remember your name. So Yah Boo Sucks to you TPTB!

Besides, across from 12 complex was this nice building called Turners, as that was the name of the company that built RAF Mount Pleasant and maintained it. A story I like is that Turners built this fancy accommodation and the RAF officers went, 'Right, that can be the Officer's mess.'

To which Turners replied, 'Push off. That's where our people are going to live.'

So the officers took over the Sgt's mess and everyone got pushed down the line. Tee Hee.

The reason I mention this is that every Tuesday night Turners had a Bingo night which was open to everyone. And they served spirits at the bar which made a nonsense of the 'No spirits for lower rankers' anyway. The watch and I went over a couple of times but we found out we could live without drinking spirits.

The beer that was available was in cans only, nothing on tap. The cans were about half pint size and they only sold two types, Red or Green. Red were Tennants Bitter and the Green was Lager, Heineken or Carlsberg, can't remember which. You could buy the cans individually or they would sell you a "slab". That was the cardboard container they came in with the plastic removed. Due to the drinking culture, people were often fined a slab for transgressing certain rules. The guilty party may have only received too many letters at mail call but some bozo would always shout out that he had to buy a slab to be shared out.

The annoying thing was that every can they sold had to be opened by the bar staff, so we naughty boys couldn't take them back to the room and stockpile them. If you did buy a slab the beer was going flat by the time you had worked your way through it. If you asked for a glass to drink it out of, they gave you a half-pint, plastic container; as if we held a real glass we would instantly go mad and start attacking everyone around us.

***

The Falklands is a funny place. People had to find a way to get through their 4 month tour, no matter what it was, otherwise they'd crack up. I always said, 'You have to do what you have to do, to make it through.' Some people spent all their time down the gym, some had affairs but most of the rest, including the watch and I, spent most of their off-time in the NAAFI or at section bars around Mount Pleasant.

We were lucky, we actually worked with women. Some guys who were posted there and spent all of their time at one of the mountain-top radar sites could go through their entire tour without even seeing a woman. We had them on our watch! And what's more, they socialised with us. Which meant that we had open invites to all the parties around the camp, as long as we brought the women along.

Our watch always stuck together out of work. Even nights when we didn't go boozing if we were working next day, we would congregate somewhere like the NAAFI and just have a quiet drink and something to eat. We used to call it "Spotting", short for "Train spotting", which meant someone who was a saddo and would go trainspotting as they had nothing better to do in life. We adopted the phrase to refer to our "quiet nights in". Even if we only sat there and shot the breeze, the main point is that we were all there.

Not to say that we were all great mates and loved each other, no, in fact me and the younger navy guy didn't get along. I'm not a big one for standing on ceremony and insisting that everyone pays due deference to my rank. And I know that the navy live in such close quarters on ships that there is a lot more informality amongst them, I get that, but this navy lad kept ordering me around and telling me what to do (which I ignored) and I got a bit miffed about it after a while. It showed a lack of respect for me and my rank. I didn't kick off about it but it raised a barrier between us. But the point is … neither of us made a big deal about it and kept things under wraps for the sake of harmony on shift. We were both big enough to put it to one side so that we could all hang out together without any animosity. And we weren't the only ones but everyone, for the most part, put their personal feelings aside and looked at the bigger picture, and I'm rather proud of the whole watch for that.

We worked and played well together. So much so, that the navy WO who was in charge of the place took a shine to us. He used to tell us that the rest of the watches all worked quietly and got on with their jobs whereas we were always laughing and joking, besides doing our work well. The place was more fun when we were on watch, he said. He knew that we would go boozing on our time off but we would always show up for work and do a good job. I'm not making this up. We arranged a trip to Port Stanley for a couple of days, and the WO even rearranged his end of tour 4 days R&R, so he could come along with us.

It seems strange to me that the RAF would continually ignore my brilliance and refuse to promote me when other services thought highly of me. Even the Major who ran JCUFI did. I was at a booze up at the JCUFI bar one night and stepped outside for a smoke. The major was there puffing on his pipe (briar not hookah) and he said to me, 'Why are you still only a corporal? You deserve to be at least a sergeant by now.'

What could I say? 'My face doesn't fit.'

In the same bunch of RAF assessment forms I acquired during the writing of this memoir was my end of tour report from the Falklands which I didn't see at the time but was put on file at RAF Gutersloh. Both the Major and the Captain serving under him recommended me for promotion to sergeant. (I have the documentation to prove it if anyone doubts me.) So how come I left the RAF still a corporal?

***

'Okay, move back just a little more so I can get a good shot.'

There was nothing in the way of entertainment (except for one ENSA show that turned up), no TV, so the only amusement was listening to BFBS radio. As it happens Kevin Costner's *Robin Hood Prince of Thieves*, was out in the cinemas and the accompanying Bryan Adams song, *Everything I do, I do it for You*, was in the charts. This went on all the time I was down south. One day the BFBS DJ said to his companion on the radio, 'Imagine if you were detached to the Falklands for four months while this song was popular. You could have done your whole tour while this song was number one.' Well, that was me! I was that airman. I did spend four months listening to that blasted song week after week.

To be fair though, when I was on disembarkation leave from the Falklands I did go to see the film to see what all the fuss was about and I must admit I enjoyed it.

***

This next bit is going to sound a little weird. When I went to the Falklands I felt that I was not going to come back alive. I just had the strangest feeling that I was going to pop my clogs. That's not as crazy as it may sound, we were regularly losing people down there, mainly to road traffic accidents. Some fool had got the measurements wrong about how deep the snow was in winter and the road to Port Stanley was about 2-3 feet off the ground, so skidding off it in winter was not uncommon.

A lot of the walkways between the buildings had been built too high as well, around knee-height. Coming back from the Engineers bar one night, there were no lights, no moonlight and it was the one time I had forgotten to bring my torch with me. I'm edging along the walkway gingerly, trying not to fall off and I turned where I thought the junction between walkways was. Next thing I know, I am lying sprawled across the bonnet of a Land Rover. That's how high they were. Imagine trying to explain to people that I had tripped over a Land Rover in the dark!

At least I wasn't injured. Unlike the time I slipped over in the snow and landed directly on my right elbow. Gave me trouble for years afterwards that did.

We actually lost 3 people while I was down there. A Phantom aircraft went into the sea and the pilot and navigator drowned. Also there was a navy guy on one of the sites, he was helping to unload a big, rubber ball filled with fuel (which is how they transport it by helicopter) and it broke loose, rolled down the hill and crushed him.

So it's perhaps not that crazy to think that I might not make it back in one piece, but I obviously did as you're reading this book.

Or did I??

Maybe there is some kind of "Sixth Sense" thing going on here and I really am dead. Who knows? Spooky!

***

When I was going through my divorce I used to write poetry as a way of getting things off my chest (well it worked for Phil Collins, didn't it?) Don't worry, I'm not going to inflict them on you now but here is one that I wrote while I was in the Falklands to describe my time there.

A Benny is a Falkland Islander. Named after a rather dim character that used to appear in a popular soap-opera "Crossroads".

THE FALKLAND ISLANDS

I'm sitting down here in the Falklands,
Wondering where I went wrong.
The days are too f**king boring,
The nights are too f**king long.

There's nothing to do in this hell-hole,
Except work and sleep and drink beer.
This may not be "The End of the World",
But you can certainly see it from here.

The place is bleak and windy.
There's not a tree to be found.
The view's just as bad from up in the air,
As it is from here on the ground.

The highlight's a day trip to Stanley,
Big eats and beer in a glass.
Where you can drink shorts 'til they come out your ears,
And they kick you out on your ass.

Or you can go to the "Benny Bop",
Drink lager and act like a lout.
Pick a fight with some of the locals,
Now that's what I call a day out!

I'll really be glad to get out of this place,
Back to the UK, and to freedom.
They can keep all their sheep and their penguins and seals,
Because I don't f**king need 'em.

To the people back there, that posted me here,
To spend four months, getting plastered.
I'd like to offer these few friendly words,
'Get me out of here ...You B**tards!'

Eat your heart out, Byron!

***

While I was there I bought this nice plaque of the Falkland Islands, metal relief on a wooden frame. *This is nice*, I thought, *I'll keep this safe until I get home to the UK and I'm living in my own house. I won't be able to go back to the Falklands and buy another one.* (Well, I could have but it wasn't worth another four months there just to buy a plaque, know what I mean?)

So, on my return to Germany, I kept it in the protective cardboard cover, with a clear, plastic front. Every time I had to move blocks I wrapped it up carefully and transported it by hand to avoid it getting damaged.

Finally I made it back to the UK when my tour in Germany finished, and I was able to move back into my own house and live like a human being again, instead of a battery hen.

Once I'd unpacked everything, to celebrate being back home, I decided to hang the plaque on the wall. I carefully unwrapped it, took it out of its cardboard case, turned it over and read the label on the back, *Made in Burford.* Just a few miles down the road from where I was presently standing. I could nip down there anytime and buy a new one! Globalisation eh?

***

So the time finally arrived when I became the FOG. I picked up my replacement at the airport, introduced him to the watch, etc. finished my packing and had one last booze up with the shift.

Arrived at the terminal next day, all ready for the off but there was a slight snag. Some weeks earlier a volcano had erupted in Peru, covering everywhere with that fine pumice dust. We had been warned not to go jogging outdoors or to spend long periods working outside because of the air quality.

The flight the day before had made it in safely as my replacement had arrived but they were having serious doubts as to whether it would be safe to fly out again. For those who don't know, the big fear about flying near erupting volcanos is that the dust will be sucked into the jet engines, where the intense heat will turn the dust particles to glass, which will obviously seriously damage the aircraft.

That volcano had been sitting there for countless millions of years but it waits for ME to be in the area before it decides to blow its top! Unlucky or what? Who says the universe isn't out to get me?

And to add insult to injury they showed us "Top Gun" while we waited in the terminal. As if to say, 'This is what flying looks like but you won't be seeing any today.'

But I guess the coin came down Heads, as they decided to fly after all and it was with great relief we took off and made our way back to jolly old England.

To my great regret, as this was my only time in the southern hemisphere, in all the time I was there, I forgot to check if the water in the toilet bowl actually does swish the other way round when you flush.

***

I can't quite remember where this photo was taken.

The ONLY good thing that can be said about a tour in the Falklands is that the RAF don't charge you for food and accommodation while you are there as it is such a sh*thole. As there is hardly anything to buy down there, you spend very little of your wages. So when I came back from down South, I had amassed £2000 in my bank and I had 2 weeks leave before I was due back to Germany. I had made arrangements with Nato Cars to pick up my new motor, a Vauxhall Astra, so I spent my time visiting friends around the UK until it was time to catch the ferry back to Germany.

***

Returned to RAF Gutersloh 14 October 1991

Alas, by the time my tour and disembarkation leave had ended, our Sgt, Rory Berry, had been posted back to the UK. I never got chance to say goodbye to him but he left me a copy of the annual write up that he had given me (just in case somebody decided to change it) and it was a good one.

In his place we got a new sergeant who I shall call Sgt Dartman, as that is all he ever talked about, playing darts in the Families club or the bar in the families apartment block. He wasn't really popular with any of the troops but we tolerated him. He had this crazy habit of making out the watch lists with all different colours for the different watches (enough to give you a migraine) then he would photocopy it and it would come out in all different shades of grey.

***

I got into skiing while I was out in Germany. Like many people I had always wanted to try it but never had the nerve. Here in Germany the RAF actively encouraged such activities and even ran their own courses down in southern Germany, staffed by RAF Physical Training Instructors. So I signed up for one but it was some months away.

Before that course came around, Bali's section were arranging a skiing trip and he asked if I wanted to go along, so I signed up for that as well. I had a terrible time, we didn't have a very good instructor IMO and I hurt myself a couple of times. It put me off skiing for life and I vowed I'd never do it again.

One good thing that came out of it was that we were near Castle Neuschwanstein which is the castle you see in *Chitty Chitty Bang Bang*, so we took a day trip there. Lovely place, well worth a visit if you're ever in that area.

Anyway, the RAF course came around, I knew it would cause me problems if I dropped out at the last minute, so I went on it. We were staying in or near a place called Garmisch-Partenkirchen. One day we visited nearby Oberammergau. That's where they hold the Passion Plays every 10 years. It's also famous for having a shop that sells Christmas decorations all year round.

I've got to admit that I'm a terrible skier. I'm all right at first but once I build up some speed I get unsteady on my feet so I tend to take wider sweeps across the face of the slope to keep my speed down, while everyone else is pointing their nose downslope and going for it.

I would always be the last one to make it to the chairlift, falling over on the cable drag and so on and I'd also hurt my knee so had to keep stopping to rest it, basically I was holding everyone back. So eventually my instructor handed me over to a Flt Sgt instructor to spend time with, to give the rest of the group a fair chance.

Best thing that could have happened! I figured that we would just bimble about on the nursery slopes but no ... this FS wanted to go skiing and he was taking me with him! He took me up as far as the chair lifts and cable drags would take us, right to the top of the mountain and then we skied down again. Great fun. As there was only me and him and we didn't have to follow a schedule, we could take our own sweet time and go where we liked. My skiing certainly improved with this one-to-one training. I found that left to myself I wasn't very good, but if I just followed this guy, kept in his tracks, I could scoot down the slopes far faster that I normally would have. I ended up having a much better time than anyone else in my group, with my own private ski instructor.

Of course, being a RAF course they had to control what we did off the slopes as well, so they made us do compulsory swimming one night. I groaned about it but it turned out to be a fascinating experience. The local swimming baths had the usual pools and water slides but they had a hot pool as well. I don't mean a hot tub but a pool with the temperature like bath water. You could swim around in it inside but at one end they had those plastic strips hanging down like they have on warehouse doors, so that vans can drive through. If you went through those strips, then the pool extended out into the open air. We were there at night so you were out under the stars in mid-winter. It was great! Your head would start to get cold after a couple of minutes but you just dunk it underwater and you were fine again.

Some of the PTI's would show off by getting out, rolling in the snow and then diving back into the pool but that's PTI's for you.

It was a great time and renewed my interest in skiing,

which I did for many years after leaving the RAF.

***

Do you remember that I told you about that odd incident where I KNEW that my posting to North Luffenham had been cancelled, only to find out subsequently that it had? Well I had another "spooky" thing happen to me, when I was at Gutersloh.

Every year the WRAF held a barbecue for charity and sold tickets to attend. It was held around the open-air swimming pool which was situated in a triangle of land, between 3 roads. The triangle held a swimming pool, some buildings and the rest was trees, surrounded by a chain link fence.

The week before the barbecue, I had a dream about it. I was standing by the wire fence, on my right was Paul Thornton, on my left one of the Air Traffic Control guys who everyone knew as "Shadwell" and opposite me was a civvy who, it turned out as the conversation progressed, was a Meteorological officer. (Most flying stations have a civilian Met Office attached to the ATC.) We weren't doing anything special; we were just standing there by the wire fence, chatting and drinking beer.

Anyway, the day of the barbecue came and I went along. At one point I found myself standing by the fence, Paul Thornton was on my right, Shadwell was on my left and opposite me was a civvy that I had never seen before. We were just standing there drinking beer and chatting.

I looked around me and suddenly had this overwhelming sense of Déjà vu. Then I remembered why it was so familiar. I told the others that I had dreamt this exact same scenario, just the week before. Of course they didn't believe it and accused me of imagining it, drinking too much, etc.

'All right then, I'll prove it,' I replied, pointing at the civvy, 'He's a Met man. How do I know that? You didn't tell me when you introduced us, so how do I know? I've never laid eyes on him before.'

'Go on then, how do you know?' one of them asked.

'Because I dreamt it last week, that's what I'm trying to tell you!'

Of course they couldn't explain how I did know, and they didn't believe me, so we left it at that.

I wish I could say that the face of the civvy was the same as that in my dream but I couldn't be sure, you know what dreams are like.

Yes okay, the more cynical amongst you could say that subconsciously I had worked out that as the Met Office is attached to ATC, if you see a civvy with an ATC guy then an educated guess might be that he is a Met Officer. Maybe that is what happened but it would have to have been subconsciously, because I wasn't aware of that thought process taking place. Who knows? It just struck me as damned weird and has stuck in my memory ever since.

***

Some people in the services say the worst rank is sergeant. I disagree, I think it's corporal. It's all about "Us" and "Them" and the poor old Cpl is stuck in the middle as he is considered "Them" by both sides. To present my argument, let me simplify things by using the situation that used to be in many unaccompanied overseas postings, such as Gan, Masirah and, when I was there, the Falklands, where the junior ranks live in their barrack blocks, eat in the Airman's mess and drink in the NAAFI. The senior NCO's live/eat/drink in the Sgt's Mess.

Now then, come the time when dirty work has to be

done, say, clean the camp up for AOC's inspection, the NCO's band together and from the WO down, issue the orders to make things happen. It comes all the way down the chain of command to the Cpl who is the one that actually has to issue the orders, no matter how unpopular, 'Clean the toilets' or 'Scrub the dustbins' etc. At that point he is considered one of Us by the NCO's and one of Them by the SAC's and J/T's.

And that's all fine and dandy, the ones who "rule", i.e. the ones who give orders, are one big happy family and the "ruled" mutter curses under their breath and then go and clean the toilets.

Until it comes to the end of the day.

All the Senior NCO's toddle off back to the Sgt's Mess and the poor old Cpl is left standing out in the street on his own, as at this point he becomes one of Them, as far as the SNCO's are concerned. He has to go back to the block where all the junior ranks live, then eat in the mess with the juniors and drink in the same bar as them. But to the juniors he is still one of Them. So poor old Cpl Bloggs is stuck in No Man's Land, without friends on either side.

Sure you could say he can drink in the Cpl's Club if there is one, but that is just a drinking club, he still has to eat in the Airman's mess and live in the barrack block.

That's why I think the corporal rank is the worst – all the responsibilities of rank but none of the perks (cheap booze and better living accommodation in the Sgt's mess). Dumped on from above and resented from those below.

It can happen with assessments too. Although technically it is the Sgt who is the first reporting officer on an assessment, in practice it is usually the Cpl's who give their opinion and the Sgt bases his write-up on that.

At Gutersloh, some didn't like the assessments that

Sgt Dartman gave them but at the end of the day, the Sgt and the other 2 Cpl's went home to their wives and I got shunned socially by one or two airmen in the block, because they didn't like their assessments.

C'est la vie.

***

In 1993 RAF Gutersloh was handed over to the army and became Princess Royal Barracks.
For the second time in my career, the RAF station I was serving on was given away to the army. I must be some sort of Jonah.

***

I used to have a lot of respect for the civilian police (this was back in the 90's). It's a dangerous and dirty job dealing with the public and protecting the civilian population against the worst that criminals have to offer – "The Thin Blue Line" and all that.

That is until Tony Blair and his Labour Government politicised them and now they spend all their time and millions in tax-payers money investigating historic sex-crimes *supposedly* carried out by members of the Tory establishment like Edward Heath, Leon Brittan and Harvey Proctor, while turning a blind eye to the multitude of rape gangs, in many major UK cities, run by "Asian Men" (as the media call them).

Refusing to come and investigate burglaries if your house has an odd number (Leicestershire police) due to man-power shortages and yet have teams of officers trawling Twitter and Facebook looking for people being "nasty" to each other. It's like they all have a Common Purpose, Ha Ha. (*Hint, Google Common Purpose.*)

However, I never had any time for the military police. I knew a few and they were all right as individuals but as organisations they always struck me as incompetent. The RAF Police wore white, peaked caps so were called "Snowdrops". The army police wore red, peaked caps and were called "Redcaps".

When they began the process of handing over RAF Gutersloh to the army, the Redcaps took over responsibility for the security of the base. Your average Redcap was quite capable of handling day to day stuff, drunken squaddies fighting or someone breaking into the NAAFI, but anything more seemed to be beyond them.

For example: At one point the base had been taken over by the army but there were still plenty of RAF chaps around. My Commcen was still manned by RAF personnel for example. After one of the Disco nights in the NAAFI, a teenage girl went missing. Some of my guys from the Commcen were questioned by the Redcaps. (Not because they were in anyway connected to it, I hasten to add. They worked on the NAAFI committee and were round and about that night, working the music system and so on, so might have seen something.)

The local German police offered to step in and take over the investigation but under the Allied Powers "We Won the War so you Germans Can F**k Off – Act of 1945" the army police decided to run the investigation themselves. Alas, the poor girl's body was found about a week later, off camp, wrapped in a duvet cover.

The Redcaps have their own investigation branch like the CID, called the Special Investigation Branch (SIB). Presumably the SIB took over the investigation at some point, so it isn't as if it was the guys who normally guard the gate who were carrying out the investigation.

SIB tracked the duvet cover back to a certain squaddie who claimed that the duvet *was* his but it had been stolen when he washed it and hung it out to dry. Said squaddie was duly arrested and in time court-martialled where he was found NOT GUILTY.

A year or two later when the girl's father was posted back to Scotland, he took out a private prosecution against the squaddie in question (which he was allowed to do under Scottish law) but he was once again found "not guilty", or "case not proven" or whatever legal term the Scottish courts use.

<u>Now then, just to be clear and for my own legal protection</u> ... I am NOT saying that the squaddie who was accused was guilty of the crime or even involved in it in anyway. All right?

What I am saying is that murder is not that common in the military (thankfully) so one would assume that SIB put their best people on the case, and yet ... whoever did do it GOT AWAY WITH MURDER! And that is all down to the Redcaps. Useless bunch of t*ssers!

***

It's often said that when Station Warrant Officers retire they last about 6 months and then die. I thought this was an urban myth until I saw it happen for myself. I was one of the latter RAF people to leave Gutersloh, so I was still around when it happened.

When we handed over the camp to the army, the first ones to be replaced were the people who actually ran the camp day-to-day, such as the police and the General Duties people, headed by the SWO. The SWO decided to retire locally instead of being posted elsewhere, and to settle in the Gutersloh area. Within 6 months and before I left Germany, he was dead.

I guess what they say is true; you take someone as powerful and important as the SWO and then just push them out the door. They've gone past the age where they can start another career. They go away and potter about in the garden but it must be a tremendous comedown for their ego. From running a flying station containing thousands of people, they no longer have any responsibility and must lose their sense of worth, I guess. Whatever the reason, they don't last long.

I should point out that this only seems to happen to SWO's. Warrant Officers of other trades, such as my own, TG 11, don't seem to have any problems. Steve Knight for example has gone on to have a successful career in civvy street. I guess people of my trade have transferable skills whereas General Duties staff don't.

***

One of the things that has annoyed me over the years is Admin clerks who don't tell you what you're entitled to claim for. Sometimes if you are doing a particularly hard or dirty job (like can happen when you're on TCW) you are allowed to claim compensation for it.

We don't know that, we're communicators, but often you only find out by word of mouth from your fellow workers. Often if you challenge the clerks on why didn't they tell you, they reply it's not their job to inform you of all the latest regulations. Well, yes, it is their job to keep us up to speed. How are we meant to find out otherwise? We don't have access to the regulations.

Even worse are those who actually deny that you have an entitlement when you do, as if it is their own money that they are trying to avoid dishing out.

Example:

For as long as I knew of, up to my time of leaving Gutersloh, only married personnel were allowed to claim Disturbance Allowance when they were posted. Then suddenly, thinking changed. (Obviously one of the Air Staff must have tried to claim this and when he got told he couldn't, he got the rules changed. It's the only reason I can explain why some enlightenment crept into our entitlement rules.) They decided that single people, who were returning to the UK and would be moving straight into their own house, were allowed to claim Disturbance Allowance. The crucial point here was that you had to have your own house, you couldn't just say, 'Oh, I will rent a place when I get home.' It had to be a place that you already owned.

Sgt Fiona Evans was like me, we owned our own homes back in England, and as singlies were living in the blocks while we were in Germany. She told me about the Disturbance Allowance, so joyfully I skipped along to General Office to put in my claim, only to be told by the clerk that there was no such thing, and I not was entitled to claim it.

Disheartened, I went back to the Commcen and the next time I saw Fiona I told her that she must be mistaken. 'Oh no,' she said, 'I know it's true because Sgt Whatnot from General Office is in the same boat as us. He lives in the Mess and he's moving back into his own house when he gets back. It was him that told me about the allowance.'

Next day I went back to General Office and as it happened ended up speaking to the same clerk. 'Look, I told you,' he said. 'Single people are not entitled to Disturbance Allowance, so you can't claim it.'

'Oh really?' I replied. 'Then perhaps you can tell me how he …' I pointed across the office to where Sgt Whatnot was sitting at his desk, '…is claiming this "non-existent" allowance? Because I know for a fact that he is.'

The clerk went and had a word with him, came back

very red-faced and dug out the right forms for me. (I shall refrain from any personal comment about the clerk or his professionalism. No doubt they punished him severely by giving him a fairly rapid promotion, compared to my trade.)

***

Of course the guys and gals in the Commcen were getting worried about being posted and to where. Some of them had outstanding loans that that had taken out on the understanding that they would be doing a full 3 year tour. As the most recent in post and with the longest left to do of a standard tour, Sgt Dartman's posting came through first. He was posted to RAF Gatow in Berlin. He was crowing about it and never gave a thought for the rest of the staff who were sweating on theirs. He kept going on about it and rubbing everyone's noses in it. We were glad to see the back of him when he left.

I wasn't bothered about being short-toured. If I did a full tour I would have a little over a year left of my time in the RAF. As a "final tour of duty" the RAF do their best to send you wherever you request, so you can get settled in the area before you leave the mob. As I would likely be going back to Brize where I had a house, it didn't make that much difference to me whether I spent a year or 18 months there before I became a civvy.

The squadrons relocated to other sites in Germany and our work load dropped to practically nothing. We had a few army guys come in to the Commcen to learn the ropes but for the most part everyone sat around playing Scrabble.

Slowly everyone got their posting and left the place until there was only Fiona Evans and myself left. It's really annoying being the last in line as you chip in to everyone's else's leaving present and go to their Gazomie do's but when it's your turn, there is no one left to contribute to yours.

The HQ of the Defence Communication Network (HQ DCN) used to have awards that they gave out to Commcens that had passed signal traffic for period, like a month, with no errors or corrections. They were called COMSTARs. It stands for

COMmendation for
Signals
Transmitted
Accurately and
Rapidly

Gutersloh had a few of these hanging on the wall that the Commcen had won in the past, so as each of our people left we gave them a COMSTAR to take with them as a memento, as we didn't want to leave them for the army. I've got one hanging on my office wall even now.

Finally our time in the Commcen came to an end and Fiona and I emptied the stationary cupboard (still not leaving anything for the army) and moved out. I went to PBX to cover for my last month at Gutersloh. Not sure what Fiona did but she left around the same time as me because we hired a van and took our stuff home together and returned to finish our tour.

***

Sgt Dartman gave everyone assessments before he left. He left them with the WO GRF who interviewed us all later. He gave me 8 for Trade Proficiency, 7 for Supervisory Ability, 7 for Personal Qualities and a generic write up but the Warrant Officer above him disagreed and bumped them up to 8 - 8 - 7. This is on a scale of 1 – 9 but traditionally nobody gets 9 for anything, the RAF won't allow it. Guy Gibson wouldn't have got 3 x 9's after the Dam Busters raid. I tell a lie though, my mate Steve Knight did get 3 x 9's once. He was on a NATO tour and the Dutch officer he worked for gave him 3 x 9's. Once it hit the RAF side of things though it got knocked down to 3 x 8's.

As I was on the way out of the RAF I wasn't too concerned about my assessments. But remember those assessments as they crop up later, when I'm back in the UK.

The only thing of note that happened in my last month was an Army Air Corps Sgt trying to cheat the system. Nobody likes a cheat. As someone once said to me, (*to* me, not *about* me) 'It's okay to ask for the moon, it's when you try to steal it that people get annoyed.'

One of the two civvy women that worked in the PBX told me that most nights this AAC Sgt would ring up from the Sgt's mess and ask for a service call back to the UK. Any of them can ask for a private call and it is charged to their mess bill, but when it is a service call (which means it's work related) it is of course free. However, the PBX op had got suspicious so she listened in on some of the calls and they were of a private nature. She billed him but he still refused to pay claiming they were service in nature.

She told me about this when I took over PBX and asked what to do. So I told her to give him the calls but to start recording them, which she did. It turns out that not only were they private calls and NOT service but they were to *someone else's wife!*

Now excuse me but when you're doing something you shouldn't be doing, surely you don't draw attention to it by doing other wrong things as well, in case they bring everything to light. I mean, if you were shop-lifting in a store, you'd be foolish to light up a cigarette and draw attention to yourself.

Anyway, I'm not the vindictive sort who enjoys dropping someone in it, but this guy was kicking the *rse out of it. I mean if he'd have just shut up and paid his bill, none of us would have said a word but he was sticking two fingers up to us.

I went over to our Warrant, explained the situation and handed over the tape. Left him with it. Never found out for certain what happened but I bet that Sgt paid up.

A short while later I packed up the Astra and headed off to dear old Blighty.

And that, Dear Reader, was the end of my time at Gutersloh.

81 SU Bampton Again

"Swan Song"

Arrived 01 September 1993 81 SU Bampton

Demobbed 11 December 1994

I arrived back in the UK. Fortunately for me I had got the posting of my choice, 81 SU again. As I had a house in the area the RAF would have done their best to post me there but that could have meant Brize Norton Commcen or even TCW as they could always fit another body in there. I could have managed TCW but I would need to be arranging resettlement courses and possibly even job interviews over the next year and I couldn't do that properly if I was being sent on exercise all the time. For me 81 SU was the best choice.

Although 81 SU was my unit, RAF Brize Norton was my parent unit and I would have to start my arrival procedure there. However, I didn't want to do anything to jeopardise my qualification for the Disturbance Allowance (the rule being you had to move straight into your own house) so I made sure I never even set foot on the camp, not even for one night, until my disembarkation leave was over. Remember that point because it becomes important later.

That was not a problem though as my old mate Steve

Smart was still stationed at Brize so he put me up until I could pick up my house keys from the rental agency.

Also Steve Knight had been posted to TCW and had a quarter at Brize. There was something kind of fitting about sharing my last posting in the mob with someone who I had shared my first posting with. Sort of completing the circle, as it were.

***

When my leave was over I turned up at 81 SU. I fully expected to be shoved on days (and become "Mr Pie Man" again) as I only had a year left but not so. I met the Warrant running the place, WO Wilce. (Never met him before but he turned out to be a decent bloke as I shall explain later.)

Bill Currie was still there as the Flt Sgt of the Planning and Coordination cell and he had already told the Warrant that I was "a good egg" and experienced in STCICS. Consequently the Warrant put me on shift almost immediately. Result!

It worked out even better as shortly afterwards the Sgt of the watch was detached to Rudloe Manor and I was put in charge of the shift for the (almost) next 6 months. I say almost as if you do the job of a higher rank for a full 6 months or longer, then you are entitled to be paid the salary rate for their rank. If I'd have done 6 months covering for him I would have been on Sgts pay for the rest of my time in the RAF but sadly, in the typical RAF way, they bought him back just short of the 6 months. Oh well, I got to be in total charge for a while so that was fine.

***

One day the Warrant called me into his office and told me that my posting assessments had turned up from Germany and I needed to sign them.

'I think there's been some mistake, sir,' I said. 'I've already been interviewed for those assessments and I was given 8, 8, 7.'

'Those aren't the numbers on this form, they've been lowered,' he replied.

Now then, I could have just said, 'All right then,' and signed them as I was leaving and it really didn't matter to me, but someone, somewhere was trying to pull a fast one and I didn't think they should be allowed to get away with it. Besides, if they were doing it to me, were they doing it to the other ex-Gutersloh staff as well?

So I told him that it wasn't right and I wasn't signing the form. I explained what had happened and bless his heart, he believed me. He could have just grumbled and said it wasn't his problem but no, he backed me up! Which I thought was a nice thing to do, trusting me on such a short acquaintance.

He contacted the Chief Clerk at Brize, who contacted the Chief clerk at Gatow, who contacted Sgt Dartman, who admitted to everything and the whole story came out. Apparently the sequence of events went something like this. After I had been interviewed by the WO at Gutersloh, the forms were sent on to Sgt Dartman, who then passed them on up the line of HIS new chain of command. When they reached the desk of Flt Lt Im-a-wally, he said, 'This write up doesn't justify the marks you've given. You need to rewrite it or drop the marks.' Dartman dropped the marks. So, we had an officer at a station I had never served at, who didn't know any of us, changing our assessments, which had already been agreed on and signed for.

I'm happy to report that this all got kicked into touch

and checking the photocopy of the F6442, it appears that all the signatories were Gutersloh based, so they must have re-instated the original form.

***

Before I left Gutersloh, while I was in the PBX, a guy named Colin Smith phoned me up. I had served with Colin in JISC in Cyprus, back in the late 70's. He was now a shift sergeant at 81 SU and had read that I was due to be posted in. He was organising a skiing trip to Germany after I had returned to the UK, and wanted to know if I was interested in coming along. I had got the taste for skiing by then so happily agreed to join the trip. So before I had even left Germany I had arranged my skiing holiday BACK there again.

We went skiing and stayed at Oberammergau (remember, Passion Play and Christmas shop? Do keep up) and we had a great time but what made it memorable was our visit to the "Zauberstub'n" or as we call it in English, "The Magic Bar".

It is owned and run by a magician named Vlado. He serves beer in the bar and if you plead with him and cajole him, he will do a magic trick for you. (Of course he will, otherwise people would drink elsewhere. They come for the magic and stay for the beer.)

He does this close up magic like Dynamo does, so it's all sleight-of-hand not trapdoors and doves. I was lucky; I got to see him performing a couple of tricks. A few of us were standing at the bar and he took the Flt Lt's wedding ring, did something with it (hid it in a bag or a box or something) and when the Flt Lt opened it up, the ring was missing. After a few minutes of embarrassed, 'Sorry, I don't know where it's gone,' and the Flt Lt getting quite irate, Vlado turned round, took a box off the shelf behind him, tied up with a bow and handed it to the Flt Lt. When he opened it up, his ring was inside.

Later in the evening he did a trick for our WRAF's, so I went over to watch. They were sitting at one of the bench tables. You know, the kind that has the bench seats attached to the legs of the table, you normally see them in parks and barbecue areas. So the WRAF's and he were sitting normally on the seats, facing each other across the table, whereas I sat astride the bench, facing his side. He was doing a floating napkin trick and even sitting right next to him I couldn't see how he did it, until I leaned my elbow on the table which put me at *just the right angle* to see the light reflecting off the incredibly thin piece of fishing line that he was using to make the napkin dance. Otherwise I would never have known how he did it. Incredible.

***

I kept up my skiing even after I left the RAF, for many years until I had a few medical problems which made getting around difficult, let alone skiing.

What I did have though, even after I stopped, was the same mental attitude that had made me take it up in the first place. An IT colleague of mine who was also a skier defined it as, 'There are two types of people in the world, those who "ski" and those who don't.'

I understood perfectly what he meant. He wasn't necessarily referring to people who actually strapped on skis and slid down mountains. Rather, he meant there are those people who are willing to go outside their comfort zone and try something different, and then there are those whose idea of an exotic holiday is two weeks in Benidorm.

I've lost count of the number of times I've said to

people, 'I'm off skiing next week.'

'I've always wanted to go skiing.'

'Well, why don't you?'

'Oh, I could never do that.'

When you press them they always use the same excuses:

'Costs too much.' One week skiing costs about the same as two weeks in the sunshine.

'I don't have the right clothing.' You don't have to have "the right clothing" to go skiing; there are no fashion police patrolling the resorts. I've seen people going down the slopes in just jumpers and jeans.

There was a place in Germany where you could buy a black bag of second-hand clothing for 10 Deutsch Marks (about £3). They also sold individually priced items of used clothing, so I got my first pair of salopettes (skiing trousers) for 10 Deutsch Marks. I just wore my normal winter coat and we all have woolly hats and gloves. The most expensive outlay was for a pair of ski goggles, but most of the time I just wore sunglasses.

People who "ski" will go for an activity holiday in Croatia, maybe hill-walking in the Pyrenees or a winter adventure in Finland. People who don't "ski" will go to Marbella or Ibiza.

Personally, one time I hopped on a plane by myself and spent a week going round all the theme parks in Florida. Another year I went to Jersey for the 800 year celebrations of unity with England. (The UK didn't exist 800 years ago, so I'm not being nationalistic.)

Nowadays I'm not as adventurous (getting old and don't like travelling any more) so I stay in the UK and do things like rent a cabin in the woods. It doesn't matter what you do, just do something different, that you've never tried before.

***

As I approached the end of my time in the RAF I had to start planning for the future. The services are very good about that sort of thing and supply a variety of resettlement courses to retrain people for their future life outside the services.

I say future life and not second career as some people are too long in the tooth for that and just take something that will aid them in their retirement. Which is why you see Group Captains and the like, learning to be plumbers or brick-layers. At first you think *what?!* Then you realise it's so they can maintain their retirement homes and not to get a job on a building site.

Personally I was always interested in computers. I knew how to run spreadsheets and word processing programs on my Amiga but I wanted to know how to actually work a *real* computer. At Marham the techies had to come over and install programs for me.

Being "A Bear of Very Little Brain", I had not been able to teach myself to that level, so I took this opportunity to remedy that. I chose a month long course at Aldershot on how to build PC's from scratch and install operating systems and programs on them. This was back in the days of MS-DOS 5.0 and Windows 3.0 was the latest thing. This stood me in good stead later after Windows 95 came out and people learned to use only that and considered themselves experts, whereas I had a deeper understanding of what went on behind the scenes and how to identify and fix problems.

I did this for my own benefit and not necessarily future job prospects as I understood it was hard to get into IT because of the age old Catch-22 situation. No one will give you a job because you have no experience – but you can't get any experience because no one will give you a job.

I didn't really know what I would do after I left the mob. I was open to most things but sort of figured that due to all the message logging and filing experience in a Commcen I might end up in some sort of office job (indoor work, no heavy lifting) but was open to whatever was on offer, I even interviewed as a proof reader at a publisher one time.

I thought that the more training I had under my belt the better. By this time the phone system (Meridian) that I had done all the planning for at Marham, had entered service in the RAF and they now taught courses on managing it, at RAF Locking, where the training school for my trade had moved to, from Cosford.

I contacted everyone at Brize and Locking that I had to and got everyone's permission to trade 2 weeks of my demob leave for a course on the Meridian phone system. I promised I'd sit quietly at the back of the room in civvies and I would provide my own accommodation. I booked myself into a bed and breakfast in Weston Super Mare.

When I got to Locking on the first day I met Mick Apps from Gutersloh who was an instructor there now. Luckily for me, he was in charge of a barrack block and had spare rooms so I cancelled my bed and breakfast and spent the fortnight in the block. Bought meals tickets at the Airman's Mess, so I wasn't cheating anyone.

And it did actually come in useful years later when I ended up in charge of the Voice Over Internet Protocol (VOIP) phone system we had installed at Oxfam, that was based on the old Meridian.

***

My tale is nearly done but I just have to mention the RAF

having one last dig at me. I really thought I was getting away free and clear but the RAF couldn't resist one last opportunity to F*ck me about!

I had planned to go on the Meridian course starting the following Monday, so I arranged to pick up my "blue card" and clear from Brize Norton/81 SU on the Thursday/Friday of the week before. Some of the sections that you clear from have to be done in a particular order, ending up at the General Office. I got rid of all the trivial places like the library and the Forms Store. The next one on my card was the Bedding Store but that was closed until the following Monday.

Of course I skipped that one (remember I had made a specific point of never setting foot on this camp or living there when I arrived back in the UK?) and went to the next on the list, the Guardroom where I came up against SAC Jobsworth.

'I can't sign that, you haven't been to the Bedding Store,' he told me.

'I don't need to go there, I don't live on camp.'

'Nevertheless I can't sign it until you do.'

'No listen, I don't live on this camp. I have never lived on this camp. There is no way I would ever have signed out anything from the Bedding Store. I don't need to go there. Besides, it's shut until next Monday.'

'Well you'll have to go back there Monday and get it signed.'

'I can't. I'm supposed to be at Locking on Monday, on a resettlement course.'

'Sorry.'

The more devious amongst you will ask, 'Why didn't you just sign that bit yourself?' But obviously the Guardroom would have known that the Bedding Store was shut that day and given the type I was up against, I would have just been making trouble for myself. Not worth the risk when I was so close to freedom.

I went to General Office and asked to speak to the Chief Clerk. I explained the situation about Locking and he must have been in a sympathetic mood that day because he said, 'It's okay. Tell them they can ignore that and just sign their bit.'

Heartened, I went back to the Guardroom, explained what the Chief Clerk had said and offered up my blue card for signature.

'Sorry, I can't sign that until you've been to the Bedding Store.'

'Didn't you hear what I just told you? The Chief Clerk said it was okay.'

'Not signing it.'

'Okay, I want to speak to your corporal'

They let me into the Guardroom and this time I spoke to a *Cpl Jobsworth* who said. 'I can't sign that until you've been to the Bedding Store.'

'But the Chief Clerk …'

'Doesn't matter.'

'Can I borrow your phone?' I phoned General Office and got the Chief Clerk on the line. Told him what was going on and handed the phone over to the Cpl. After he came off the phone he begrudgingly took my card and signed it, as if he was signing the release form for me to take away his children. And the Guardroom staff wonder why they aren't liked.

Although I didn't really finish with the RAF until I'd finished the course at Locking, the story above ended with me handing my ID card back to the RAF and walking out of RAF Brize Norton for the last time.

So you sign on for 6 years and then 22 years later you're walking out the main gate minus ID card and uniform and asking yourself, 'Wait, what just happened? Where have the last 22 years gone?'

***

I did get one last dig back at the RAF though. A WRAF Sgt I knew was stationed at RAF Neatishead and she invited me up for their Christmas do. We kept it quiet that I was still in the RAF and she booked me a room in the Sgt's Mess as a civilian, which they're allowed to do with visitors. Little did they know that I was still serving at the time so I got the last laugh by sleeping in the Sgt's Mess as a Cpl. Ha, Ha! Revenge!

***

You look back, 24 years after leaving the Air Force, and wonder where it all went. I used to be young and pretty once … now I'm on medication for high blood pressure, I have to get up at least once in the night to go to the toilet and when I do, I'm peeing in Morse code. (Well at least I had a head start on that.)

Ah, farewell, sweet bird of youth.

As I look back over my career as a communicator I realise that I have no idea how the military does its communicating these days. Probably all on social media, texting or Facebook. At least when they had to pass messages through Commcen staff we could rein in their more obvious security blunders. Can you imagine it nowadays?

Tweet - 'Sorry, can't make officer's dining-in night as my squadron is bombing Syria that day. LOL. Should be totes amazeballs!'

Good luck to them.

***

Having done a PC course for my resettlement, I was lucky enough to get the chance to go into Information Technology. I found that having been in the forces gave me a good grounding for my future career in civvy street. In fact, some of the traits that held me back in the RAF were *precisely* the things that were considered positives by my later employers, such as being willing to stand up to the bosses and tell them the truth about a problem instead of trying to sugar-coat it or spread the blame around. If a project was being mis-managed, underfunded or undermanned, I told them. I think they came to appreciate my honest, "doesn't do bullsh*t" attitude. They knew that I would always give them the truth of the situation, good or bad. They also appreciated me being willing to work unpaid overtime should it be required, 'You work to the job, not to the clock,' as one boss told me. He was ex-RAF too.

Although some of my civvy work colleagues didn't understand me sometimes. When we were planning something, an upgrade to the system perhaps, I would always be the one that would say, 'But what do we do if the equipment doesn't turn up?' or 'What if we don't finish this in time?' They chided me for being gloomy and pessimistic but another ex-serviceman would have understood exactly what I was doing. The forces methodology is to 'Hope for the best but plan for the worst.' You should always have a Plan B, followed by a Plan C, a Plan D … and so on. I was just pointing out to them that we needed contingency plans in case the worst happened.

These attitudes gave me a solid grounding and a good work ethic which is why after leaving the mob, apart from a year on the dole before I found a job, I stayed in permanent employment for the next 14 years. Okay, despite being in IT I didn't make a fortune. I wasn't like those City boys who drank champagne and snorted cocaine off a hooker's breasts. (More like, drank Brown Ale while snorting Lemsip off of Doris, from the chip-shop.) But I made a good living and was able to retire early at 55, so I can't complain.

***

Well, that was my life, my service career anyway. I hope you weren't too bored by it but if you were, think about me, I had to live through it!

Apologies to those I haven't mentioned – can't remember you all – met some good people but lost touch with them. Reconnecting with them due to Facebook. To the good ones who I served with thanks for all the good times – if you are one of the others who made my time not so fun, you can do one!

Bye Bye now!

Tony Rattigan

July 2018

Other books by this Author:

Split Infinity

Hair of the Dog

The Speed of Dark

The Londum Omnibus Volume One

A Londum Yuletide

Snake Eyes

Quantum of Solstice

The Great Game

Snowfall (Second Edition)

Winter Shorts

Foothold

The Londum Omnibus Volume Two

For more information about these books and characters go to www.tonyrattigan.co.uk
    If you enjoyed this book then please feel free to leave a review at the online shop where you purchased it and help to spread the word. It would be most appreciated.

About the Author:

Tony Rattigan* is the author of a series of books about an alternate Universe, one of many different Universes that make up a Multiverse.

After 22 years in the Royal Air Force, 5 years in the National Health Service and 10 years at one of the UK's largest charities, Tony decided he'd done enough for Queen and Country and he was about due some 'me' time.

Consequently he took early retirement in 2010 to work on his writing. He lives in Oxfordshire UK with his Albatross and a pet monkey. (No, not really. That's just a vain attempt to sound interesting.)

*Tony Rattigan is the founder member of the Anti-Reincarnation Society, whose motto is – "Once is Enough!" All members carry a card that reads, 'If found dead - please do not reincarnate'.

34086306R00188

Printed in Great Britain
by Amazon